Beppe Finessi
ベッペ・フィネッシ

su Mangiarotti
マンジャロッティの世界

建築・デザイン・彫刻
72プロジェクト・227未発表資料・3論文

監訳　マンジャロッティ・アソシエイツ・ジャパン

建築技術

日本版出版にあたって

ミラノ・トリエンナーレ2002年の特別企画展として、主会場のパラッツォ・デ・ラルテの2,000m²を使用した「アンジェロ・マンジャロッティ展」が催され、大好評を博した。この展覧会に平行して企画・出版されたのが本書である。オリジナル版はイタリア語と英語の併記で編集されている。この日本版はオリジナル版をベースに、イタリア語のみを日本語に置き換えたもので、その他の構成はほぼオリジナルのままである。翻訳はマンジャロッティ事務所OBの有志が分担し(日本文の末尾に各担当者のイニシャルを付す)、筆者が監修をさせていただいた。

マンジャロッティ事務所には、1959年イタリア政府留学生であった河原一郎法政大学名誉教授を皮切りに、デザイナー川上元美を含め、現所員堀川絹江まで、40数年間途切れることなく、20数名の日本人建築家・デザイナーが学んでいる。われわれOB有志は、上記「アンジェロ・マンジャロッティ展」を日本に誘致すべく、河原一郎を委員長に「マンジャロッティ展実行委員会」を2002年に設立し活動を展開してきた。幸い日本での「アンジェロ・マンジャロッティ展」(2004-9-10〜11-13)を「ギャラリー・間」が引き受けて下さり、それと平行して本書の出版を株式会社建築技術の橋戸幹彦氏が快諾してくれました。本書の実現にあたっては多くの方々のご協力を得ましたが、とりわけ忙中の閑を縫いボランティアで翻訳を担当してくれたマンジャロッティ・アソシエイツ・ジャパンの有志各位と全体に目を通して、いくつかの迷訳を明訳に正していただいた会議通訳の名人田丸公美子氏、的確な助言とともに編集作業をリードしてくれた橋戸幹彦氏と編集を担当しながら、われわれの無骨な文章を滑らかな日本語に誘導してくれた後藤由希子氏に心から感謝します。同時に出版の便宜を整えてくれたマンジャロッティ氏とオリジナル版の発行人であるレナート・ミネット氏の寛容な配慮に深謝したい。

濱口オサミ

su Mangiarotti
by
Beppe Finessi

copyright © 2002 by Editrice Abitare Segesta spa, Milano
Japanese Translation by Mangiarotti Associates Japan
Published 2004 in Japan
by Kenchiku Gijutsu
ISBN4-7677-0101-5 C3052

まえがき

〈もう1つの〉マンジャロッティ論の企画を実現するにあたって、以下の方々から格別の協力を得られたことを感謝とともに書き留めたい。

マンジャロッティ事務所のステファノ・コルツァーニ、堀川絹江、エンリコ・マッリ、アンナ・マンジャロッティ、キアーラ・パンポ、それにラウラ・パストーレ、彼らの温情と惜しみない協力に深く感謝します。

カルラ・ルッソは、常にこの企画を真近で支えてくれると同時に、フランシワ・ブルクハルトのテキストの翻訳を担当した。ガブリエラ・オルランディは原稿の校正を、スティーブ・ピッコロはすべての翻訳を迅速かつ正確に成し遂げてくれた。

フランソア・ブルクハルト、ルチアーノ・カラメル、そしてグイド・ナルディはこの企画に賛同し、新たに論文を寄稿してくれた。ステファノ・コルツァーニは情熱をもって私に同伴してくれた。膨大なマンジャロッティの資料についての知識と彼の惜しみない協力がなければ、この本の多くの資料が陽の目を見なかったことだろう。アレッサンドロ・ベルッフィは忍耐強く協働してくれた。エレーナ・トゥリウンヴェーリは原稿の校正のための貴重な助言を提供し、専門性と優れた判断力を必要とするこの本の編集を取りまとめてくれた。

形式ばらない、より新鮮な本が実現する可能性を信じ続けてくれたアビターレ・セジェスタ出版社とアントネッラ・ミネット社主に感謝したい。イタロ・ルーピはこの本のアートディレクターを務めただけでなく、この本の出版企画全体の共同者でもある。

そして、アンジェロ・マンジャロッティは、友情と人生全般にわたる数々の教えとともに、多くの時間を私に提供してくれた。イタロとアンジェロには、どんなに感謝しようともし過ぎることはない。

ベッペ・フィネッシ

7	アンジェロ・マンジャロッティ "幸せは的確な仕事によりもたらされる" ベッペ・フィネッシ
20	バランザーテの教会／ミラノ，1957年
28	スプリューゲン・ブロイ社倉庫／メストレ（ヴェネツィア），1962年
32	モラスッティ社倉庫／パドバ，1958年
36	海の見本市展示館／ジェノヴァ，1963年
44	ガヴィラーテ通りの集合住宅／ミラノ，1959年
48	クアドロンノ通りの集合住宅／ミラノ，1960年
54	ピオンビーノの集合住宅計画／リヴォルノ，1961年
58	モンツァの集合住宅／ミラノ，1972年
60	アロジオの集合住宅／コモ，1977年
64	ムルロンゴの休暇のための集合住宅／ヴェローナ，1971年
68	アヴォーラの漁業施設再生計画／シラクーサ，1997年
70	貯水塔計画，1961年
72	都心センター計画，1965年
74	傾けられた塔状集合住宅計画，1985年
76	第14回ミラノ・トリエンナーレ展の展示場計画，1968年
80	マルチャニーゼの工場と従業員用の集合住宅／カゼルタ，1962年
86	ファチェブ社による構造システム，1964年
90	チニゼッロ・バルサーモのアルミタリア社屋／ミラノ，1968年
94	構造システム U70 ISOCELL，1969年
98	構造システム BRIONA，1972年
102	グリッド状の巨大架構計画，1975年
104	ファチェブ社による構造システム，1976年
108	マイアーノ・デル・フリウリのズナイデロ社オフィス／ウディネ，1978年
112	カラーラのIMM社オフィス，1991年
116	構造体S99のためのスタディ，1999年
118	チェルトーザおよびロゴレードの鉄道駅／ミラノ，1982年
122	地下鉄ヴェネツィア駅とレ・ププブリカ駅／ミラノ，1982-98年
130	パレルモのサッカー競技場計画，1987年
132	カターニアのサッカー競技場計画，1987年
134	リオ・マッジョーレの歩道橋計画，1997年
136	**建築について　グィド・ナルディ**
138	時計：セクティコン，1956年
142	自動車のスタディ，1961年
144	ラジオのプロジェクト，1966年
145	ポータブル・テレビのプロジェクト，1966年
146	鋳型成型と旋盤加工によるブロンズ製花器シリーズ，1962年
150	躍動する花器，1964年
151	灰皿：バルバドス，1964年

152	ガラス質磁器による小品，1968年
154	テラコッタ製組合せ植木鉢，1968年
156	切削加工による大理石の花器，1971年
158	照明器具：コンドットーレ・ディ・ルーチェ（光の伝導体），1962年
160	照明器具：レスボ，1966年
161	照明器具：サッフォ，1966年
162	吊り構造の照明：V+V，1967年
166	屋外照明器具：チェメンタ，1971年
167	照明器具：エジーナ，1979年
168	クリスタルガラスの小品のシリーズ
174	テーブルウェアーシリーズ：エルゴノミカ，1990年
175	コーヒーメーカー，1991年
176	レバーハンドルのプロジェクト
178	椅子：シカゴ，1983年
180	屋外用椅子：クリーツィア，1990年
182	テーブルシリーズ：エロス，1971年
186	テーブルシリーズ：インカス，1978年
188	テーブルシリーズ：アゾロ，1981年
190	テーブル：モアー，1989年
192	曲げ成型合板による家具，1955年
193	マンゾーニ通りのアパート／ミラノ，1957年
194	ビニャルディ通りのアパート／ミラノ，1952年
196	システム家具：ジュニア，1966年
200	システム：CUB8，1967年
204	システム：IN/OUT，1968年
208	書棚：エストゥルアル，1981年
210	書棚：イプシロン，1996年
212	化粧用突き板：IN/IN，1981年
215	化粧用突き板：ネヴァー・ザ・セイム，1993年
218	指輪：ヴェラ・ライカ，2000年
220	**デザインについて　フランソア・ブルクハルト**
222	天空の円錐，1987年
226	プレゼンツェ（存在），1999年
228	ギャラリー／マリーナ・ディ・カッラーラ（マッサ・カッラーラ），1999年
230	軌跡／マリーナ・ディ・カッラーラ（マッサ・カッラーラ），1999年
232	労働戦死者のモニュメント／アプリチェーナ（フォッジャ），2000年
234	サンタンナの虐殺／サンタンナ・ディ・スタッゼマ（ルッカ），2000年
238	**彫刻について　ルチアーノ・カラメル**
240	一体型システム，2000年

v

翻訳者一覧 （順不同）

(M.K): 川上元美　川上デザインルーム

(M.T): 竹居正武　ダムダン空間工作所

(M.O): 奥田宗幸　東京理科大学教授

(C.I): 石井千歳　アトリエ・メビウス建築設計事務所

(O.H): 濱口オサミ　濱口建築・デザイン工房

(Ka.M): 三井一成　日本設計

(Ke.M): 諸角 敬　諸角敬建築・デザイン研究室　Studio A

(Y.T): 豊島夕起夫　豊島夕起夫建築アトリエ

(N.M): 元良信彦　モトラデザインスタジオ

(I.M): 宮川 格　イタルデザイン

(T.K): 河合俊和　河合俊和建築設計事務所

(K.H): 堀川絹江　Studio MANGIAROTTI

マンジャロッティの世界

発行
2004年9月17日

著者
ベッペ・フィネッシ

監訳
マンジャロッティ・アソシエイツ・ジャパン

発行者
橋戸幹彦

発行所
株式会社建築技術
〒101-0061
東京都千代田区三崎町3-10-4　千代田ビル
TEL 03-3222-5951
FAX 03-3222-5957
http://www.k-gijutsu.co.jp
振替口座00100-7-72417

日本語組版デザイン
赤崎正一

印刷・製本
三報社印刷株式会社

落丁・乱丁本はお取り替えいたします。
ISBN4-7677-0101-5　C3052
©マンジャロッティ・アソシエイツ・ジャパン

Beppe Finessi

su Mangiarotti

**architettura design scultura
72 progetti • 227 inediti • 3 contributi critici**

grafica di Italo Lupi

contributi critici

François Burkhardt

Luciano Caramel

Guido Nardi

Abitare Segesta Cataloghi

Abitare Segesta Cataloghi

Editore
Renato Minetto

Direttore Editoriale
Enrico Morteo

Coordinamento editoriale
Antonella Minetto

Progetto grafico
Italo Lupi
con Alessandra Beluffi • Studio Lupi

Coordinamento redazionale
Elena Triunveri

Ricerche iconografiche
Beppe Finessi
con Stefano Colzani (Studio Mangiarotti)

Traduzioni
Steve Piccolo

Studio per una gru, 1975

© Editrice Abitare Segesta spa, Milano
Tutti i diritti riservati
Finito di stampare nel gennaio 2002
da Galli e Thierry, Milano
ISBN 88-86116-45-4

Distribuzione: Edizioni Corraini
Maurizio Corraini srl • via Madonna della Vittoria, 5
46100 Mantova • tel. +39 0376 322753 fax +39 0376 365566
edcorraini@tin.it • www.corraini.com

La realizzazione di un progetto di "altre" monografie necessita di complici speciali che ricordo e ringrazio. Un ringraziamento particolare va a Stefano Colzani, Kinue Horikawa, Enrico Malli, Anna Mangiarotti, Chiara Pampo e Laura Pastore dello studio Mangiarotti per la disponibilità e l'ospitalità. Carla Russo – che continua ad essere vicina a questo progetto editoriale - ha curato la traduzione del testo di François Burkhardt, Gabriella Orlandi ha collaborato alla revisione dei testi, Steve Piccolo ha tradotto tutto con celerità e raffinatezza. François Burkhardt, Luciano Caramel e Guido Nardi hanno aderito al progetto con contributi critici originali. Stefano Colzani mi ha accompagnato con entusiasmo nella conoscenza dell'immenso archivio Mangiarotti e senza la sua determinante collaborazione molti di questi materiali non avrebbero visto la luce. Alessandra Beluffi ha lavorato con pazienza e complicità. Elena Triunveri ha coordinato la redazione del libro con professionalità ed estrema competenza prodigandosi in consigli preziosi per la revisione dei testi. Grazie ad Antonella Minetto e alla casa Editrice Abitare Segesta che continuano a credere nella possibilità di realizzare libri meno ingessati e più freschi. Italo Lupi non è solo l'art director di questo libro ma il co-autore dell'intero progetto editoriale. Angelo Mangiarotti mi ha regalato molto del suo tempo oltre che amicizia e insegnamenti di una vita intera. Per Italo e Angelo non bastano i miei grazie. B.F.

L'editore ringrazia Angelo Mangiarotti per aver gentilmente concesso il materiale iconografico che illustra il volume.

Referenze fotografiche
Aldo Ballo • Gabriele Basilico • Bitetto • Rodolfo Facchini • Foto Casali • Foto Masera • Angelo Mangiarotti • Lionel Pasquon • Studio G • WeShoot

L'editore è a disposizione degli aventi diritto per le eventuali fonti iconografiche non identificate.

7	**ANGELO MANGIAROTTI "LA FELICITÀ VIENE DALLA CORRETTEZZA"** Beppe Finessi
20	CHIESA MATER MISERICORDIAE A BARANZATE, 1957
28	DEPOSITO SPLUGEN BRÄU A MESTRE, 1962
32	DEPOSITO MORASSUTTI A PADOVA, 1958
36	PADIGLIONE PER ESPOSIZIONI ALLA FIERA DEL MARE A GENOVA, 1963
44	CASA IN VIA GAVIRATE A MILANO, 1959
48	CASA IN VIA QUADRONNO A MILANO, 1960
54	PROGETTO DI UN COMPLESSO RESIDENZIALE A PIOMBINO, 1961
58	CASA A MONZA, 1972
60	CASA AD AROSIO, 1977
64	CASE PER VACANZE A MURLONGO, 1971
68	PROGETTO DI RECUPERO DI UNA TONNARA AD AVOLA, 1997
70	PROGETTO DI UN SERBATOIO IDRICO, 1961
72	PROGETTO DI UN POLICENTRO, 1965
74	PROGETTO DI UNA TORRE INCLINATA, 1985
76	PROGETTO DI UN PADIGLIONE ESPOSITIVO ALLA XIV TRIENNALE DI MILANO, 1968
80	STABILIMENTO E ABITAZIONI A MARCIANISE, 1962
86	SISTEMA COSTRUTTIVO FACEP 1964
90	STABILIMENTO ARMITALIA A CINISELLO BALSAMO, 1968
94	SISTEMA COSTRUTTIVO U70 ISOCELL 1969
98	SISTEMA COSTRUTTIVO BRIONA 1972
102	PROGETTO DI UNA MEGASTRUTTURA A MAGLIA QUADRATA, 1975
104	SISTEMA COSTRUTTIVO FACEP 1976
108	UFFICI SNAIDERO A MAIANO DEL FRIULI, 1978
112	UFFICI IMM A CARRARA, 1991
116	STUDIO DELLA STRUTTURA S99, 1999
118	STAZIONI FERROVIARIE CERTOSA E ROGOREDO, MILANO, 1982
122	STAZIONI FERROVIARIE SOTTERRANEE VENEZIA E REPUBBLICA, MILANO, 1982-98
130	PROGETTO DI UNO STADIO A PALERMO, 1987
132	PROGETTO DI UNO STADIO A CATANIA, 1987
134	PROGETTO DI UN PONTE PEDONALE A RIOMAGGIORE, 1997
136	**SULL'ARCHITETTURA** Guido Nardi
138	OROLOGI SECTICON, 1956
142	STUDI PER AUTOMOBILI, 1961
144	PROGETTI DI APPARECCHI RADIO, 1966
145	PROGETTO DI UN TELEVISORE PORTATILE, 1966
146	VASI IN BRONZO FUSO E TORNITO, 1962
150	VASI TREMITI, 1964
151	PORTACENERE BARBADOS, 1964
152	OGGETTI IN VITREOUS-CHINA, 1968
154	VASI COMPONIBILI IN TERRACOTTA, 1968
156	VASI IN MARMO FRESATO, 1971
158	LAMPADA CONDUTTORE DI LUCE, 1962
160	LAMPADA LESBO, 1966
161	LAMPADA SAFFO, 1966
162	LAMPADA A SOSPENSIONE V+V, 1967
166	LAMPADA CEMENTA, 1971
167	LAMPADA EGINA, 1979
168	COLLEZIONE DI OGGETTI IN CRISTALLO
174	POSATE SERIE ERGONOMICA, 1990
175	CAFFETTIERA, 1991
176	PROGETTI DI MANIGLIE
178	SEDIA CHICAGO, 1983
180	SEDUTA PER ESTERNI CLIZIA, 1990
182	TAVOLI EROS, 1971
186	TAVOLI INCAS, 1978
188	TAVOLI ASOLO, 1981
190	TAVOLI MORE, 1989
192	MOBILI IN COMPENSATO CURVATO, 1955
193	APPARTAMENTO MANZONI, MILANO, 1957
194	APPARTAMENTO BIGNARDI, MILANO, 1952
196	SISTEMA JUNIOR, 1966
200	SISTEMA CUB8, 1967
204	SISTEMA IN/OUT, 1968
208	LIBRERIA ESTRUAL 1981
210	LIBRERIA YPSILON, 1996
212	IMPIALLACCIATURE IN/IN, 1981
215	IMPIALLACCIATURE NEVER THE SAME, 1993
218	ANELLO VERA LAICA, 2000
220	**SUL DESIGN** François Burkhardt
222	CONO-CIELO, 1987
226	PRESENZE, 1999
228	LA GALLERIA, 1999
230	IL PERCORSO, 1999
232	MONUMENTO AI CADUTI SUL LAVORO, 2000
234	MASSACRO A SANT'ANNA, 2000
238	**SULLA SCULTURA** Luciano Caramel
240	MONOLITE

- 7 **ANGELO MANGIAROTTI "HAPPINESS COMES FROM CORRECTNESS"** Beppe Finessi
- 20 MATER MISERICORDIAE CHURCH IN BARANZATE, 1957
- 28 SPLÜGEN BRÄU WAREHOUSE IN MESTRE, 1962
- 32 MORASSUTTI WAREHOUSE IN PADUA, 1958
- 36 TRADE FAIR PAVILION FOR THE FIERA DEL MARE IN GENOA, 1963
- 44 BUILDING ON VIA GAVIRATE IN MILAN, 1959
- 48 APARTMENT HOUSE ON VIA QUADRONNO IN MILAN, 1960
- 54 PROJECT FOR A RESIDENTIAL COMPLEX IN PIOMBINO, 1961
- 58 RESIDENTIAL BUILDING IN MONZA, 1972
- 60 RESIDENTIAL BUILDING IN AROSIO, 1977
- 64 VACATION HOMES AT MURLONGO, 1971
- 68 PROJECT FOR THE REUTILIZATION OF A TONNARA AT AVOLA, 1997
- 70 DESIGN FOR A WATER TANK, 1961
- 72 DESIGN FOR A MULTIFUNCTIONAL CENTER, 1965
- 74 DESIGN FOR AN INCLINED TOWER, 1985
- 76 DESIGN FOR AN EXHIBITION PAVILION, 14TH MILAN TRIENNIAL, 1968
- 80 PLANT AND HOUSING IN MARCIANISE, 1962
- 86 FACEP 1964 CONSTRUCTION SYSTEM
- 90 ARMITALIA PLANT IN CINISELLO BALSAMO, 1968
- 94 U70 ISOCELL 1969 CONSTRUCTION SYSTEM
- 98 BRIONA 1972 CONSTRUCTION SYSTEM
- 102 PROJECT FOR A SQUARE-GRID MEGASTRUCTURE, 1975
- 104 FACEP 1976 CONSTRUCTION SYSTEM
- 108 SNAIDERO OFFICES IN MAIANO DEL FRIULI, 1978
- 112 IMM OFFICES IN CARRARA, 1991
- 116 STUDY FOR THE S99 STRUCTURE, 1999
- 118 CERTOSA AND ROGOREDO RAIL STATIONS, MILAN, 1982
- 122 VENEZIA & REPUBBLICA UNDERGROUND STATIONS, RAIL BYPASS, MILAN, 1982-1998
- 130 DESIGN FOR A STADIUM IN PALERMO, 1987
- 132 DESIGN FOR A STADIUM IN CATANIA, 1987
- 134 DESIGN FOR A FOOTBRIDGE IN RIOMAGGIORE, 1997
- 136 **ON THE ARCHITECTURE** Guido Nardi
- 138 SECTICON CLOCKS, 1956
- 142 STUDIES FOR AUTOMOBILES, 1961
- 144 DESIGNS FOR RADIOS, 1966
- 145 DESIGN FOR A PORTABLE TELEVISION, 1966
- 146 VASES IN CAST TURNED BRONZE, 1962
- 150 TREMITI VASES, 1964
- 151 BARBADOS ASHTRAY, 1964
- 152 OBJECTS IN VITREOUS CHINA, 1968
- 154 COMPONENT FLOWERPOTS IN TERRACOTTA, 1968
- 156 VASES IN MILLED MARBLE, 1971
- 158 CONDUTTORE DI LUCE LAMP, 1962
- 160 LESBO LAMP, 1966
- 161 SAFFO LAMP, 1966
- 162 V-V HANGING LAMP, 1967
- 166 CEMENTA LAMP, 1971
- 167 EGINA LAMP, 1979
- 168 COLLECTION OF OBJECTS IN CRYSTAL
- 174 ERGONOMICA FLATWARE, 1990
- 175 COFFEEMAKER, 1991
- 176 DESIGNS FOR HANDLES
- 178 CHICAGO CHAIR, 1983
- 180 CLIZIA OUTDOOR SEATING, 1990
- 182 EROS TABLES, 1971
- 186 INCAS TABLES, 1978
- 188 ASOLO TABLES, 1981
- 190 MORE TABLES, 1989
- 192 CURVED PLYWOOD FURNITURE, 1955
- 193 MANZONI APARTMENT, MILANO, 1957
- 194 BIGNARDI APARTMENT, MILANO, 1952
- 196 JUNIOR SYSTEM, 1966
- 200 CUB8 SYSTEM, 1967
- 204 IN/OUT SYSTEM, 1968
- 208 ESTRUAL BOOKCASE, 1981
- 210 YPSILON BOOKCASE, 1996
- 212 IN/IN VENEERS, 1981
- 215 NEVER THE SAME VENEERS, 1993
- 218 VERA LAICA RING, 2000
- 220 **ON THE DESIGN** François Burkhardt
- 222 CONO-CIELO, 1987
- 226 PRESENZE, 1999
- 228 LA GALLERIA, 1999
- 230 IL PERCORSO, 1999
- 232 MONUMENT TO WORKPLACE CASUALTIES, 2000
- 234 MASSACRO A SANT'ANNA, 2000
- 238 **ON THE SCULPTURE** Luciano Caramel
- 240 MONOLITE

ANGELO MANGIAROTTI
"LA FELICITÀ VIENE DALLA CORRETTEZZA"

アンジェロ・マンジャロッティ "幸せは的確な仕事によりもたらされる" ベッペ・フィネッシ

アンジェロ・マンジャロッティの仕事は、「ハンマーをふりかざした労働者が自らを守る構造物を組み立てている」この絵に象徴されている。つくり方はごくシンプルで、多大な経費や特殊な技術が使われているわけではない。

このハンマーは、建築やデザインを構成するエレメントとの直接的で親密な関係を意味する。マンジャロッティは、作業する人、職人や工房の親方の重要な役割をよく知っている。つまり、現場で素材と向かい合い格闘する彼らこそが、純真に秘められた可能性を読みとり、決定を下し得るものである。彼の仕事はまさにここにあり、その特徴は、素材や職人の仕事に対して、強い関心と尊敬の念を抱き、そこに関係性を構築する優れた資質にある。

この素材や仕事に対する愛情は、彼の幼年期と家族にルーツがある。彼の父親は有名なパン職人の親方だった。マンジャロッティは、大げさではないが的確な動作で香ばしいパンと焼き菓子をつくる父親の様子を、今でも夢の中の出来事のように思い出すことができる。彼は、父親が小麦粉、水、酵母、油、塩、等々の材料とその性質を吟味している姿を覚えている。例えば、小麦粉にはよい小麦粉とよくない小麦粉があること、酵母にもいろいろあること、水は「あそこの水はいいから」と言って父がコモ湖まで水を汲みに行ったこと、油は「リグーリアから特別に送らせた油」を使っていると言っていたことなど、さらに、おいしいパンや焼き菓子をつくるためには、生地をつくる作業の手順や焼き時間が重要だということも覚えている。このような幼年期の体験から、父親の仕事をとおして、よいものをつくるにはよい仕事が欠かせないことを自分の体で覚えている。彼は、素材のよしあしや部材の使

ミシン（サルモイラーギ社），1956年／Sewing machine Salmoiraghi, 1956
共同者：ブルーノ・モラスッティ／With Bruno Morassutti

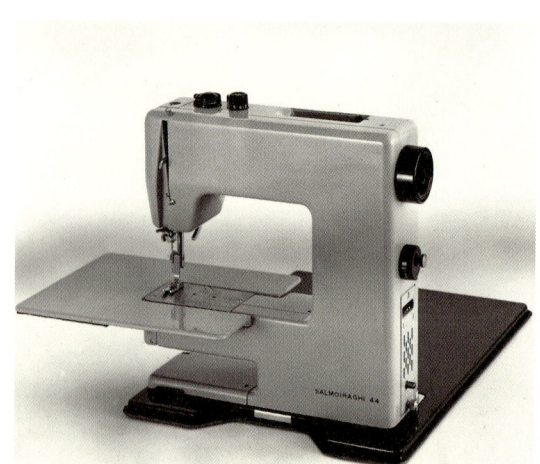

ポータブルミシン（サルモイラーギ社），1957年／Portable sewing machine, Salmoiraghi, 1957
共同者：ブルーノ・モラスッティ／With Bruno Morassutti

  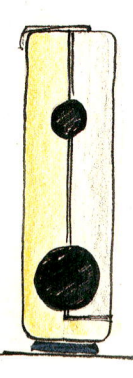

い方、もののつくり方の知識が豊富で、薄いシートメタルを曲げただけで強度を出し、それに構造的な役割をもたせた材を、パドバの「モラスッティ社倉庫」の屋根に使っている。また、彼は石材の性質にも熟知し、大理石とセレーナ石、御影石のそれぞれに異なる性質を活かしたテーブルのシリーズをデザインしている。塩化ビニル樹脂の特徴である弾力を活かした「CUB8」や「IN/OUT」のジョイントデザインも同様である。さらに、彼は工業製品でありながら自然素材のような豊かな表情をもつ、新しいインテリア素材である化粧用突板「ネヴァー・ザ・セイム」を開発している。

1980年代中頃から、彼は機械加工の新しい技術＝数値制御（NC）を活用して、大理石を加工する技術の可能性を研究し始めている。彼が考案した彫刻作品「コーノ・チエーロ（天空の円錐）」は、構造上の合理性という点ではブランクーシの「無限柱」を超えている。ブランクーシの作品では、同一のモデュールを高く積み重ねていくのに対し、マンジャロッティの作品の特徴は、テーパーをつけることで、構造上の必然性を獲得した新しい技術の成果である。

そのほかのプロジェクトにも、彼の感性、知性、能力、知識が活かされている。特にチニゼッロバルサーモにある「アルミタリア社屋」では、彼がすべての事務員、管理職、労働者に快適な環境を提供しようと腐心しているところに、彼らしさがよく表現されている。また、道路交通の積載量の新規制を契機に新しい構造「BILITH（2エレメント構成）」を考案し、梁のない大型の屋根材を可能にした仕事にも、マンジャロッティらしさがみられる。このように彼には素材がもつ可能性を引き出す力がある。例えば、連続する小さなヴォールト屋根で覆われたカッラーラの「インテルナツィオナーレ・マルミ・エ・マッキネ社のオフィス」は、まったく前例のない構法である。

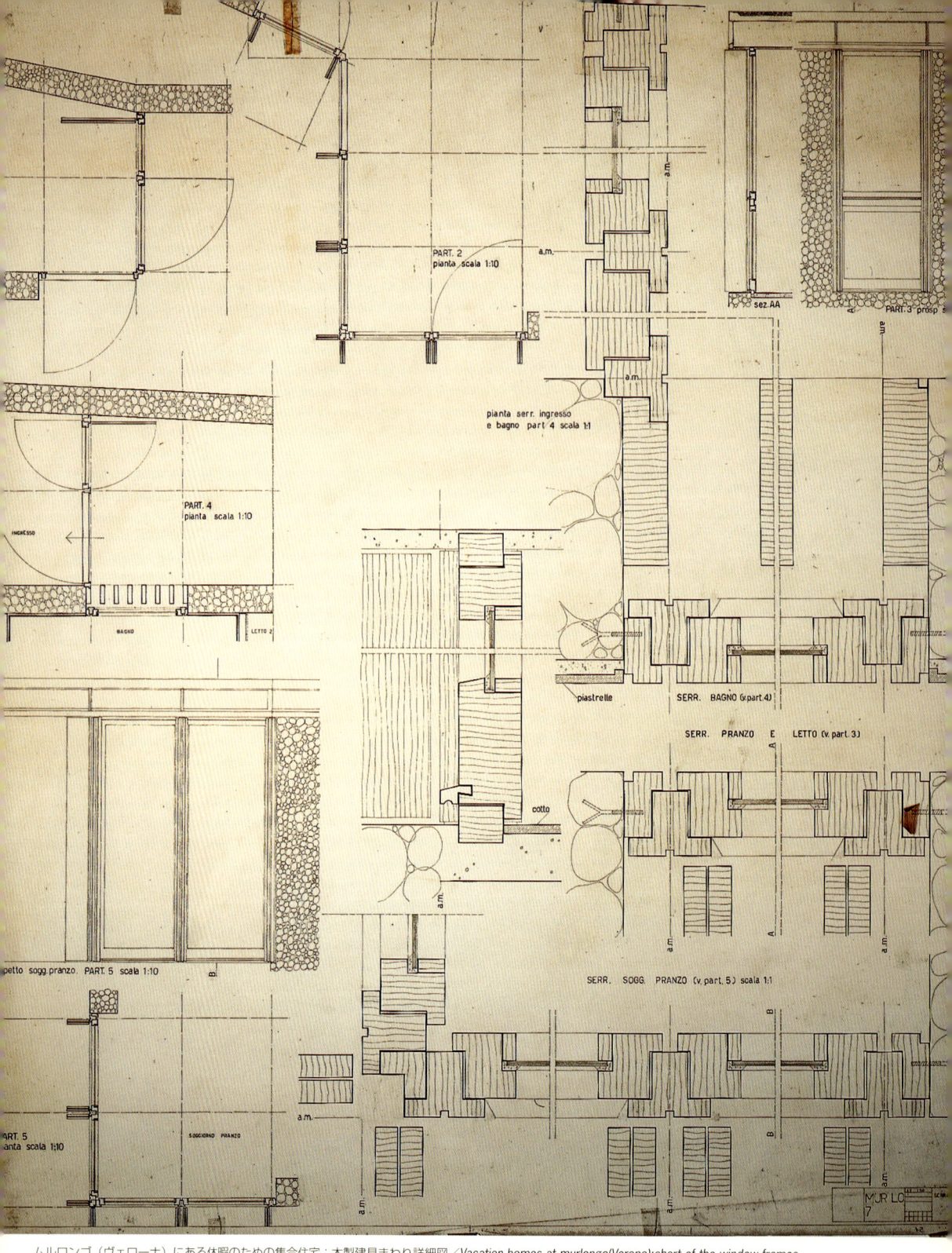

ムルロンゴ（ヴェローナ）にある休暇のための集合住宅：木製建具まわり詳細図／Vacation homes at murlongo(Verona):chart of the window frames

「クアドロンノ通りの集合住宅」では、すべての居住者の要求を満たすために、グリッドをなすモデュールの可能性を活かして、自由に間取りが変更できる住宅計画を提案している。コーヒーメーカーの設計では、すべての細部にわたって全神経が注がれている。「切削加工による大理石の花器」のシリーズでは、形を想像して楽しむために、できあがった瞬間に初めて形がわかるように工夫されている。「テラコッタ製組合せ植木鉢」では、草花の生長に応じて植替えの手間が省けるように、日常のささいなことにも配慮している。また、マンジャロッティの特徴は、試行錯誤を繰り返しながら結果を再考することにある。例えば、広範囲のガラス製品の開発では、用途に応じた機能を的確に満たすために800種ものデザインを試みている。傾けたときに氷が飛び出すことを防ぐウィスキー用グラス「アイス・ストッパー」、注ぎ口のまわりに残った油が垂れないように工夫した油さし「オルベ」、雌雄一体型の指輪「ヴェラ・ライカ」のジョイントは、結婚の結びつきに象徴されるようにそれぞれの機能が働いて、1つの指輪になるように極度に洗練されたデザインとなっている。孔をうがたれた1枚の四角いコールテン鋼でつくられたモニュメントは、「サンタンナの虐殺」をドラマティックに暗喩した表現である。

彼のクリエイティブな才能を引き出すスタディは、デザイナー特有の手段であるドローイングによって行われる。これが課題の核心とその解決法を明確にする彼の作業ツールである。彼は四六時中ドローイングを繰り返している。その線は、単純かつ明快で、情感にあふれ、正確な線である。彼のドローイングは鋭く形態を描き出し、解決する技術を明確に示している。この形態・解法・技術の根源は、素材の性質を探求することにある。言い換えると、素材が有する特徴や利点だけでなく、短所や欠点をも含めて素材の性質を深く理解することにある。そして、素材の条件にかかわらず、最適な解決策を見出すために、不適切でつじつまの合わない使い方を避けている。だか

自由な断面をもつブロンズの花器.
1979年／Free-section vases in bronze, 1979

ら彼の場合、素材の制約や限界は、決してデザインの障害ではなく、むしろ困難を克服するための刺激剤となっている。

マンジャロッティは、実にユニークなクリエーターであり、さまざまな流派（イズム）とは一線を画している。彼はより緻密でより創造的なプルーヴェであり、多様性を好むエンジニアリングのセンスをもったミースであり、融通のきく懐の広いモランディである。

彼は作家でありながら、コストパフォーマンスに対するセンスを有している。これは近代の重要な課題ではあるが、今日ではほとんど忘れかけられている。この課題はあまりにコントロールが難しく、追求することが困難なために、過去のものとして片づけられがちである。だがそれは、より質のよい建築を何千人もが働く工場に提供するためにプレファブ工法に取り組み始めたこのデザイナーにとっては、乗り越えなければならない課題である。仕事を遂行することの正しさ（幸せは的確な仕事によりもたらされる）によって満足を得るに至った巨匠の彼は、倫理と審美性のやっかいな二元論を高いレベルでの調和へと導く、類い稀な成功に到達したのである。

(M.K)

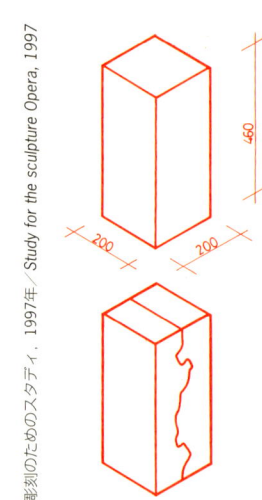

彫刻のためのスタディ、1997年／Study for the sculpture Opera, 1997

ANGELO MANGIAROTTI
"HAPPINESS COMES FROM CORRECTNESS"

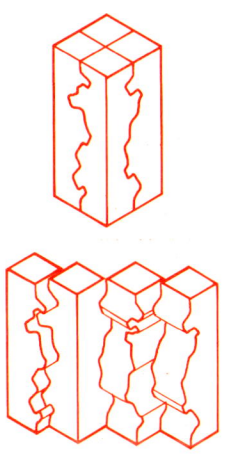

This image (page 6) sums up the work of Angelo Mangiarotti. A laborer brandishing a hammer, assembling a structure that will serve to protect him. An architecture that can be made simply, without excessive expenditure of economic resources, without exaggerated technological effort. This is the meaning of the hammer: to maintain a direct, controlled relationship with the things of architecture and design. Mangiarotti is aware of the importance of the role of the worker, the craftsman, the master builder. People from whom to steal astuteness, to whom to delegate decisions and suggest possibilities. This is his job. A capacity for relations based on extreme sensitivity and respect for materials and the work of others. A love that has deep roots in childhood and family. His father was the owner of a well-known bakery. Mangiarotti remembers, as in a dream, the small but decisive actions required to produce a work (in this case fragrant bread and pastries). Infinite reasoning on the ingredients (flour, water, yeast, oil, salt, etc) and their characteristics: there is good flour and bad, one yeast or another, and then there's the water (Mangiarotti recalls that his father went to Como for water, "because the water was good") and oil (his father spoke of "oil specially shipped from Liguria"). Then came the operations of mixing and baking, where gestures and timing are decisive for the results. All this was the experience of the need to work well to achieve good results: knowledge with which to appreciate, to utilize, to realize, to obtain. Therefore it was possible for Mangiarotti to use light

構造体のスタディ, 1975年 / Study for a structure, 1975

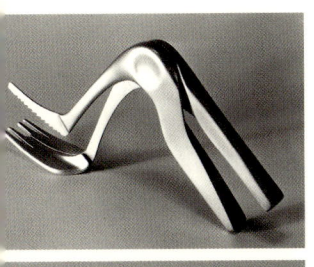
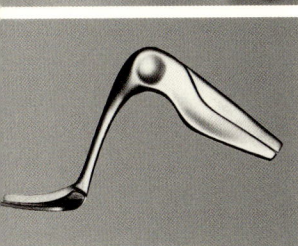

身障者のためのナイフ・フォーク, 1987年 / Knife-fork utensil for the handicapped, 1987

sheet metal, strengthened and given a structural role simply by bending, for the roofing of the Morassutti warehouse in Padua. Thus, knowing the characteristics of stone materials, he was able to design several series of tables that exploit the different characteristics of marble, pietra serena and granite. Thus, utilizing the characteristic elasticity of PVC, he was able to create the joints of the Cub8 and In/Out systems for accessorized walls. Yes, love and knowledge, also for the techniques of working and production. So he has even reinvented a semi-finished furnishing product, wood veneer (Never the same), making it variable like a product of nature, but produced by a machine. In the mid-eighties he began to reason on the possibilities offered by new numerically controlled machines for the working of marble, creating new marvels such as the sculpture Cono Cielo: an action that surpasses the Infinite Column of Brancusi, at least in terms of constructive intelligence: in the former, an identical module that rises in height without changing its dimensions, in the latter a body that tapers because it is necessary, in terms of construction, and possible in terms of production. Other projects shed light on the various shadings of his sensibility, intelligence, ability, knowledge. All of Mangiarotti is there in the Armitalia plant in Cinisello Balsamo, when he worries about offering identical conditions of comfort in the spaces for clerks, managers and workers. All of Mangiarotti is there when he invents a new structure like the Bilith which, stimulated by new regulations to facilitate road transport of large loads, leads to larger roofing segments that make it possible to eliminate the beams. There is his ability to explore the hidden characteristics of a given material, as in the offices of Internazionale Marmi e Macchine in Carrara, where the roofing is entirely made of small marble vaults, an unprecedented procedure. There is the pleasure of anticipating the desires of users, hypothesizing housing that can be easily varied, taking advantage of the infinite possibilities offered by a modular grid, as in the apartments on Via Quadronno. There's the painstaking attention to the smallest details in the design of a coffeemaker. There's the pleasure of imagining forms that find their definition only in the moment of production, as in the Variazioni vases in milled marble. There's the gauging of attention to the minimum, resolving little everyday problems, as in the design of flowerpot components in terracotta, a reaction to the problem of how to avoid transplanting growing houseplants. There's the taste for experimentation, testing, trial and error, and rethinking of results achieved. As in the extensive research on glass objects (as many as 800 designs) for precise satisfaction of different utilization needs: a glass for whiskey that keeps the ice from moving during sips (Ice Stopper glass), or an oil cruet that stops drips from reaching the sides or the grip (Olpe). And there's the extreme sophism of the male-female joint designed for the Vera Laica, a ring that functions in the relation of its two parts, like the union of marriage it represents. Finally, there is the striking narrative force of a sheet of perforated corten steel, a dramatic allusion to the massacre of Sant'Anna di Stazzema (Massacro a Sant'Anna). A creative talent whose research and reasoning are often developed through that particular tool of the designer: the drawing. A working tool with which to

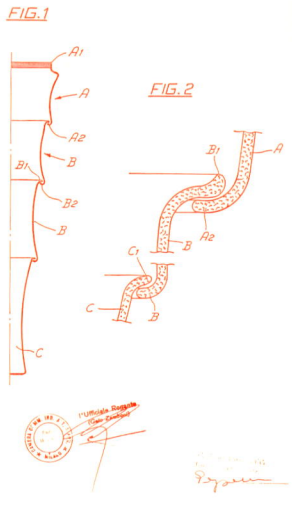

ランプ「V on V」ヴィストージ社, 1967年／Lamp V su V, Vistosi, 1967

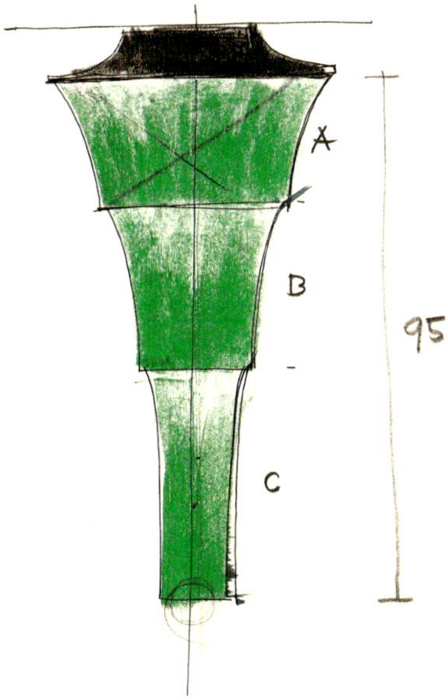

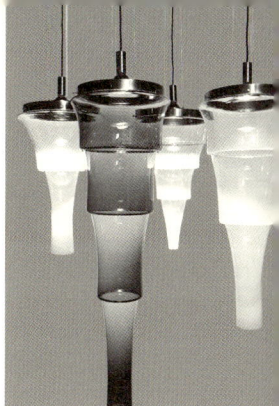

A
B
95
C

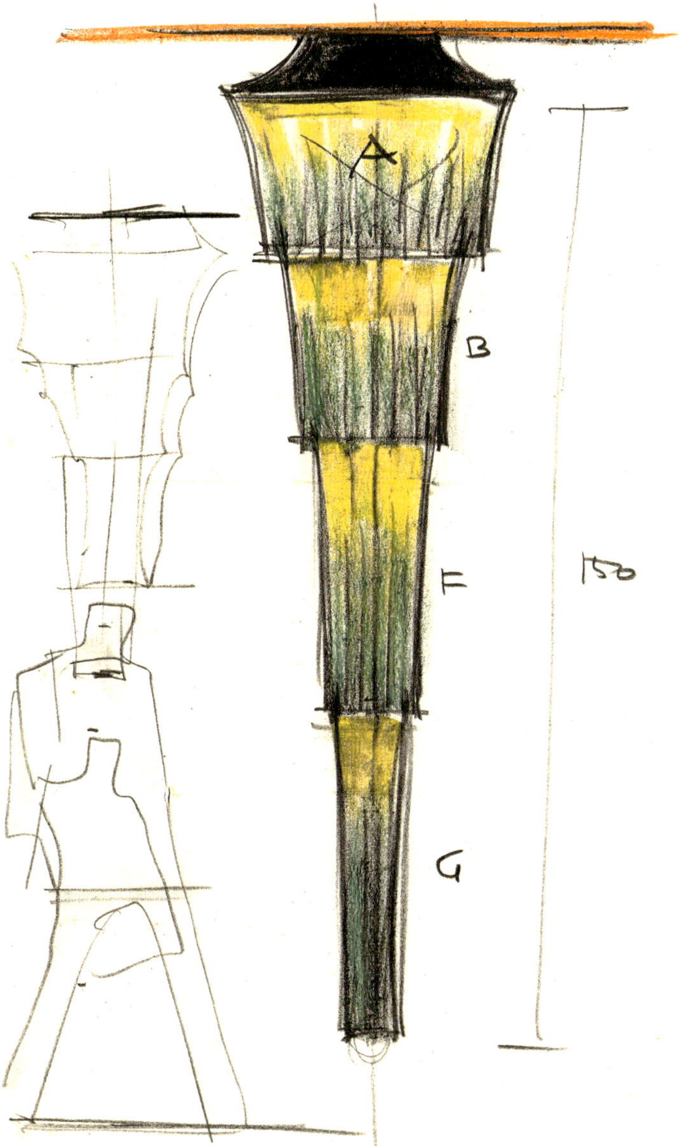

A
B
F
150
G

bring problems and solutions into focus. Mangiarotti never stops drawing, with lines that are never complicated or undecipherable, always evocative and precise. Drawings that sharply narrate forms, therefore, solutions, therefore techniques. Forms, solutions and techniques found by reasoning on the characteristics of a material, explored in depth, case by case, with the pleasure of unveiling and comprehending its qualities, but also of identifying its drawbacks and defects. And then, forgetting about those limitations (every material has some), to find correct solutions, avoiding inappropriate, inconsistent, incoherent applications. Thus the limitations are never an impediment to the project, but a stimulus to go overcome constraints. A unique creator, isolated perhaps, certainly far from all the isms. A more rigorous and creative Prouvé, a Mies with a bent for engineering and an appreciation of diversity, a more versatile, open-minded Morandi. An author with economy in mind (economy, not economics or business), that great precept of the modern, a nearly forgotten objective in this moment in history. A goal that is willingly relegated to the past, as it is difficult to control and laborious to pursue. An ideal to cherish, instead, for a designer who began to work on prefabrication to "improve the architectural quality of the factories in which thousands of people would have to work". A master who has reached contentment through the correctness of doing ("Happiness comes from correctness"), who is capable, as rarely occurs, of achieving a sublime reconciliation of the troublesome dualism between ethics and aesthetics. B.F.

エルネスト・ネイサン・ロジャース作『アンジェロ・マンジャロッティの肖像画』、1955年 / Angelo mangiarotti in a portrait by Ernesto Nathan Rogers, 1955

CHIESA MATER MISERICORDIAE A BARANZATE (MILANO), 1957

バランザーテの教会／ミラノ，1957年

この現代建築の傑作はミラノ郊外に建設されている。この建物は、鉄筋コンクリートの主要構造体と、全周を囲む二重ガラス壁による極めて明解な直方体のボリュームである。4本の柱は、2本の主要な短辺方向の梁を支え、その上に6本の梁が長辺方向に架けられている。この6本の梁は非常に特徴的なX字型の断面をもつプレキャストコンクリート部材で構成され、梁にあけられた穴に差し込まれるワイヤーケーブルにテンションをかけて順次組み立てられる。この構造の技術的解決方法は特筆に値する。6本の梁の上に載せられる屋根材は交差リブによって剛性を増している。発泡スチロールの断熱パネルをはさみこんだ二重ガラス壁は、透明なガラス面により屋根と視覚的に分節化（アーティキュレイト）されている。主礼拝堂の床レベルは建物周囲の地盤面より高く設定され、それと同じ高さのコンクリートと河原の石でつくられた周壁がこの宗教的空間を周辺地域から隔離し守っている。

(M.T)

天井伏図／Intrados plan

MATER MISERICORDIAE CHURCH, BARANZATE (MILAN), 1957. On the outskirts of Milan, a masterpiece of contemporary architecture. A load-bearing structure in reinforced concrete, with double glass panes to create a very pure volume of crystalline proportions. Four pilasters support two main beams on which six secondary beams rest. The latter are made with prefabricated blocks of reinforced concrete (strikingly characterized by their X section), assembled with prestressing cables that cross them, following the pattern of the stresses in a truly noteworthy technical-constructive solution. The roofing segments, resting on the secondary beam structure, are reinforced by crossed ribbing that "designs" the intrados. The double-pane glass walls (containing an insulation panel in polystyrene) are separated from the roofing by a narrow pane of glass. The level of the hall is raised with respect to the surrounding terrain and coincides with that of the perimeter wall (in concrete and river stones) that isolates and shelters the place of worship from the surrounding territory.

共同者:ブルーノ・モラスッティ／With Bruno Morassutti
構造設計:アルド・ファビーニ／Structures Aldo Favini

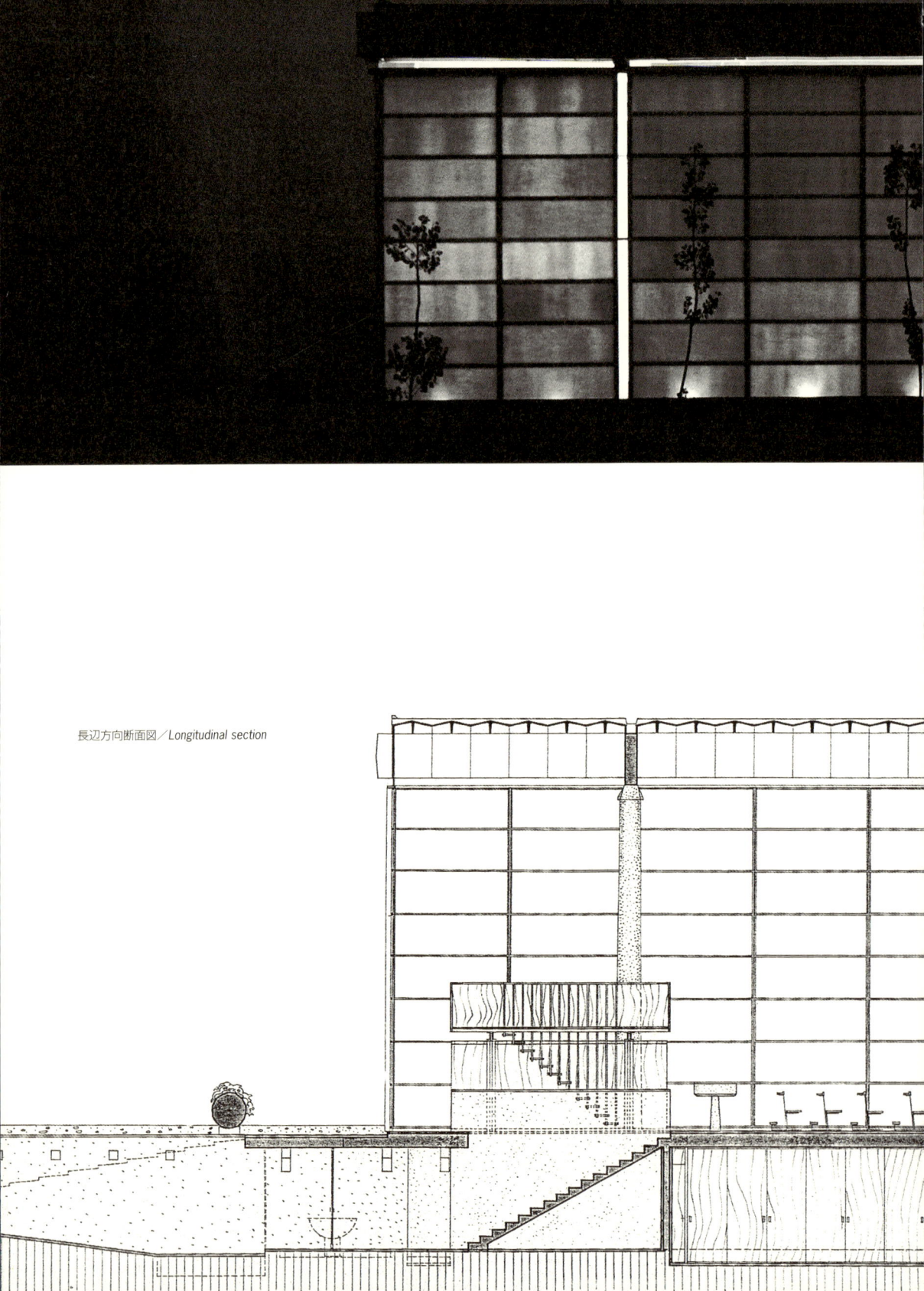

長辺方向断面図／Longitudinal section

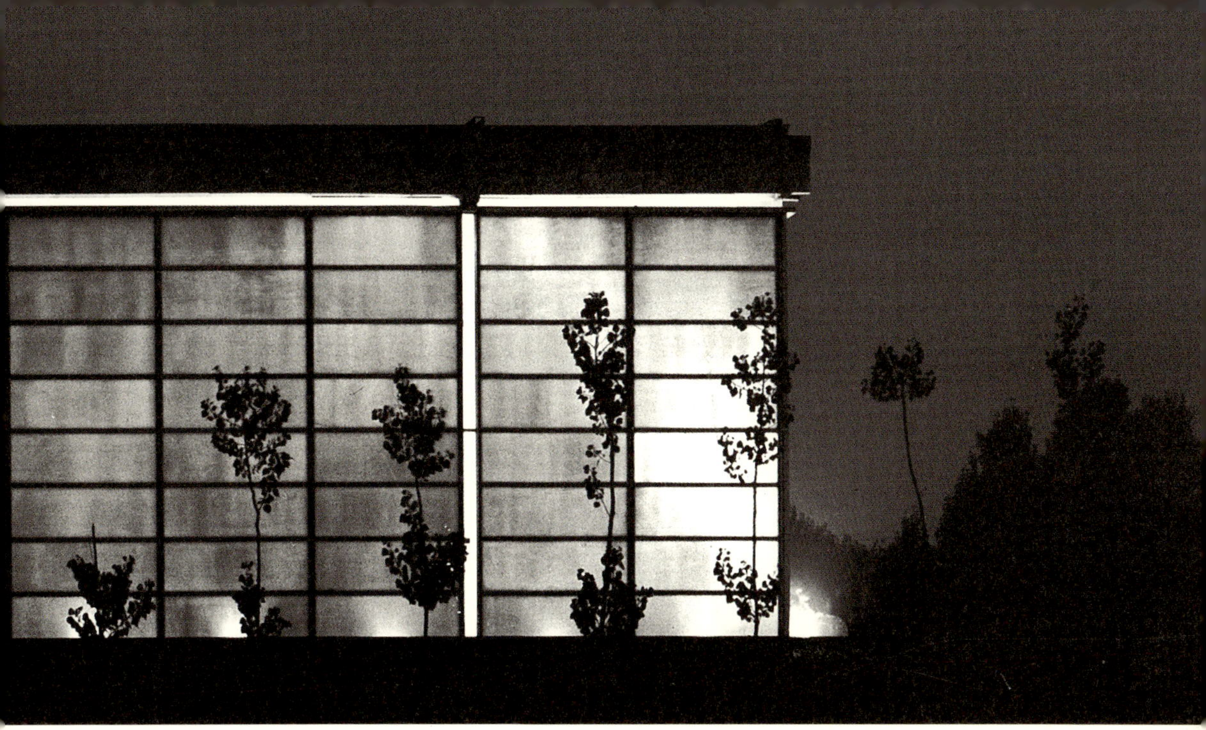

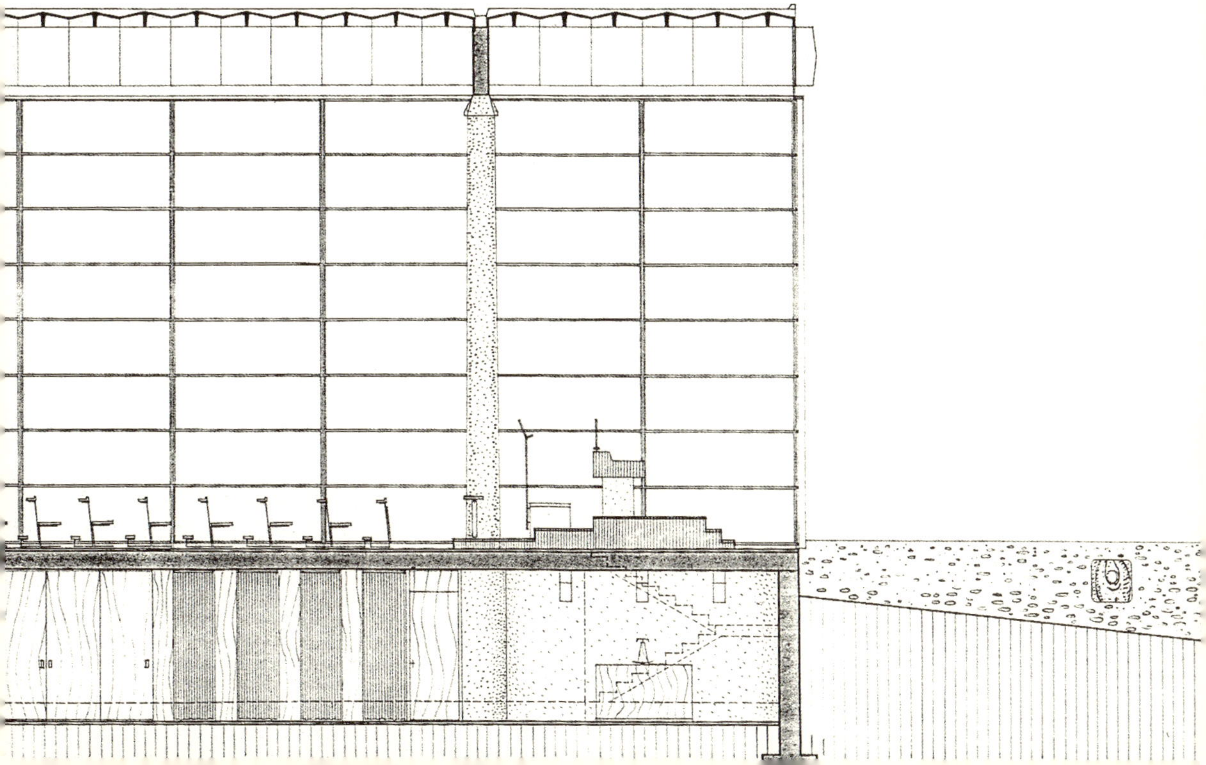

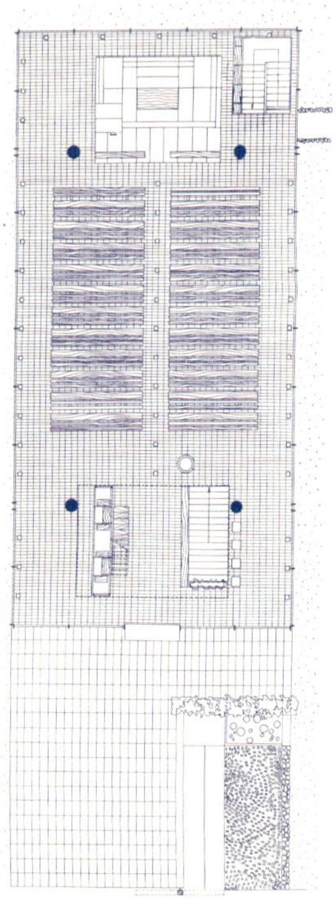

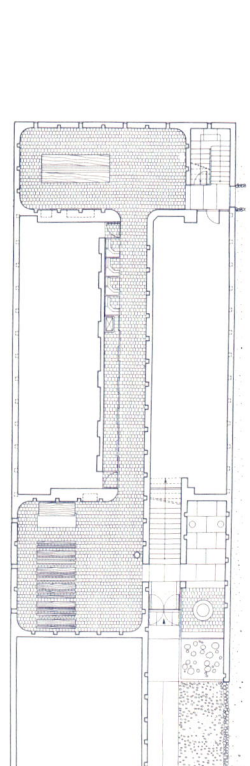

教会平面図 / Plan of the church

地下聖堂平面図 / Plan of crypt

DEPOSITO SPLÜGEN BRÄU
A MESTRE (VENEZIA), 1962

スプリューゲン・ブロイ社倉庫／メストレ（ヴェネツィア），1962年

この倉庫は、鉄筋コンクリートによるプレファブリケーションの代表例である。円形の断面をもつ4本の柱が一辺22mの正方形の屋根版を支えることで、建築的基本ユニットを構成している。正方形の屋根版は8本の梁型部材にワイヤーケーブルを通し、ポストテンションをかけることでできている。この倉庫は、2つの正方形の屋根版をつないでつくられ、川に向かって張り出した屋根が船荷の積み下ろし作業時には、キャノピーの役割を果たしている。この建物の天井は、梁上部の張出し屋根スラブとして機能し、梁下部は構造上の背骨として機能していて、それらが一体化した形態に特徴がある。生産と構造における経済性を考慮しつつ、純化したブルータリストの意匠をまとったリズムと全体構成の珠玉の美を創出している。

(M.O)

SPLÜGEN BRÄU WAREHOUSE, MESTRE (VENICE), 1962. A lesson in prefabrication of reinforced concrete. An architectural module in which four pilasters with a circular section support a square roofing slab measuring 22 meters per side. Each slab is formed by eight beams fabricated on site, connected crosswise by prestressing cables. Two modules placed side by side form this industrial warehouse where the overhangs of the roofing toward the river offer shelter for operations of loading and unloading freight. The intrados is marked by the complex of the structural ribbing of the beams (where the upper wing serves only as covering) and represents a true gem of rhythm and composition for this construction based on a brutalist language, but not a question of mannerism, because it is purified by the implicit economy of productive and structural considerations.

構造設計：アルド・ファビーニ／*Structures Aldo Favini*

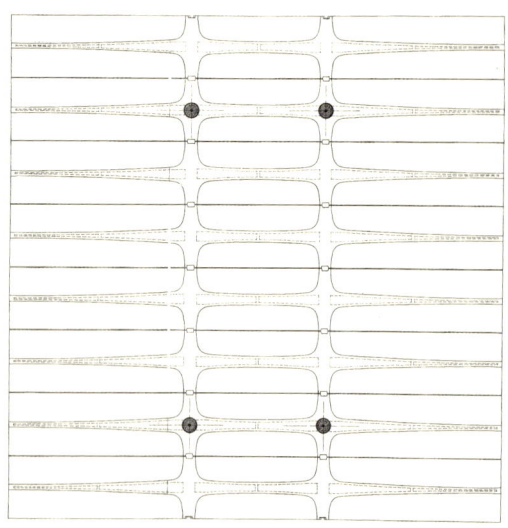

天井伏図／Intrados plan

オフィスとガレージのための建物／Building for offices and garage

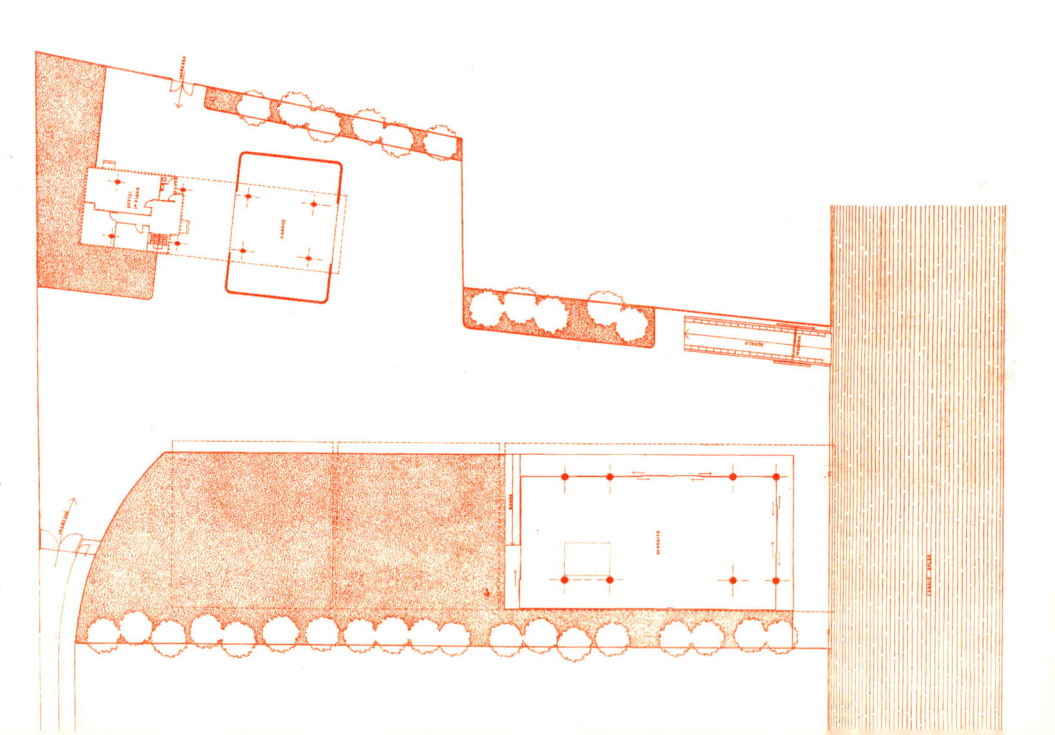

配置図／General plan

長辺方向断面図／Cross section

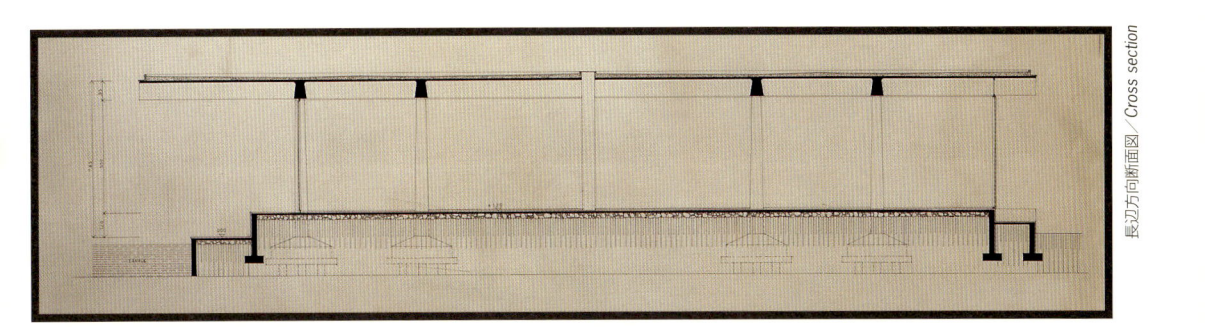

UN ELEMENTO PORTANTE-COPRENTE

DEPOSITO MORASSUTTI A PADOVA, 1958

モラスッティ社倉庫／パドバ，1958年

レンガ、アルミ、ガラスで覆われたこの建物は、現場打ち鉄筋コンクリートの柱と梁で構成され、長辺方向に二分された正方形のプランである。

この屋根は対になっている鋼板を折り曲げることで、六角形の断面をもつ梁を形成しているところに特徴がある。この形態は構造的にも大きな耐力をつくり出すことができる。自然採光は、この六角形の梁を貫通した鋼板による円筒の上に載せた透明ドームを通して建物内部に導かれる。一方、人口照明は六角形の梁の先端に取り付けられ、点灯すると屋根の軽さを強調するようにデザインされている。移動クレーンのレールとして利用できるC型形状を背中合わせにした鉄筋コンクリートの梁の造形は、巨匠フランコ・アルビーニをも感心させ、以後移動クレーンが用いられる倉庫の常套手段になった。

(C.I)

共同者：ブルーノ・モラスッティ／With Bruno Morassutti
構造設計：アルド・ファビーニ／Structures Aldo Favini

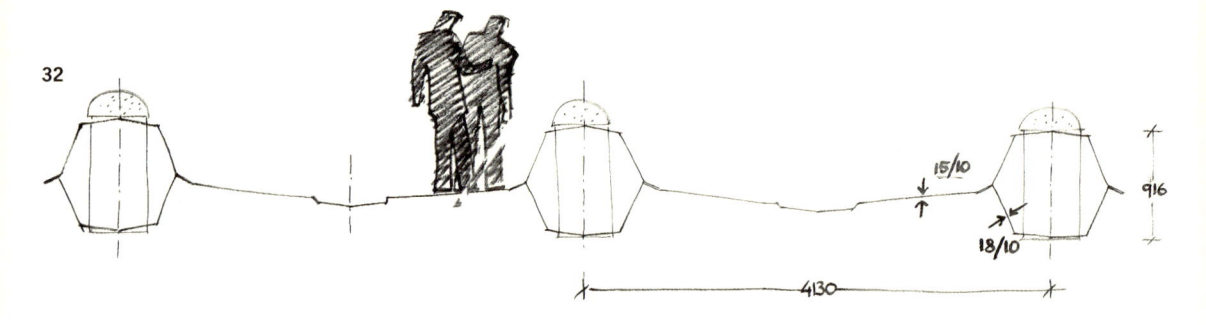

MORASSUTTI WAREHOUSE, PADUA, 1958. A building with a rectangular plan, divided into two longitudinal spans, paced by a structure of pilasters and beams in reinforced concrete, poured on site, filled with elements in brick, aluminium and glass. The characteristic roofing is formed by two coupled sheets of steel that bend to form the hexagonal-section beams: a high level of resistance obtained by means of form. Natural lighting enters through special sheet-metal cylinders (topped by transparent domes) inserted in the hexagonal beams (contributing to strengthen them), while the artificial lighting, positioned at the ends of the beams, seems to draw attention to the extreme lightness of the overall design. The double-C profile of the structural beams in reinforced concrete – now a part of collective memory, after having astonished even Franco Albini – is determined by the assembly requirements of the bridge crane utilized in the warehouse.

天井伏図／*Intrados plan*

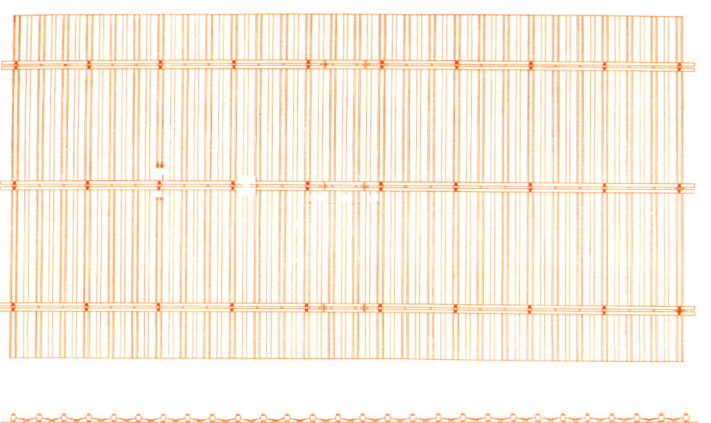

立面図／*Elevation*

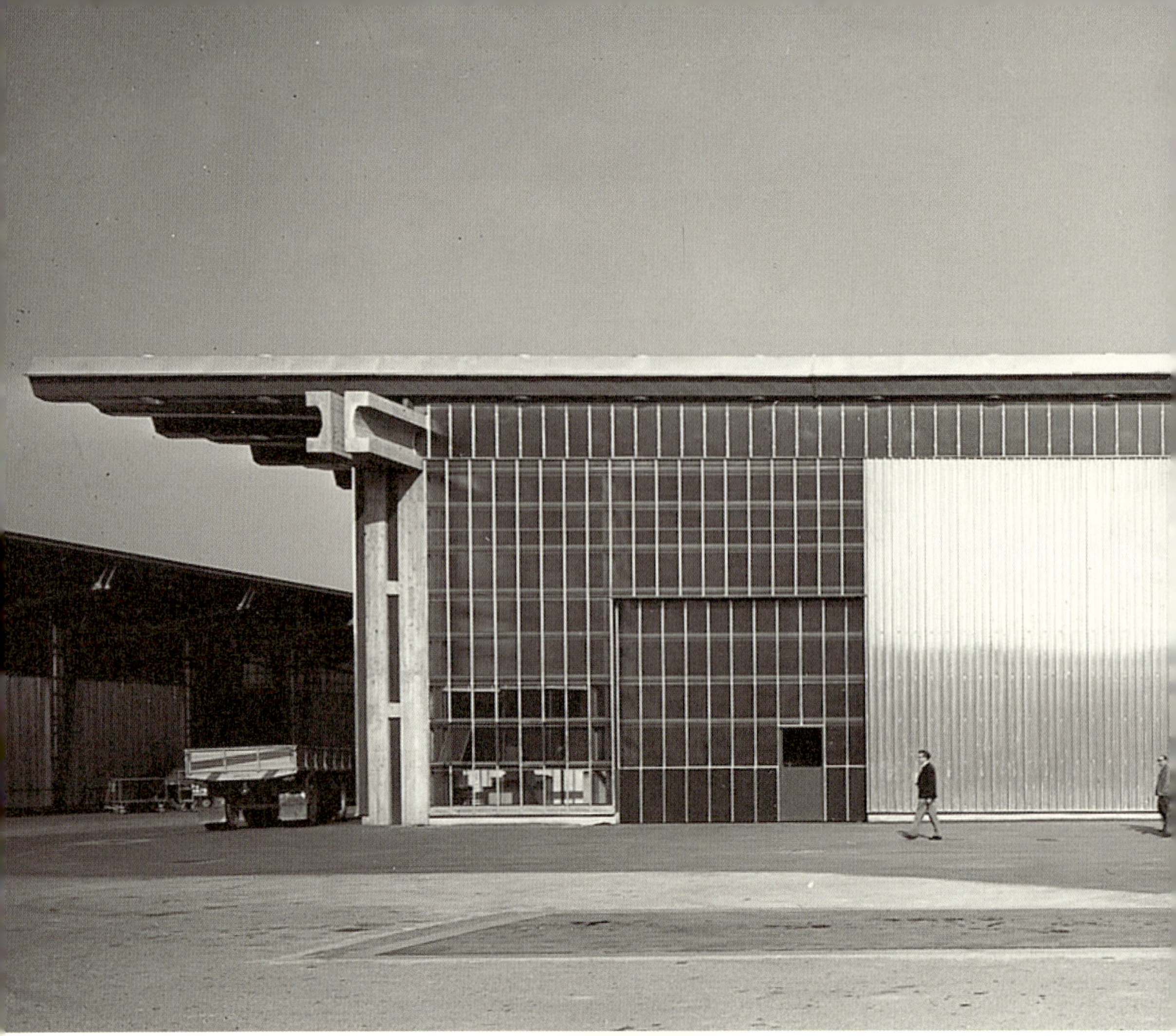

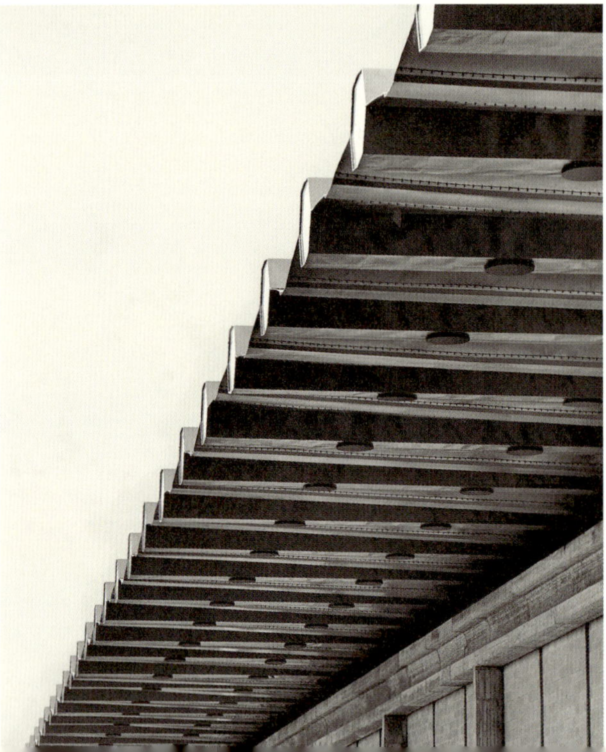

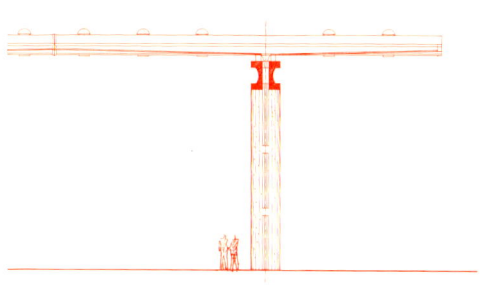

柱と梁の接合部詳細図／Details of the joint between column and beam

構造設計：メタリケ・フィンシデール構造設計事務所（ファブリーツィオ・デ・ミランダ）／Structures Costruzioni Metalliche Finsider(Fabrizio De Miranda)

PADIGLIONE PER ESPOSIZIONI ALLA FIERA DEL MARE A GENOVA, 1963

海の見本市展示館／ジェノヴァ，1963年

船の模型を展示するために設計された建物である。

マンジャロッティは「現実の船を展示する場」としてこの建物を設計した。この空間は、円錐形の4本の鋼製支柱と、それに支えられた大屋根で構成される鉄骨構造に特徴がある。大屋根は、網目状の内部構造に厚さ2mmの鋼板を上下の引張側と圧縮側に用いて、大きな凸レンズ状のフォルムになっている。それは、同時に訪問者の視線を海に向けて知覚的に拡張する作用に働かせている。反対に、屋根の下に設けられたディスプレイケースは、凹面状に向き合わせることにより、訪問者の注意を展示内容に引込む作用に働かせている。

講演会や研修のための講義室は、石で仕上げられた基壇下の地下に設けられている。ジェノヴァ滞在中に建築家でありエンジニアでもあるコンラッド・ウォッシュマンを感動させたこの建物は、保存状態がよかったにもかかわらず、2000年に取り壊された。彼の傑作の1つが消え去ってしまった。

(O.H)

基壇（展示スペース）平面図／*Plan of the platform*

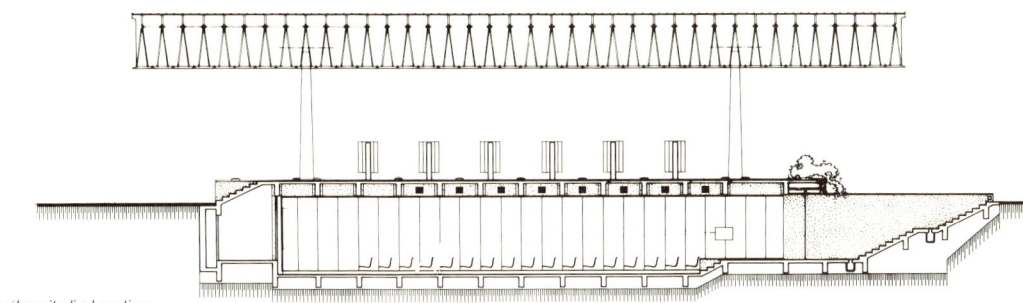

長辺方向断面図／*Longitudinal section*

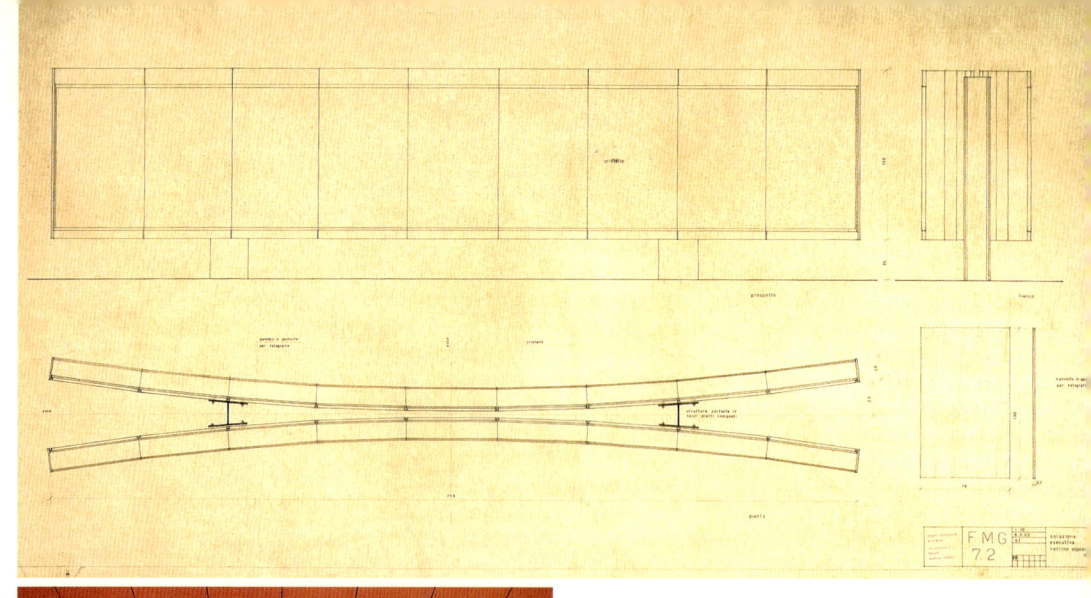

ショーケース / Display cases

lla nave

EXPOSITION PAVILION AT THE FIERA DEL MARE, GENOA, 1963. *A pavilion for the display of boats, according to the initial request of the client. An open place "in which to see the vessels as they are", according to Mangiarotti.. A space defined by a steel structure composed of four truncated cone pilasters and a large roof (made with 2-mm sheet metal held in tension by a reticular structure), with a lenticular profile that opens perception of the space and guides the*

gaze of the visitor toward the seascape. Beneath the roof, on the other hand, the concave display windows attract attention to their contents. At the lower level, beneath the base clad in stone, an auditorium is placed for presentations and conferences. In spite of the fact that it was still in excellent condition, the building – which impressed Konrad Wachsmann during his stay in Genoa – was demolished in 2000. A fallen hero.

CASA IN VIA GAVIRATE A MILANO, 1959

ガヴィラーテ通りの集合住宅／ミラノ，1959年

中央の鉄筋コンクリートの柱で支えられた最上階の大梁から吊るされた、それぞれ3つのシリンダーからなる集合住宅は、1フロア3住戸で構成されている。入居者のプライバシーを守るため、3つのシリンダーは1つのアクセス空間からそれぞれ垂直の動線でつながっている。荷重を支える中央スペースがそれぞれの住戸へのアプローチになっており、自由な平面と立面構成を可能にしている。規格化された木製パネルで構成された立面は、目隠しパネルと窓付パネルを自由に選択することが可能である。最上階にある管理人住居の平面計画は小さいながらも、設計は秀逸で賞賛に値する。屋上庭園では、周りを高く取り囲むパラペットがミラノの建築ブームに乗って建設された異常な景観や外部からの視線を遮り、広がる空を享受することができる。リチャード・ノイトラがイタリア旅行の際に立ち寄り、この集合住宅を絶賛している。

(Ka.M)

1階平面図／Ground floor plan　　　基準階平面図／Typical floor plan

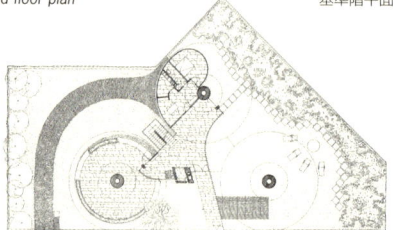

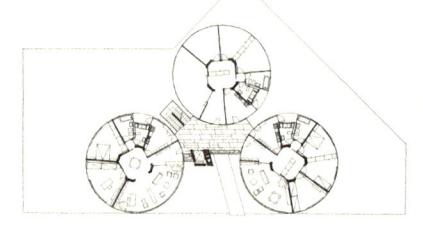

共同者：ブルーノ・モラスッティ／
With Bruno Morassutti
構造設計：アルド・ファビーニ／
Structures Aldo Favini

RESIDENTIAL BUILDING ON VIA GAVIRATE, MILAN, 1959. Three cylinders suspended on central structures in reinforced concrete, three buildings containing just one apartment per floor, in keeping with precise privacy requirements of the clients, three independent volumes joined by access spaces and vertical connections. The load-bearing structure crosses each apartment only at its center, permitting free layouts and elevations, where the external wood facing can alternate closed panels and window-frame modules. The custodian's lodging is a small planimetric gem; it would be a dream to enjoy the "sky rights" of the hanging gardens on the top level, sheltered from prying eyes by the upper cornice that completes the top of these unusual figures in the Milan of the boom years. During his trips to Italy Richard Neutra never failed to make a stop to admire this complex.

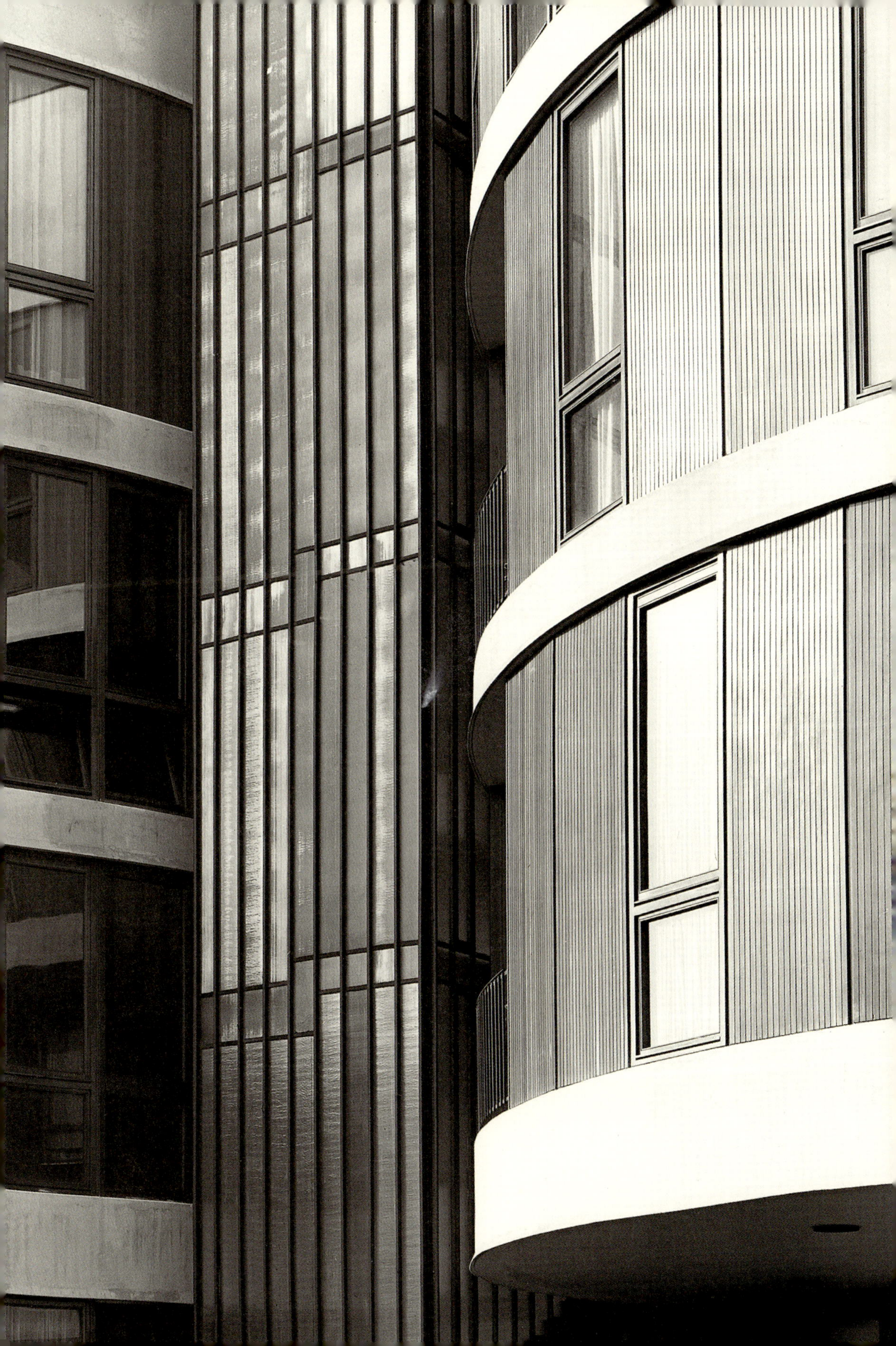

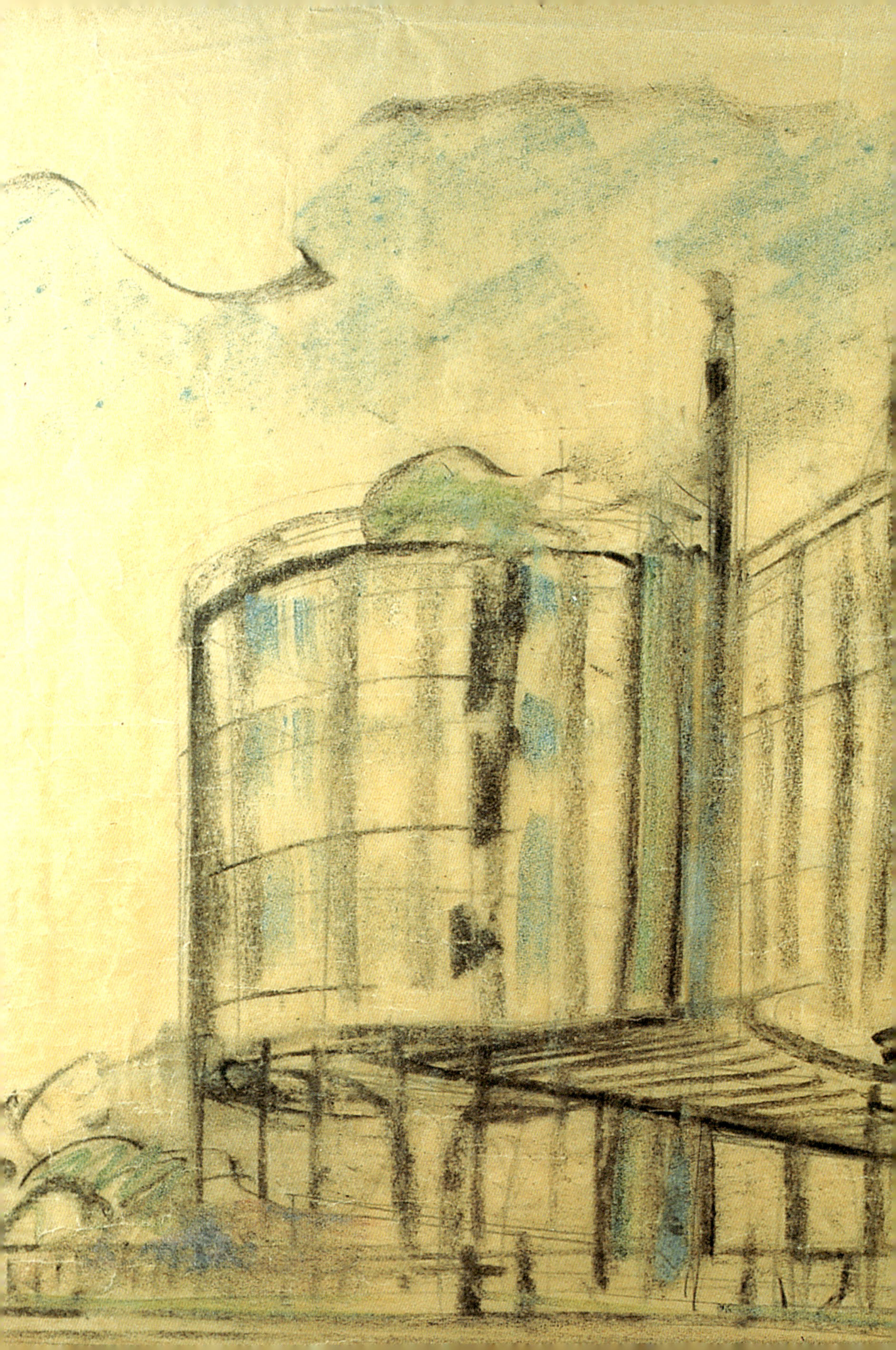

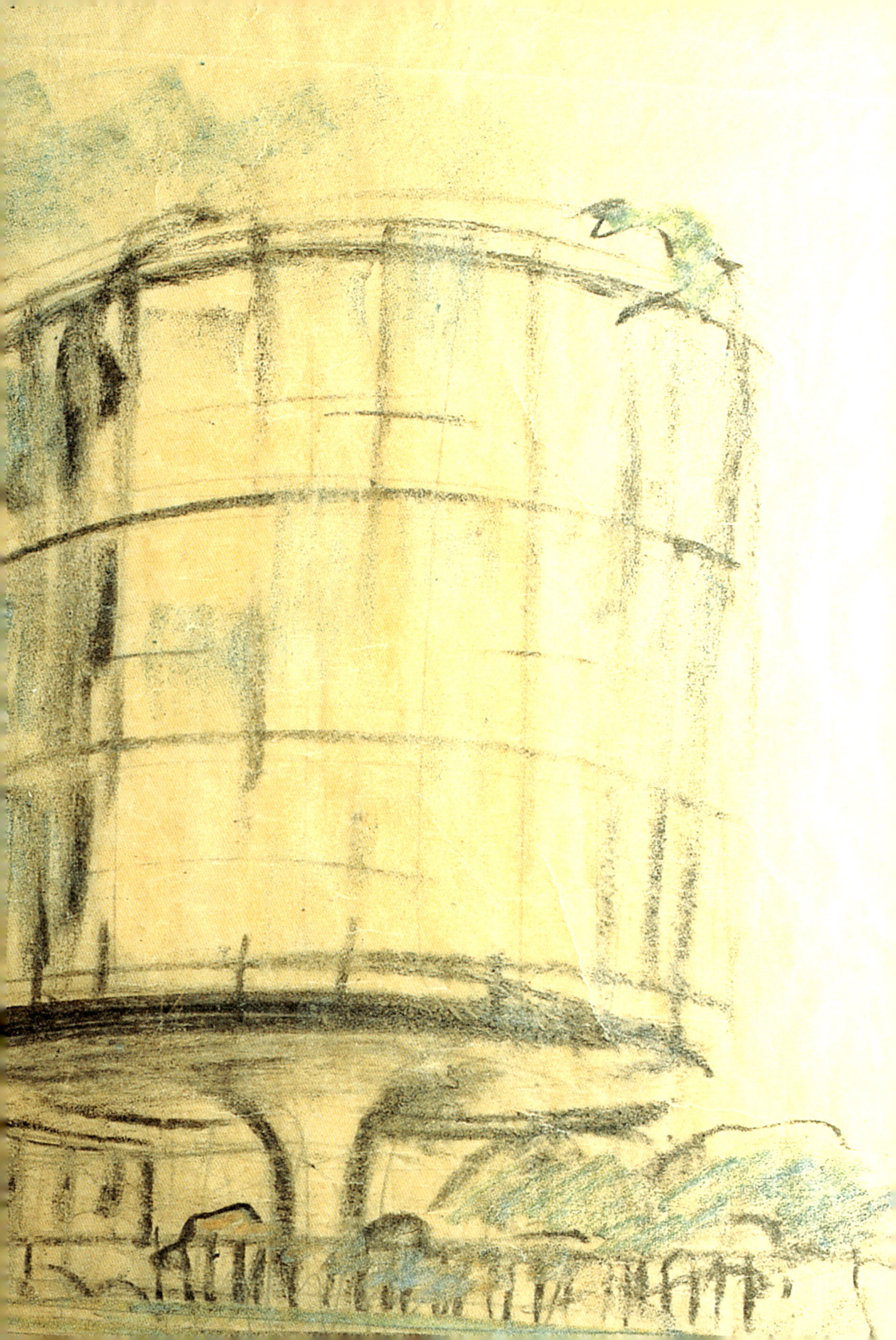

CASA IN VIA QUADRONNO A MILANO, 1960

クアドロンノ通りの集合住宅／ミラノ，1960年

この集合住宅は、イタリアだけでなく、世界中で最も称賛されている現代建築である。エレガントでダイナミック、そしてリズミカルで簡潔なデザイン（オリジナル案では2棟だった）は、伝統的な構造（鉄筋コンクリートの柱と壁）を用いて、極めて現代的なデザインになっている。居住者は、好みに合わせて自由に平面計画を選択でき、外装パネルの選択も可能である。ファサードのデザインに用いられているモデュラーグリッドは、自由な立面構成を可能としながらも調和を目指している。それぞれのグリッドは木製パネル、ガラスパネル（枠は木製）、またバルコニーにも適応でき、これらのエレメントの組合せによるさまざまなバリエーションをもっている。例えばインナーバルコニーをつくることができたり、木製目隠しパネルを窓付パネルに取り替えることができる。この集合住宅は居住者のすべての要求を満足させながら、デザインが破綻することもない。マンジャロッティは、この集合住宅において、居住者の要望をデザインに活かすという理想を実現している。

(Ke.M)

共同者：ブルーノ・モラスッティ／With Bruno Morassutti
構造設計：アルド・ファビーニ／Structures Aldo Favini

RESIDENTIAL BUILDING ON VIA QUADRONNO, MILAN, 1960. One of the most admired, best-loved examples of contemporary architecture, Italian or otherwise. Elegant, dynamic and musical, terse, the design for Via Quadronno (originally planned as two buildings) employs a traditional structure (pilasters and walls in reinforced concrete, arranged in such a way as to reduce layout constraints) to achieve an extremely modern solution: allowing each individual homeowner the possibility of choosing his own internal plan, all the way to the external facings. A modular grid for the design of the facades permits control of the composition of the elevations, simultaneously aimed at freedom and harmony. The grid is variegated by solid wooden panels, window frames (also in wood) or balconies. These elements are also designed for variation of position in time, permitting transformation, for example, of balconies into interior rooms, or windows into solid walls. A practically unsurpassed model of residential building focused on the needs of users, while avoiding the pitfalls of the uncontrollable "architecture of participation": Mangiarotti achieves results without useless utopias.

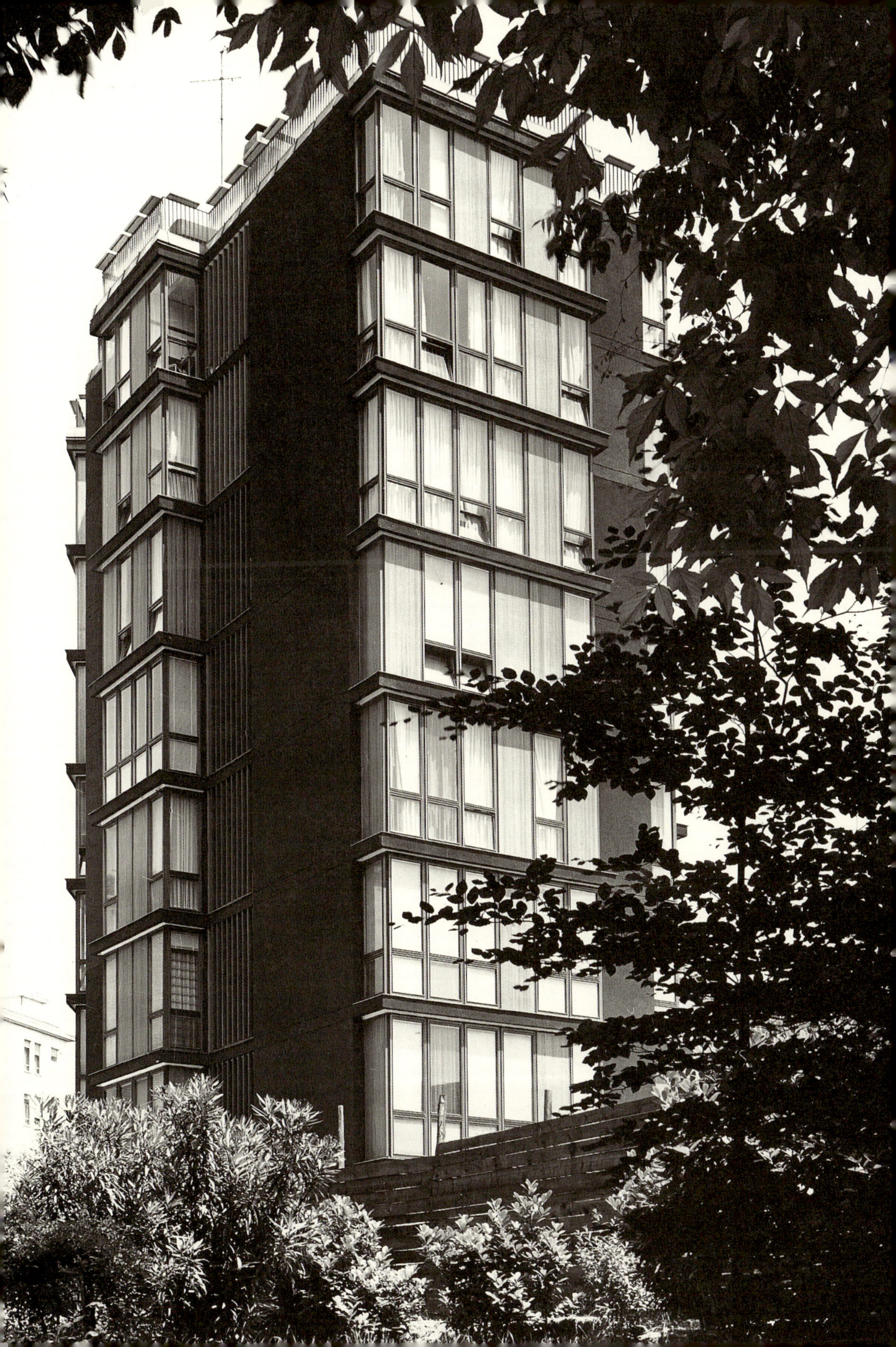

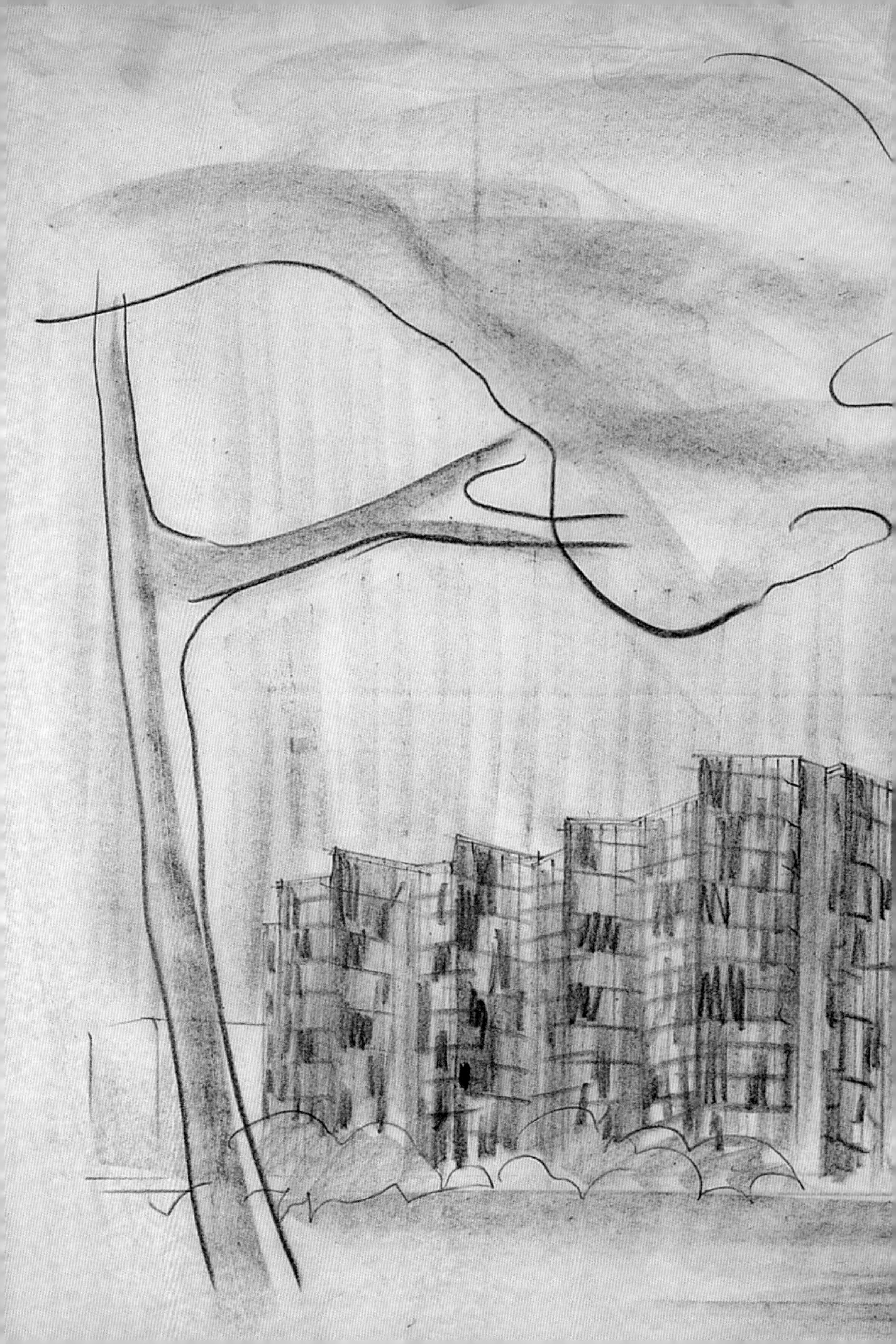

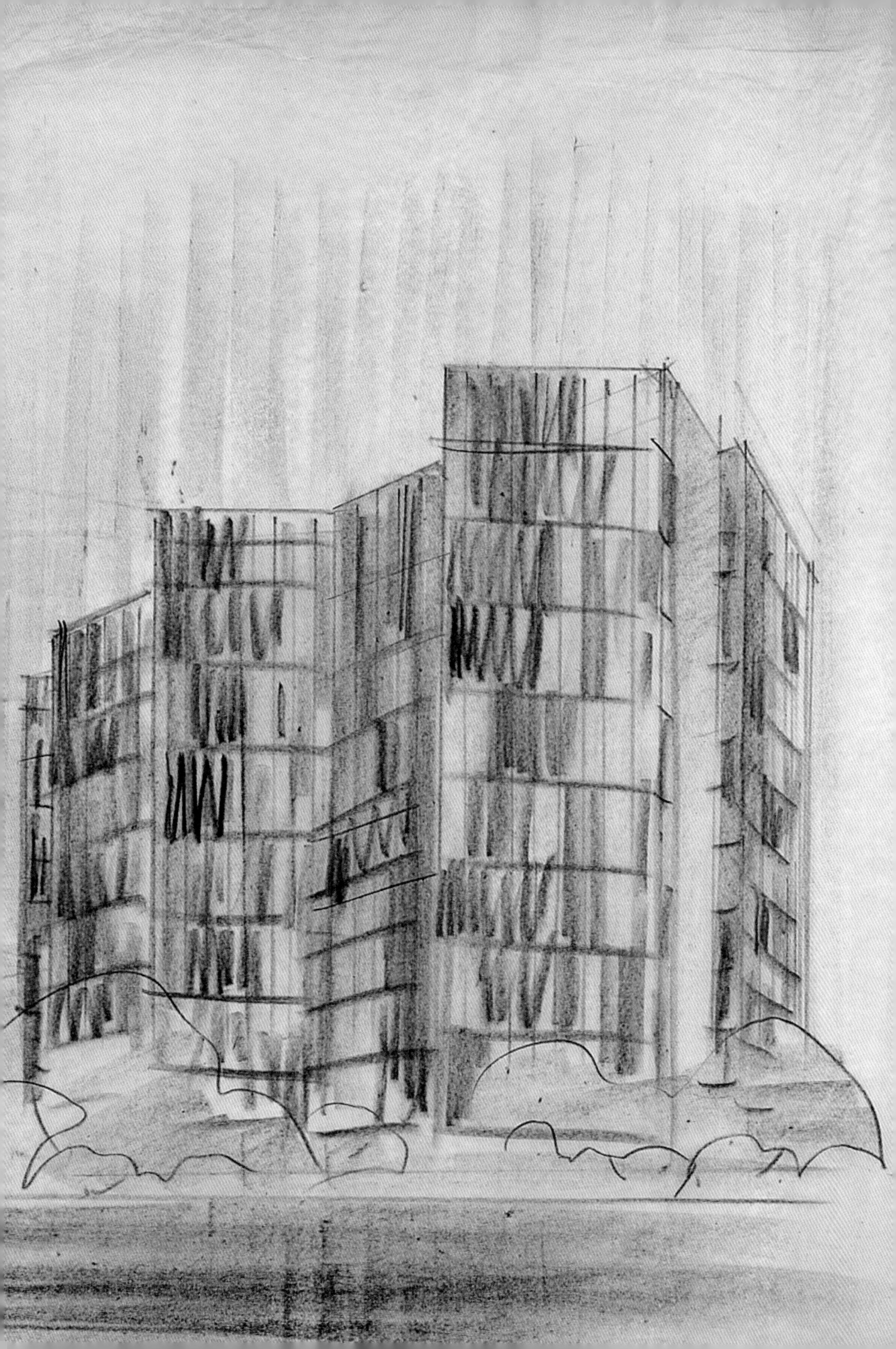

基準階平面図／Typical floor plan

ファサードにおける外装パネルの選択可能性を示す図、目隠しパネルと窓付パネル詳細図／Scheme of different methods to plug the front and detail of blind-opaque pannels

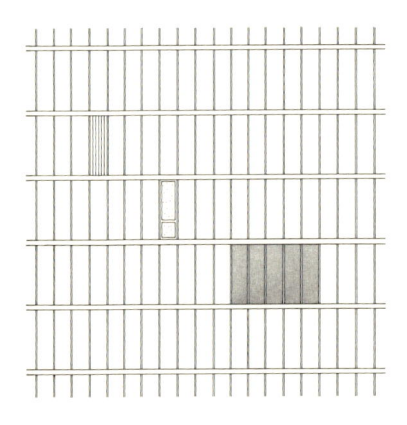

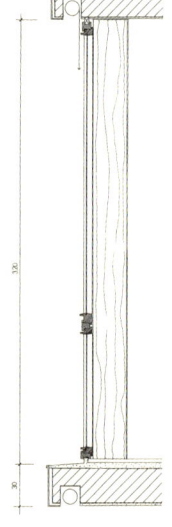

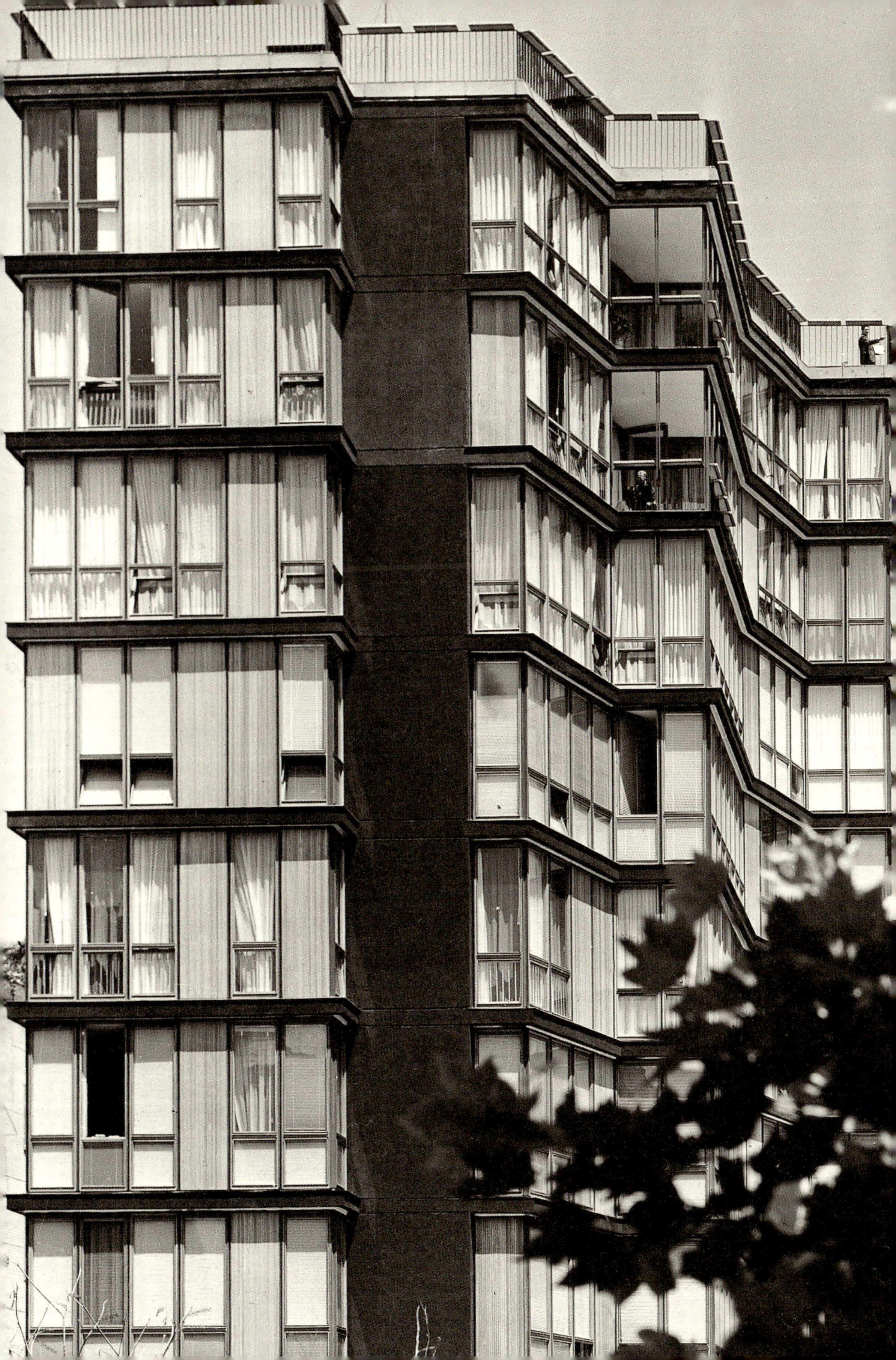

PROGETTO DI UN COMPLESSO RESIDENZIALE A PIOMBINO (LIVORNO), 1961

ピオンビーノの集合住宅計画／リヴォルノ, 1961年

2階建の9戸の家族向け戸建住宅は、海に向かって傾斜する地面に沿って扇型に配置されている。各階に住戸をもつ8階建の塔は、正方形のグリッド上に配置されている。この塔は、4本の鉄骨柱で水平スラブを支える構造形式で、その上に各住戸の平面計画が自由に展開されている。外観は鋼鉄製プレートや金属製縦格子で、すべて工場生産された外装パネルで構成されている。一方、ガラスが嵌められたパネルは1つ、あるいは複数のグリッドに合わせてセットバックし、いろいろな位置にさまざまな大きさのバルコニーを設けることも可能にしている。

(Y.T)

PROJECT FOR A RESIDENTIAL COMPLEX, PIOMBINO (LEGHORN). 1961. Nine two-storey single-family houses positioned in a fan-like array on land sloping toward the sea. An eight-storey tower with one apartment only on each level, based on a rigorous square grid. The structural solution of the tower calls for four steel pilasters to support the horizontal slabs, for free design of the layout of each apartment. The facing panels of all the buildings are in sheet steel or metal sunscreen grill, flush-mounted in the facade, while the glazed walls are set back by one module or more, creating balconies with variable sizes and positions.

構造設計：メタリケ・フィンシデール構造設計事務所／*Structures Costruzioni Metalliche Finsider*

模型写真／*Model*

高層棟のファサードのスケッチ / Study for the facade of the tower

B
C
D
A
C
D
B

配置図 / General plan

高層棟平面図／*Plan of the tall block*

CASA A MONZA (MILANO), 1972

モンツァの集合住宅／ミラノ，1972年

ミラノの「クアドロンノ通りの集合住宅」と同様に、この集合住宅の構造体は、鉄筋コンクリートの柱とテラコッタブロックを用いたスラブという伝統的な技術を用いて建てられている。集合住宅にもかかわらず、モデュールが自由な立面と平面とを居住者に提供している。同様に、外装には木製目隠しパネル、窓付パネル、バルコニーのいずれかの選択が可能になっている。クアドロンノとの相違は、プレファブリケーションの経験を積んだマンジャロッティが、室内側をポリウレタンで断熱し、外部側をヴィチェンツァ産の石を砕いて仕上げたPCによる外装パネルを採用したことにある。この解決方法は、自由度と質を伴ない、耐久性を追求する姿勢から得られた成果である。

(N.M)

RESIDENTIAL BUILDING, MONZA (MILANO) 1972. As in the building on Via Quadronno in Milan, the support structure is made with traditional techniques (pilasters in reinforced concrete, floor slabs in brick), while the modulation of the elevations (and in this case also of the layout) offers users extreme freedom in the definition of their own apartments. As in the earlier work the external facing solutions include solid panels, wooden window frames and balconies. But in contrast with the previous case, here Mangiarotti – after over a decade of experience in the field of prefabrication – specifies a system of facing panels in reinforced concrete with an inner chamber in expanded polyurethane and an external covering in crushed Vicenza stone. A solution in which liberty rhymes with quality (permitting quantity). After having taken a vow of durability.

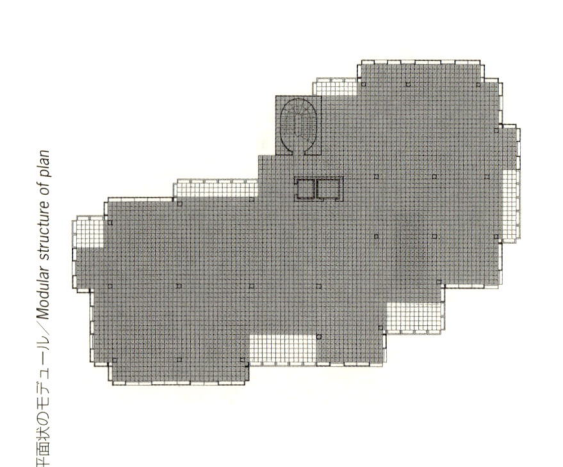

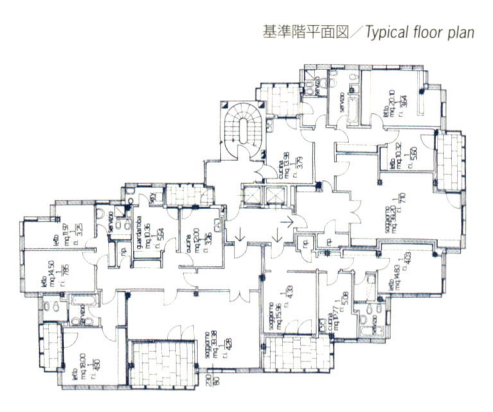

平面状のモデュール／*Modular structure of plan*

基準階平面図／*Typical floor plan*

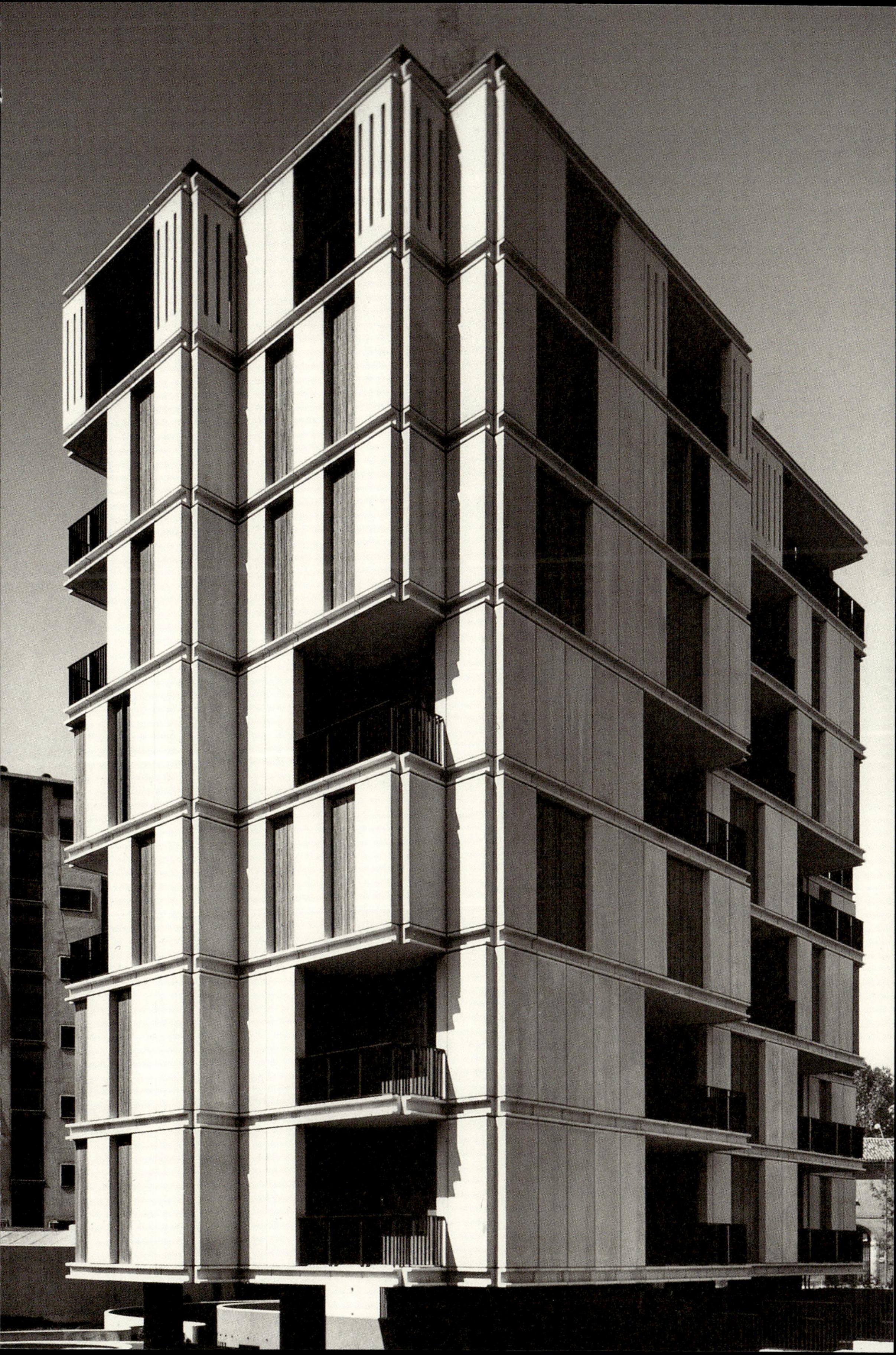

CASA AD AROSIO (COMO), 1977

アロジオの集合住宅／コモ，1977年

この建物の本質的な設計手法は、すでに「モンツァの集合住宅」で試みられたものである。非常に細かい正方形グリッドのモデュールが、ほとんど無限に近い多様な内部の平面計画を可能にしている。ファサードは、居住者のどんな要望にも対応できるようになっている。この建物は鉄筋コンクリートの柱を構造にして、外装はPCによる壁パネル、木製サッシとロッジア（バルコニー）の3要素で構成されている。

(I.M)

スタディのためのスケッチ / Working sketch

平面上のモデュール／Modular structure of plan

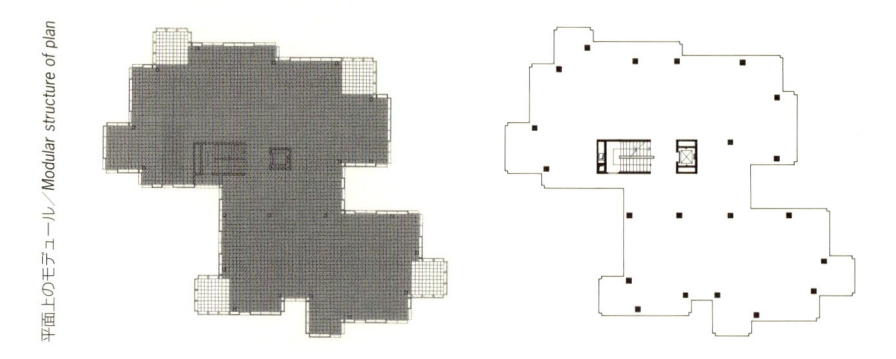

RESIDENTIAL BUILDING, AROSIO (COMO), 1977. In substance, an application of the solutions already utilized in the building in Monza. Once again the plan is based on a very dense orthogonal grid (to permit an almost infinite variety of planimetric solutions), the facade design is left free to reflect the desires of users, the structure is based on reinforced concrete pilasters, and a triad of possibilities is offered for external facings: solid panels in reinforced concrete, wooden window frames and loggia/balconies (more evident, in this case).

基準階平面図／Typical floor plan

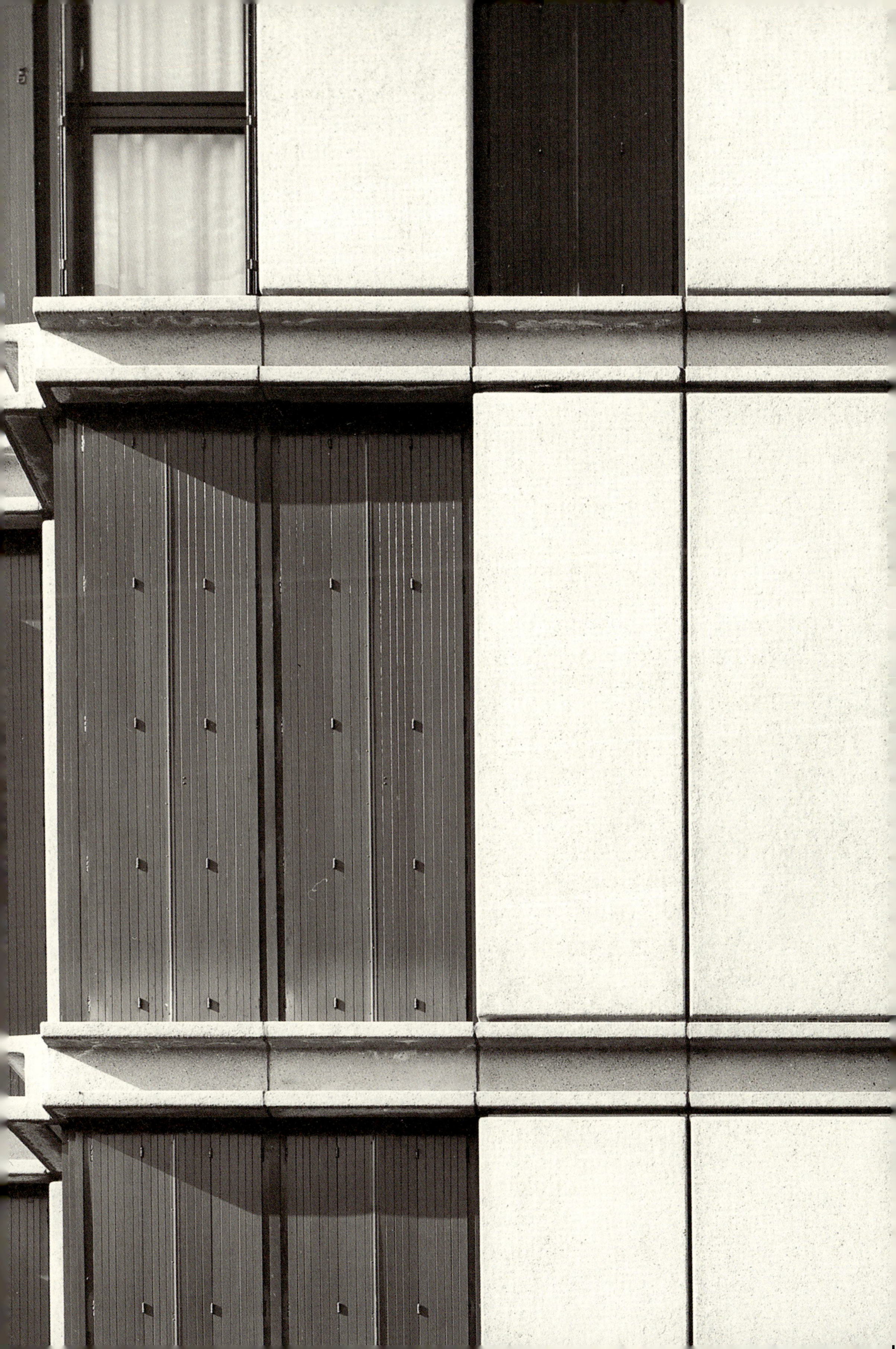

CASE PER VACANZE
A MURLONGO (VERONA), 1971

ムルロンゴの休暇のための集合住宅／ヴェローナ，1971年

当初、クライアントの要求は200戸の集合住宅を計画して欲しいというものであった。しかし、この計画では既存の糸杉を1本も伐採することなく、同時に各住戸のプライバシーの確保と景観を守りながら、地勢に沿って配列された約60住戸の集合住宅が提案されている。平屋や2階建の独立型住戸や連結型住戸が、分節化された正方形グリッドのモデュール上に、配慮の行き届いた平面計画で計画されている。壁はこの地域で採れる石を用いて無筋コンクリートで固めた職人技によるものである。木製サッシはいろいろなタイプが簡潔な意匠でまとめられている。床スラブはテラコッタとコンクリートとの複合版で、屋根には薄板鋼板が用いられている。この集合住宅はガルダ湖の丘陵地に沿って、単純な繰返しではない上品でリズミカルな佇まいを形成している。

(T.K)

VACATION HOME COMPLEX, MURLONGO (VERONA), 1971. Rejecting the initial request of the client to build as many as 200 housing units, about 60 residences were designed, positioned on the land so as to avoid cutting down the existing cypress trees, while guaranteeing fine views and privacy for each unit. Single or row houses, with one or two floors, and layouts based on the modulation of a square grid. Walls in local stone and concrete poured without reinforcement, in an artisan approach, window frames in wood, specially designed in different configurations, brick floor slabs and sheet metal roofing. Tact and discretion, but without mimesis, on the hills of Lake Garda.

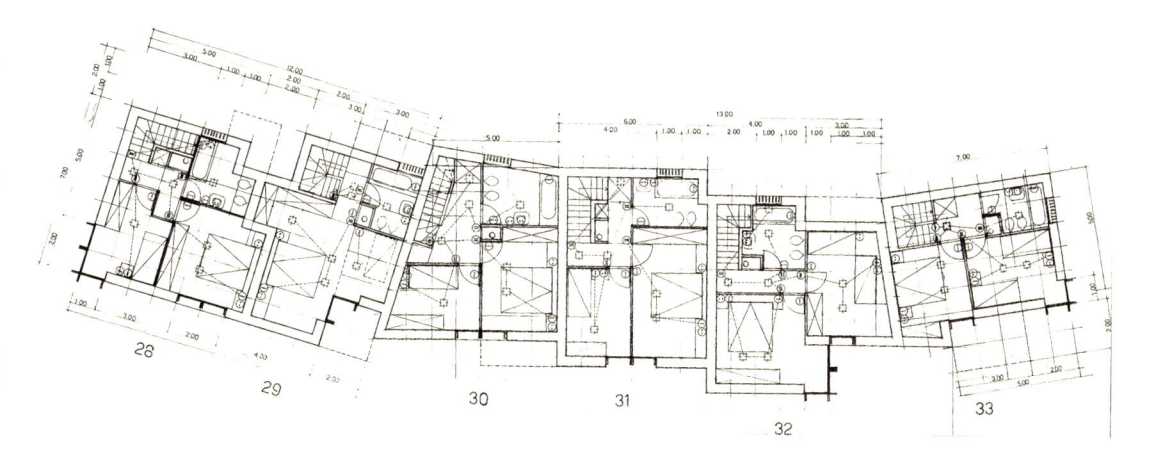

明解なモデュールによる住居平面図／Plan of the houses highlighting the modular grid

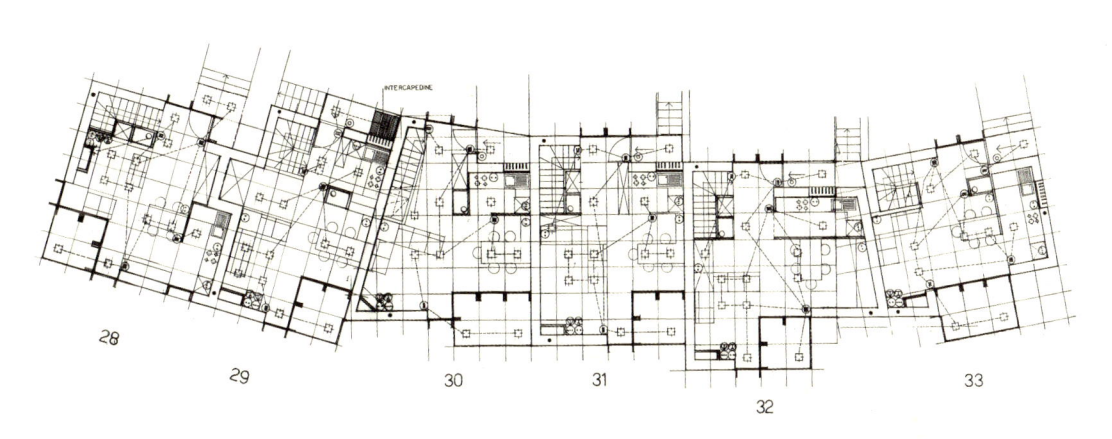

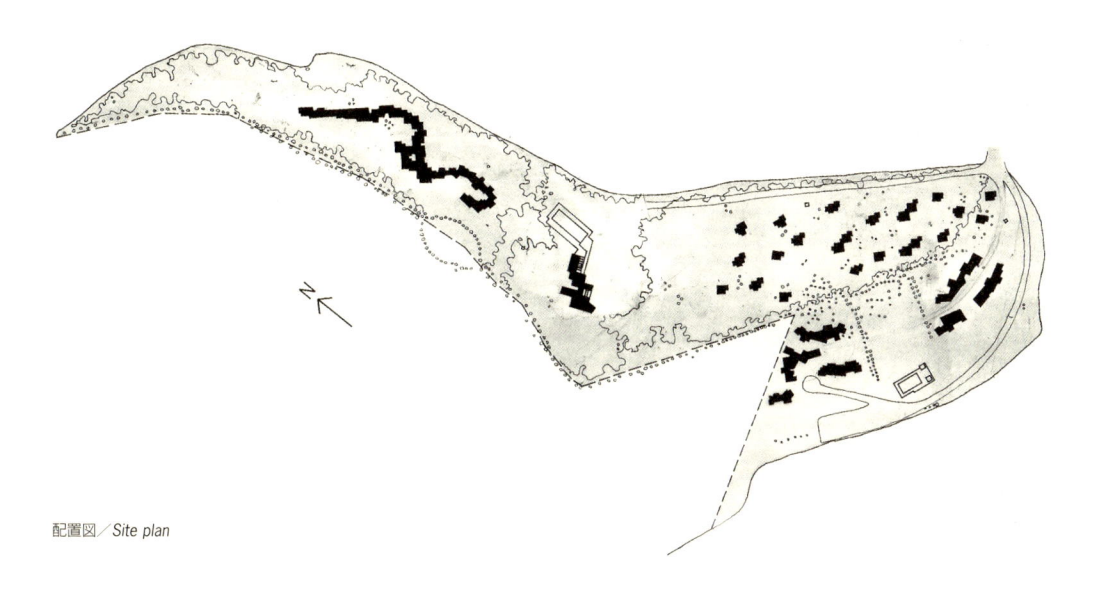

配置図／Site plan

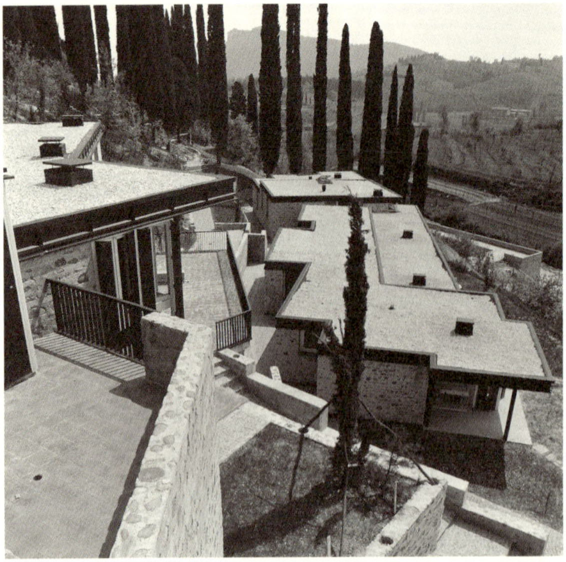

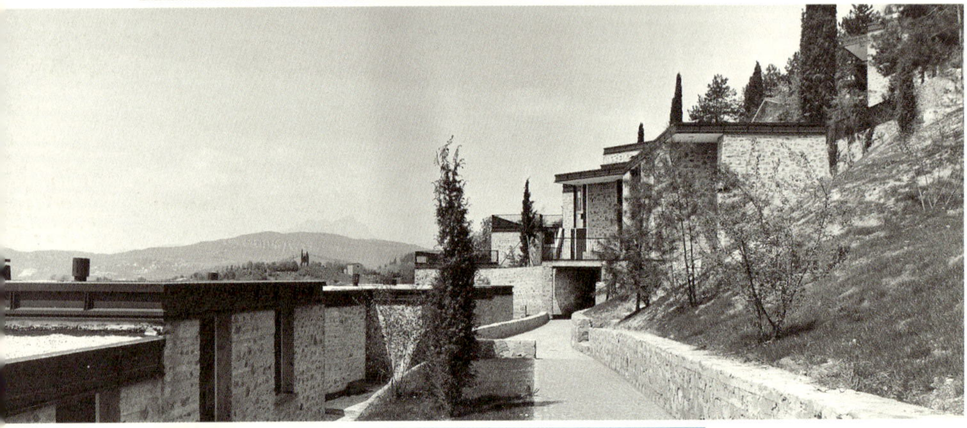

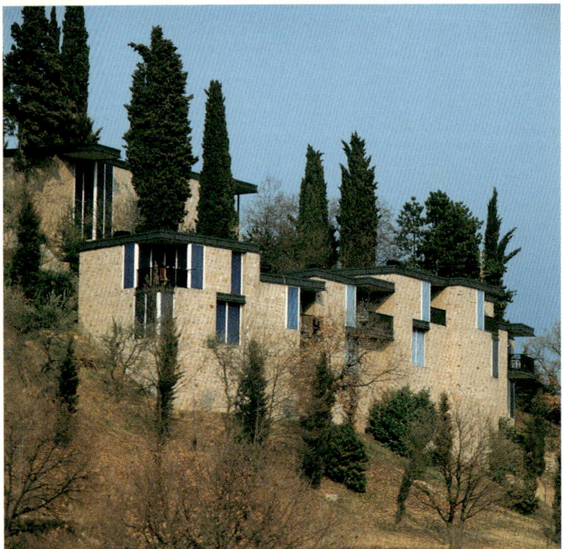

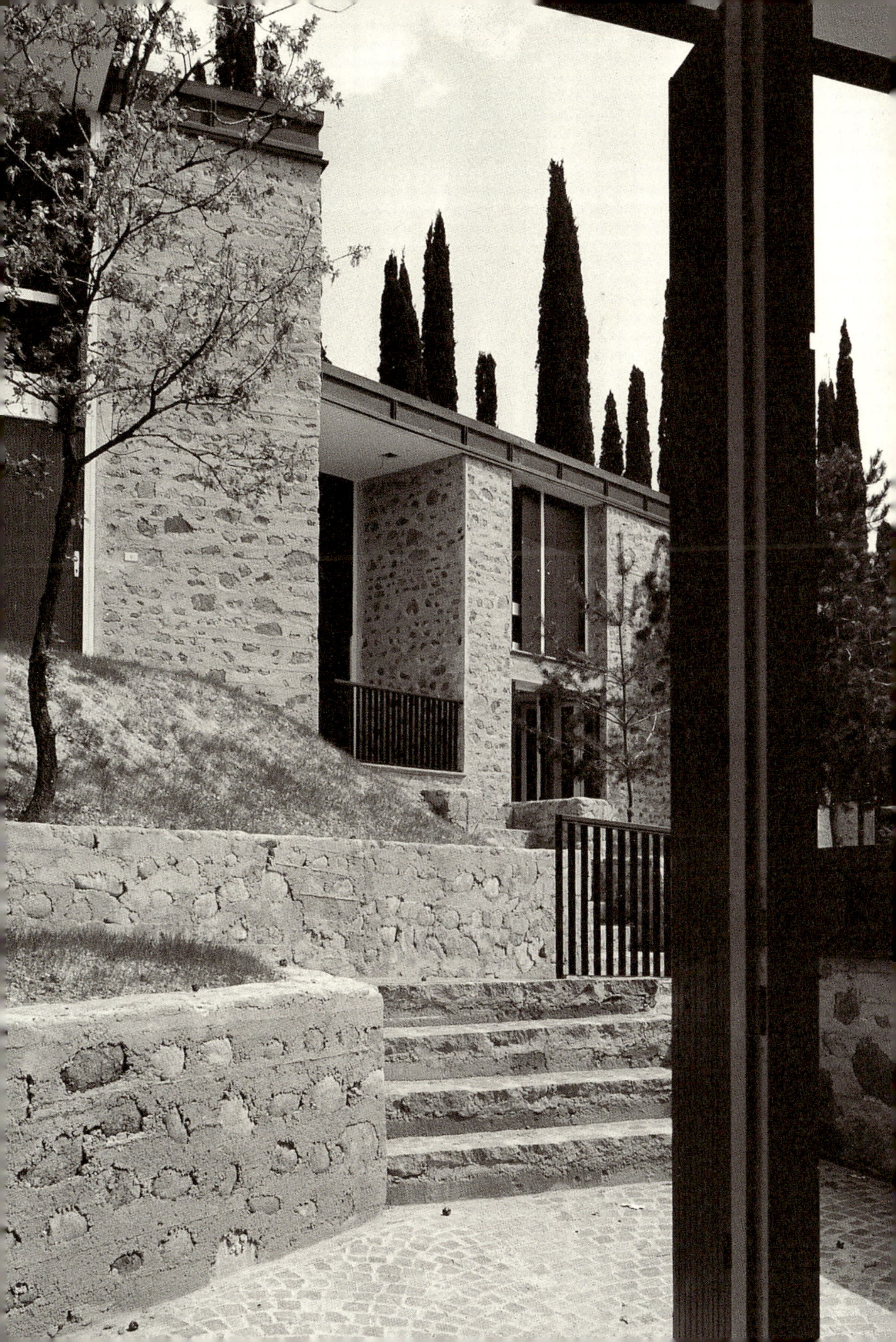

PROGETTO DI RECUPERO DI UNA TONNARA AVOLA (SIRACUSA), 1997

アヴォーラの漁業施設再生計画／シラクーサ，1997年

海に面した岩場に建つまぐろ漁のための施設が、利潤追求に走らず、その土地の魅力と、伝統的建築手法や建築法規に細心の配慮をしながら、居住施設として再生されている。　(M.T)

PROJECT FOR THE REUTILIZATION OF A TONNARA, AVOLA (SIRACUSA) 1997. An old tuna fishing complex on rocky land facing the sea is reutilized for residential purposes thanks to a project that is particularly sensitive to the charm of the site and the local construction tradition and building regulations, avoiding any form of speculation.

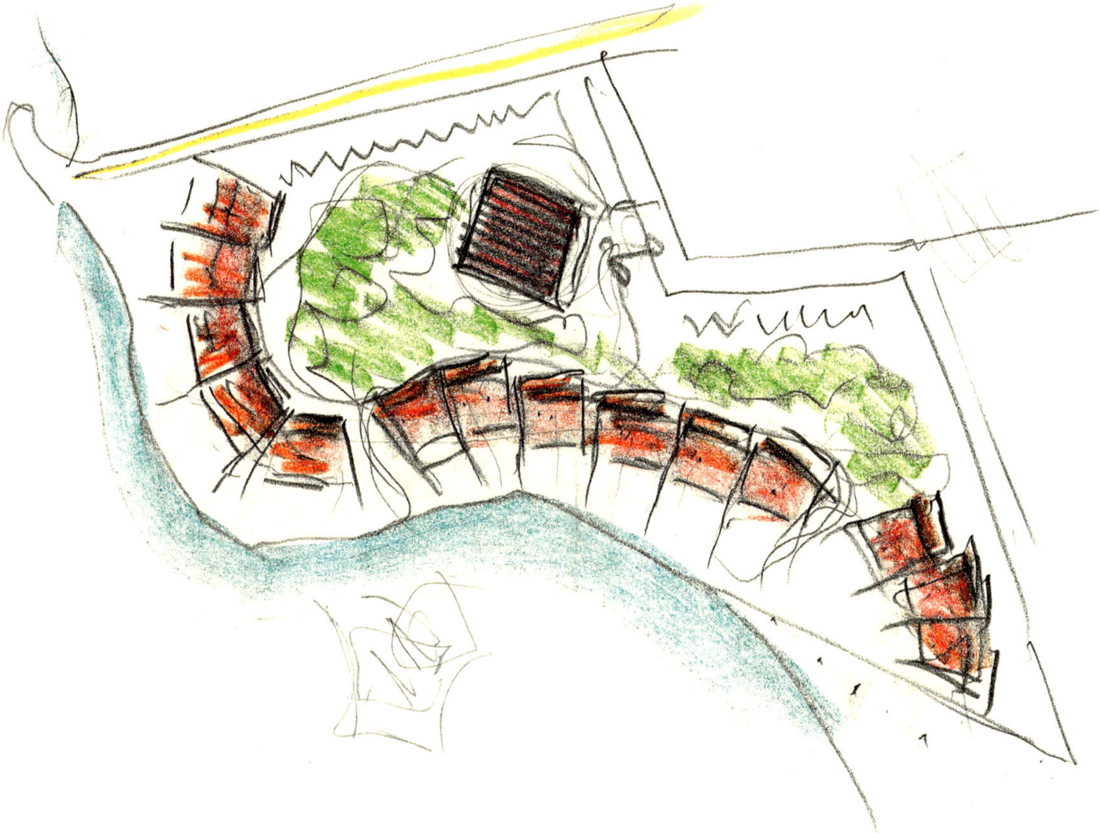

PROGETTO DI UN SERBATOIO IDRICO, 1961

貯水塔計画，1961年

高さ50mのコンクリート造の貯水塔は、宙に浮いたタンク、支持構造、そして地上階の機械スペースで構成され、エレガントな輪郭で統合されている。ローマ郊外に計画されたこのプロジェクトは、通常機能的側面だけで計画されるのに対し、建築的類型では見られない、洗練された表現力に富んだデザインで計画されている。

(M.O)

構造設計：アルド・ファビーニ／*Structures Aldo Favini*

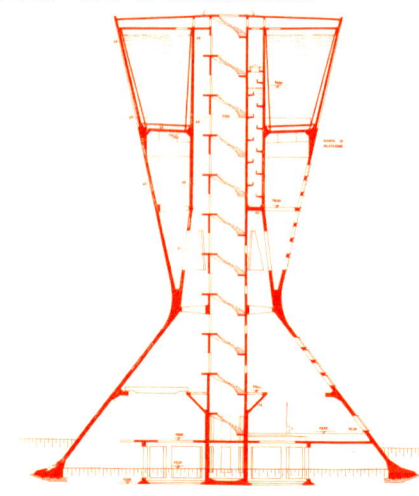

貯水槽部平断面図／*Plan of the reservoir*

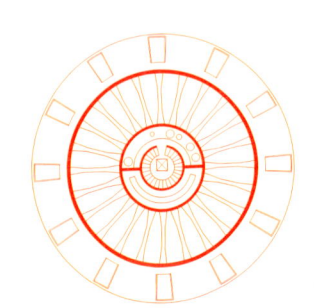

DESIGN FOR A WATER TANK, 1961. A single volume in reinforced concrete, 50 meters in height, combines in an elegant profile the suspended tank, the support structure and the ground-level technical spaces. Designed for the Roman countryside, the project is a refined, expressive unicum *in the history of this architectural typology, one that is normally viewed only in functional terms.*

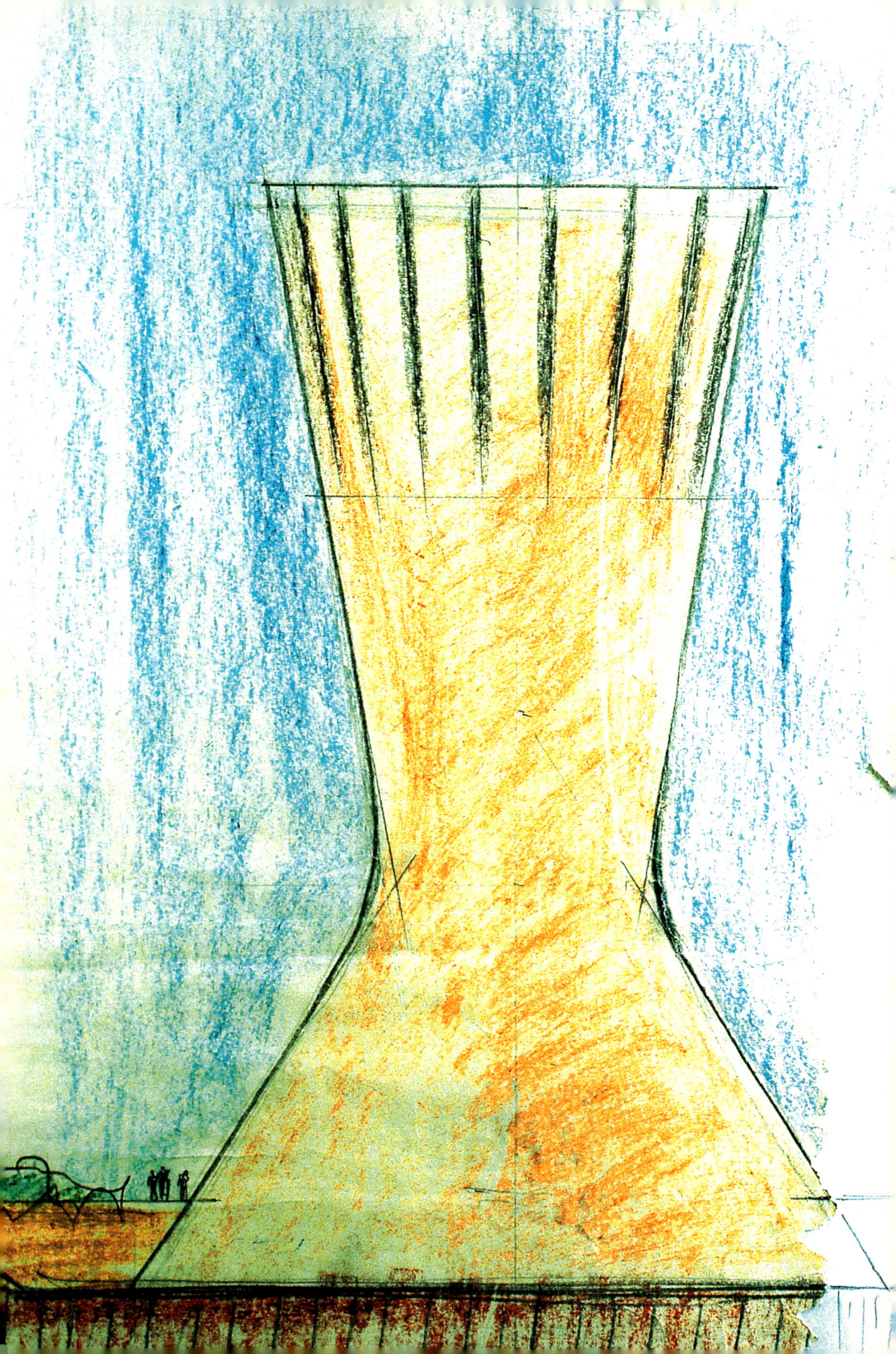

PROGETTO DI UN POLICENTRO, 1965

都心センター計画，1965年

1960年代の典型的な都市をテーマにした巨大構造物計画である。この建物は、都市、地域に必要とされる主要な機能をもち、高さ500mで計画されている。鉄筋コンクリートのコア部分と上部から吊るされたスラブからなり、各階の床面積が最大限に活用できるように計画されている。

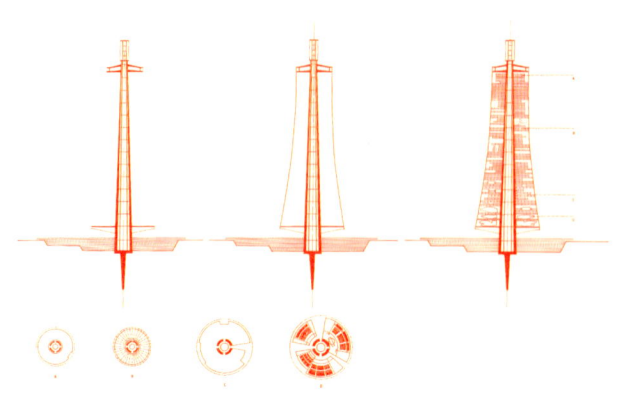

(C.I)

平面図，断面図，立面図／Plans, sections and elevation

DESIGN FOR A MULTIFUNCTIONAL CENTER, 1965. The theme of the megastructure on an urban scale typical of the research of the 1960s. A skyscraper 500 meters in height to contain community services for the city and the region, with full utilization of the space of each single level, made possible by a central structure in reinforced concrete and by floor slabs suspended from the top of the tower.

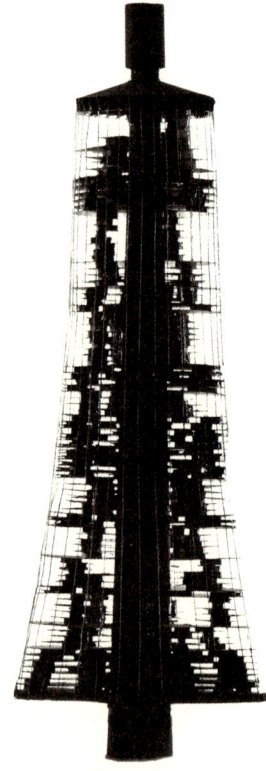

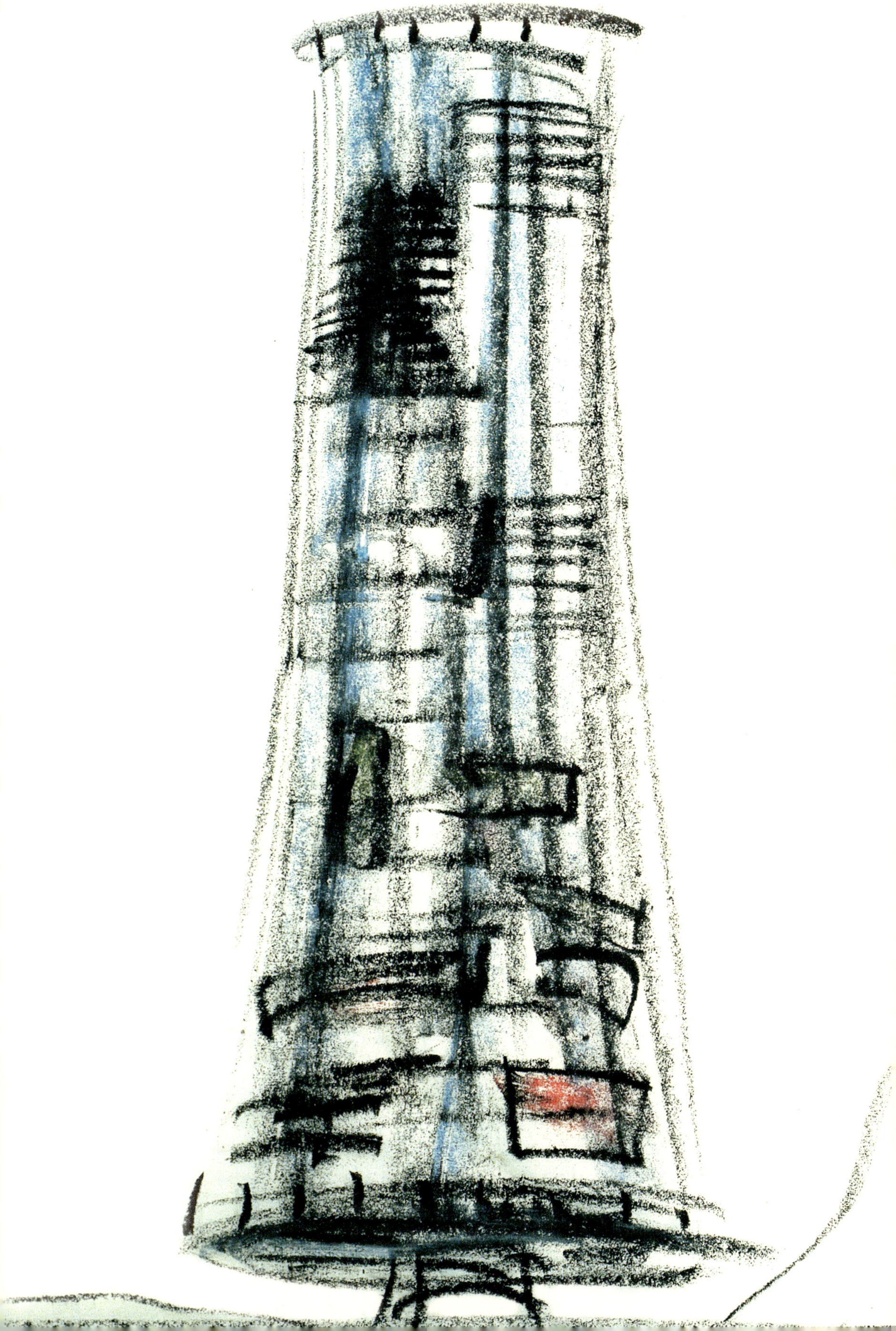

PROGETTO DI UNA TORRE INCLINATA, 1985

傾けられた塔状集合住宅計画，1985年

この計画は、ジェノヴァ近郊の山腹に位置し、上に行くほど床面積が小さく、フロア数が少なくなる5つのブロックを斜めの構造体とテンション材で重ね合わせてできている。海側は景観を堪能するために前傾し、山側は山を見上げるように後傾している。あまり見慣れないプロフィールを有する塔状集合住宅である。

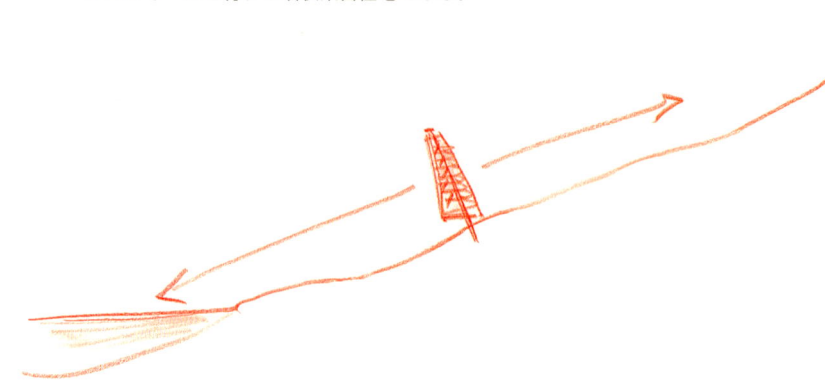

(Ka.M)

DESIGN FOR A STAYED INCLINED TOWER, 1985. For the hillside near Genoa, an inclined structure composed of five stacked, propped blocks that decrease in size and the number of storeys. A residential tower with an unusual profile extended downhill (toward the sea), also offering wider, less direct views of the hilly landscape in the other direction.

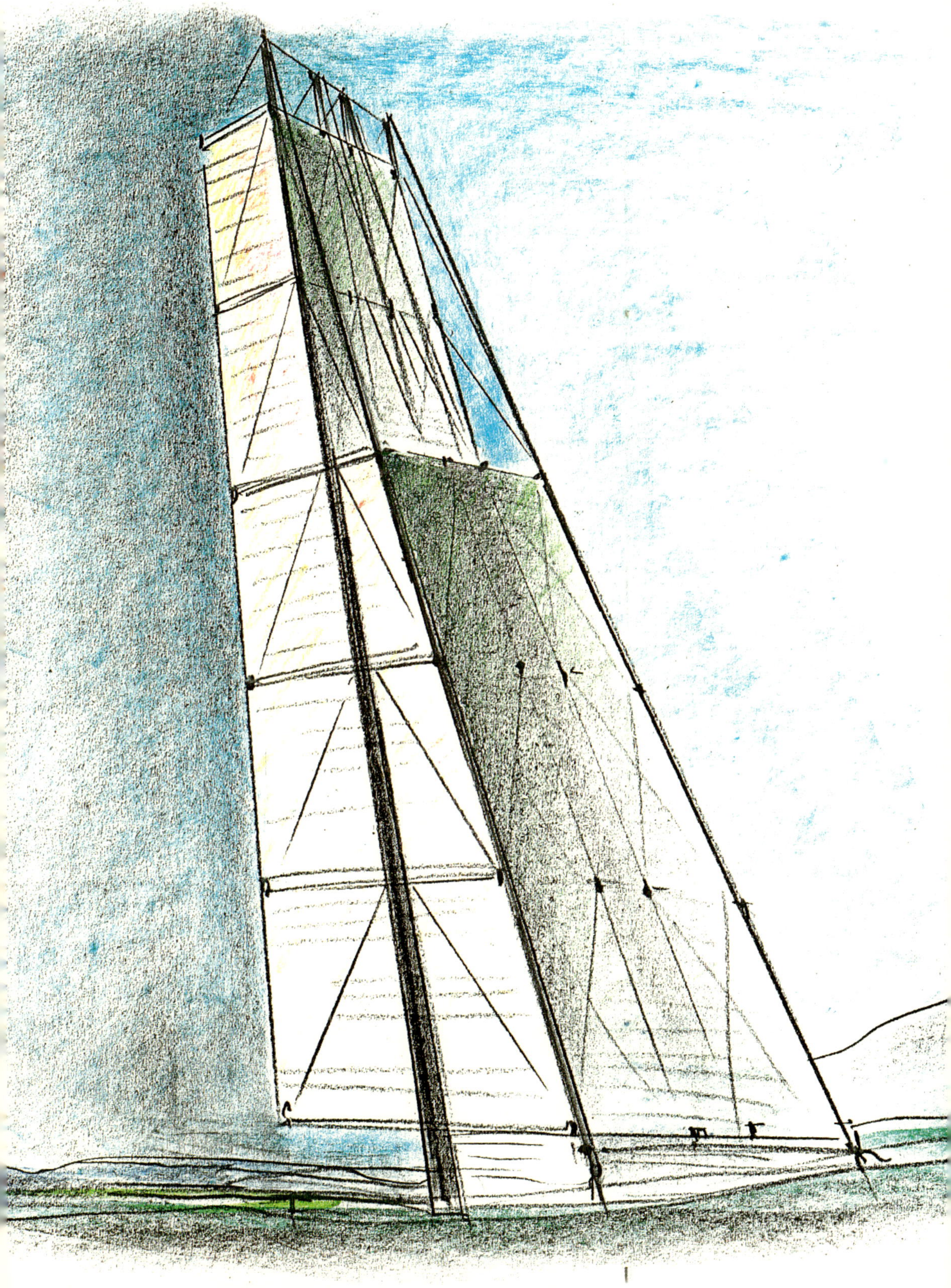

PROGETTO DI UN PADIGLIONE ESPOSITIVO ALLA XIV TRIENNALE DI MILANO, 1968

第14回ミラノ・トリエンナーレ展の展示場計画，1968年

この展示場計画は、主会場のパラッツォ・デ・ラルテの裏手に計画された、家具と照明器具のパビリオンである。波状で自由な形態は、園内の木を切り倒してはならないという設計条件から生まれている。2層のファイバーグラス補強ポリウレタン樹脂でつくられるシェル構造は、高さが変化する連続的な空間のつながりを表現している。このプロジェクトは技術的にも空間的にも斬新な提案であり、環境保護にも配慮した提案であったが、残念ながら実現されなかった。

(Ke.M)

DESIGN FOR AN EXHIBITION PAVILION FOR THE 14TH MILAN TRIENNIAL, 1968. Behind the Palazzo dell'Arte, a pavilion for the display of furniture and lamps. A sinuous and apparently free form that is the result, instead, of the precise requirement of not cutting down the trees in the park. The shell structure in two layers of polyurethane resin reinforced fiberglass (PRVF) allows for a continuous sequence of spaces of variable height. Technological and typological innovation and safeguarding of environmental factors in a project that unfortunately was never built.

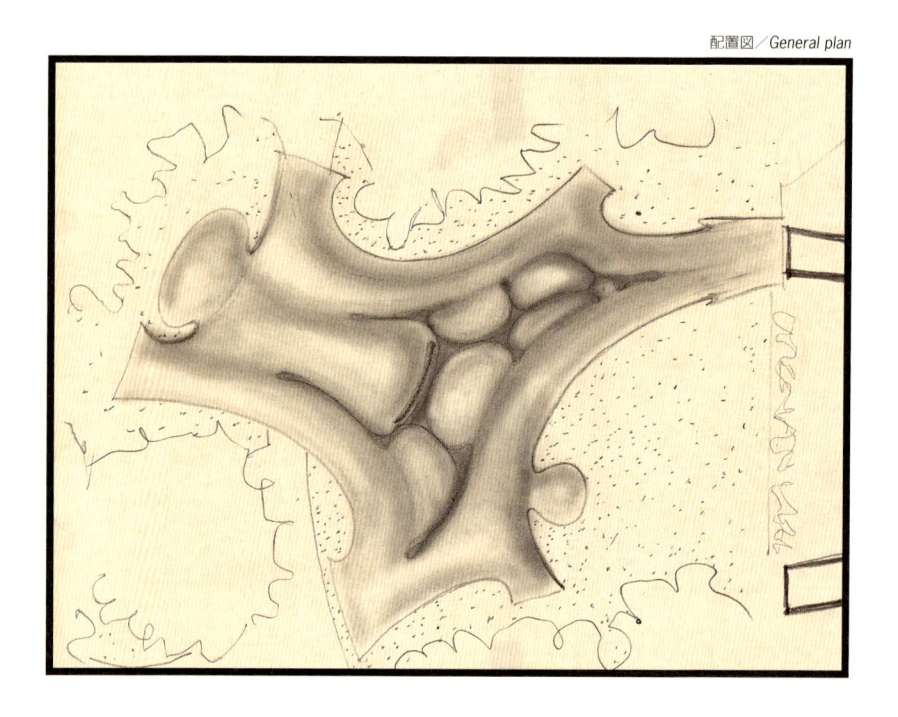

配置図／General plan

模型写真／Model

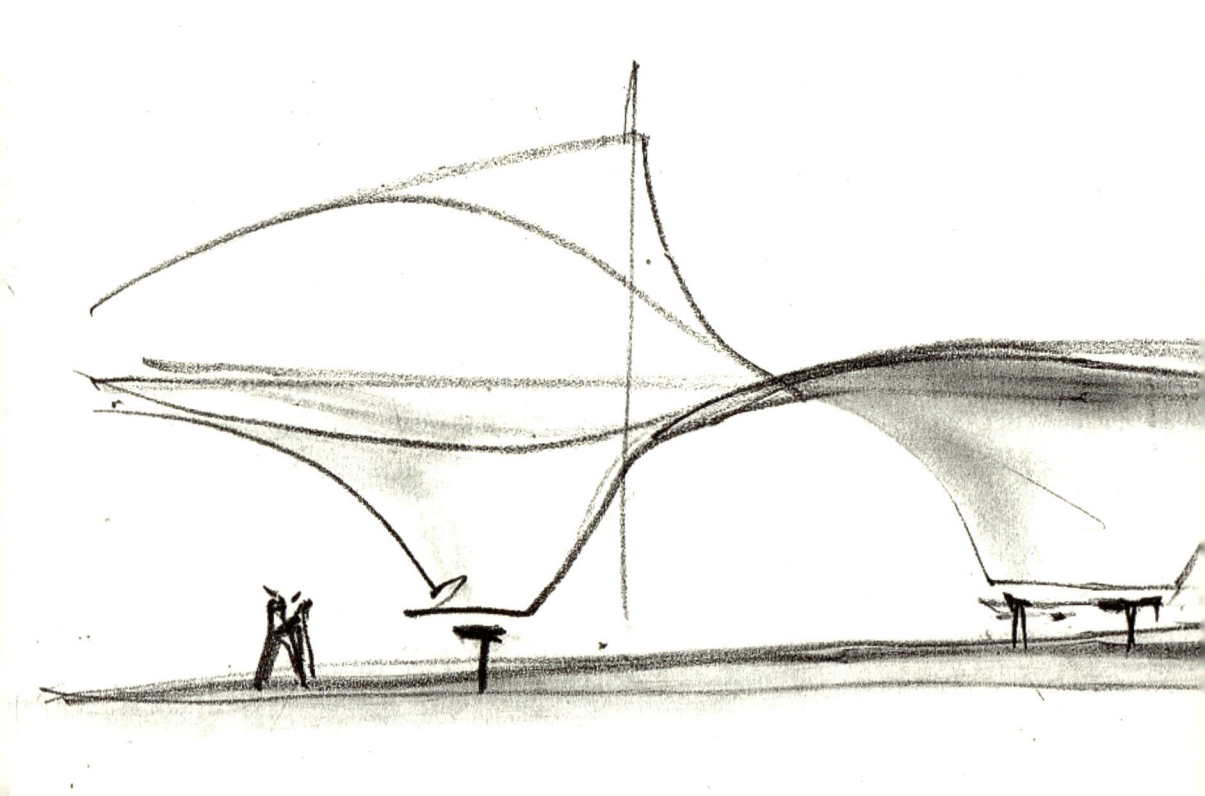

展示場内部のスケッチ / Working sketchs of interiors of the pavilion

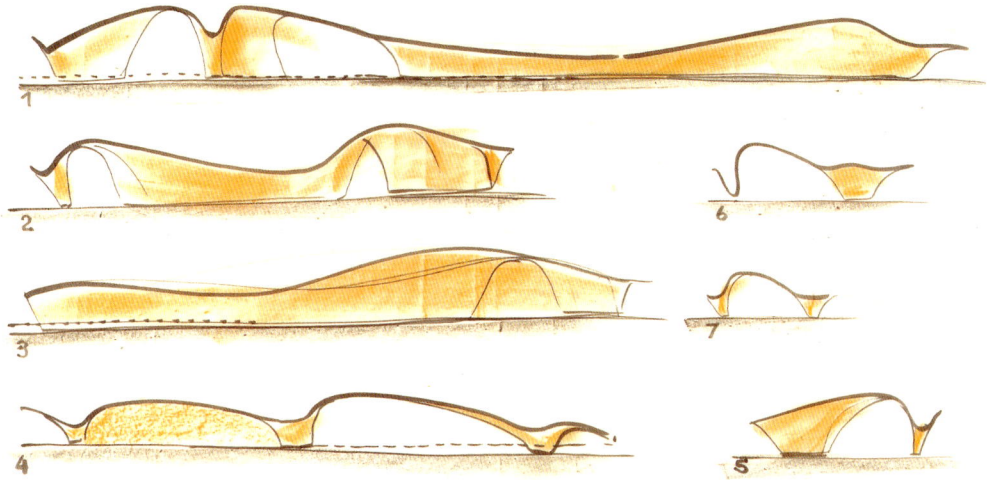

断面図／Sections

STABILIMENTO E ABITAZIONI
A MARCIANISE (CASERTA), 1962

マルチャニーゼの工場と従業員用の集合住宅／カゼルタ，1962年

「私は、ここがパーティクルボードを生産する工場のある場所だと思わせるようにすべく設計作業を始めた。その過程で、パーティクルボードを外装に利用するアイディアが生まれた」
このパーティクルボード会社は、工場と従業員用集合住宅の2棟を彼に設計依頼した。

工場は柱・梁の構造システムで、床スラブはテラコッタブロックと鉄筋コンクリートで構成されている。柱は2つの並列した薄い鉄筋コンクリートの壁柱でできていて、その2つの間は視覚的に軽く見せるだけでなく、内部に自然光を導き入れるとともに、柱上部の梁との接合を容易にする役目も兼ねている。

工場で働く従業員のための集合住宅は医務室、食堂、ガレージなどを含み、正方形のグリッド上に自由に配置されている。鉄筋コンクリートの構造体は、現場でプレファブリケートされたもので、十字形の平断面をした柱（ドレンを内蔵する）の上に大梁を載せ、それに小梁が取り付いている。各住戸は、中庭と外部の風景を見通すことができる。外壁と内壁（自社製品）は、4種類のパネル部材の組合せで多様な解決方法を可能にしている。

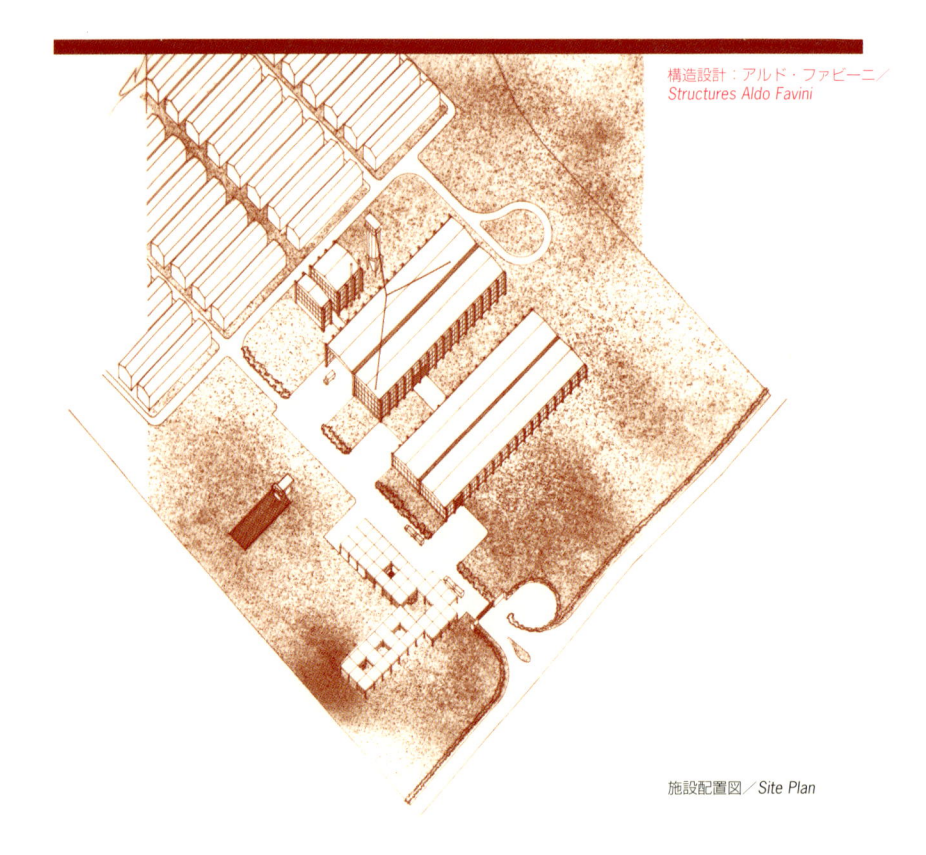

(Y.T)

構造設計：アルド・ファビーニ／
Structures Aldo Favini

施設配置図／*Site Plan*

工場外観 / View of the plant

工場内観／Interior view of the plant

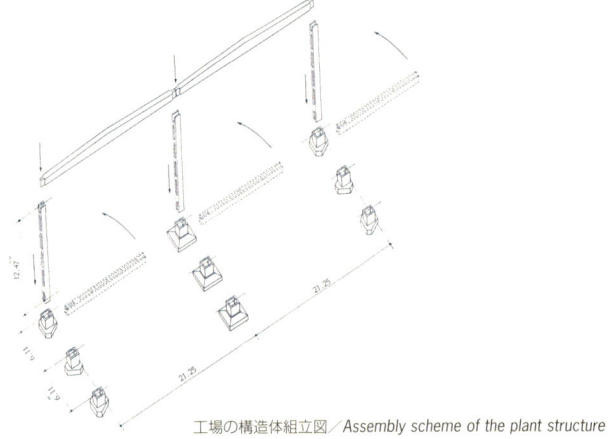

工場の構造体組立図／Assembly scheme of the plant structure

PLANT AND HOUSING, MARCIANISE (CASERTA), 1962. *"I started with the fact that a factory for the production of chipboard panels would be built here; this led to the idea of using those same panels for the facings"*. Two different episodes in this project for a manufacturer of chipboard panels. The plant is structured with a pilaster-beam system, completed by floor slabs in brick and concrete. The reinforced concrete pilaster is formed by two slender juxtaposed strips: the space between the two elements visually lightens the profile, permitting natural light to enter the interiors and offering a simple solution for connection with the beam in the upper part of the pilaster. The housing for the plant technicians and other spaces for an infirmary, a dining hall and a garage are laid out with apparent freedom on a very rigorous squared grid. The structure in reinforced concrete, prefabricated on site, is composed of cruciform pilasters (containing the drainpipes) which support the main beams; the main beams support the secondary beams. Each housing unit has a view of an internal patio and the surrounding landscape. The arrangement of the external panels and the internal partitions (produced by the client) is controlled by a range of four different elements, permitting highly diversified solutions.

住居部分外観／View of the residences

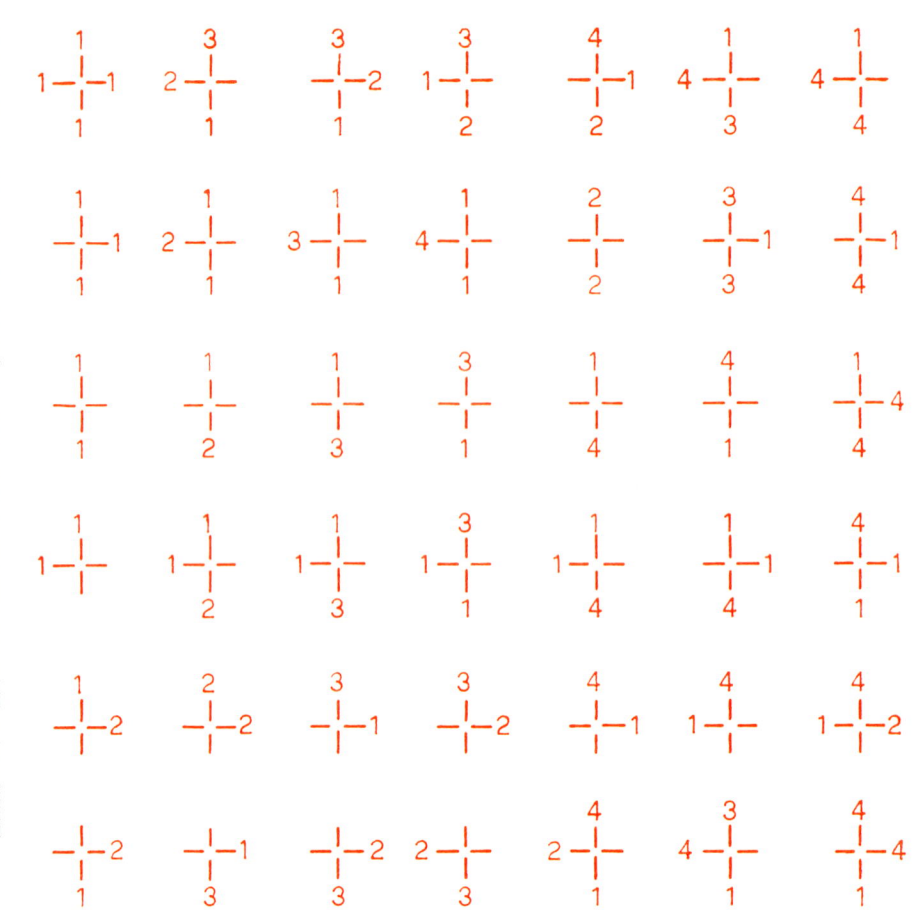

住居部分における4種類のパネルの組合せ図／Residences: chart of the possible combinations with the four types of panels

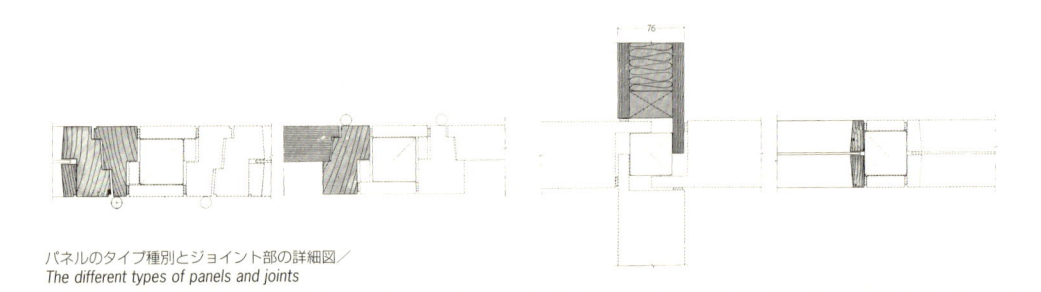

パネルのタイプ種別とジョイント部の詳細図／
The different types of panels and joints

内部に竪樋をもつ柱の平断面図／Residences: horizontal section of the pilarster with the inner drainpipe

SISTEMA COSTRUTTIVO FACEP 1964

ファチェプ社による構造システム，1964年

これは、一時代を画したプレファブリケーションの構造システムである。アンジェロ・マンジャロッティはミラノ郊外のリッソーネに2つの工場を建てるために、経済性・生産性などの諸要求を満たす有効性を再確認して、3つのプレキャスト・プレストレストコンクリートのコンポーネント（柱・梁・屋根）で構成されるプレファブリケーションの構造システムを採用した。構造システムの特徴である柱頭部のデザインは、梁と接合する部分が広がり、柱間隔より梁長を短くすることで、運送上の困難を解決している。両端が斜めの柱頭部のフォルムは、梁との接合を容易にするとともに、工場が規模を拡張する可能性も秘めている。屋根ユニット裏面にはユニークにデザインされた補強リブがあり、その補強リブのフラットな面は、外装パネルやサッシの取付けを容易にしている。かつ、表面の長手方向には、軽くむくりがついており、雨水の流れをスムーズにしている。また、屋根ユニットは、ガラス繊維で補強されたトップライト付屋根ユニットと取り替えることも可能である。

(O.H)

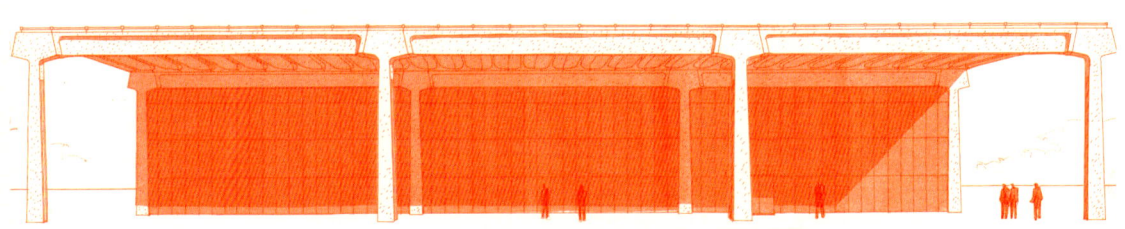

リッソーネ（ミラノ）にあるエル・マーグ社工場，1964年／Plant Elmag, Lissone(Milano), 1964

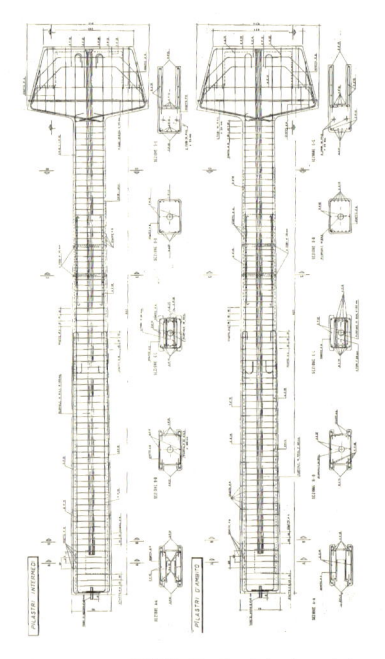

構造設計：アレッサンドロ・スブリッシャ・フィオレッティ／Structures Alessandro Sbriscia Fioretti

柱エレメントの配筋詳細図／Detail drawings of the pilasters with the reinforcement

リッソーネ（ミラノ）にあるエル・マーグ社工場, 1964年 / Plant Elmag, Lissone(Milano), 1964

FACEP CONSTRUCTION SYSTEM 1964. A construction system capable of characterizing an era. To build this industrial building in Lissone, Angelo Mangiarotti develops a prefabricated system in prestressed reinforced concrete composed of the three traditional elements of the trilithic system (pilaster, beam and roofing segment) revisited with an eye on economics. The capital of the pilaster, the distinctive feature of this design, widens at the connection point with the beam, reducing its length for the same span between the pillars and simplifying transport. Its inclined profile facilitates connection with the beam and indicates the possibility of subsequent expansion of the factory. The roofing segments have ribbing that characterizes the design of the intrados (while guaranteeing a flat surface for the attachment of the external parts in sheet metal and glass) and a slight longitudinal convexity that facilitates drainage of rainwater; they can be alternated with roofing elements in reinforced fiberglass to permit natural light to enter.

エル・マーグ社工場：木の構造システムによる拡張計画のイメージスケッチ／Plant Elmag:addition hypothesis with wooden structure

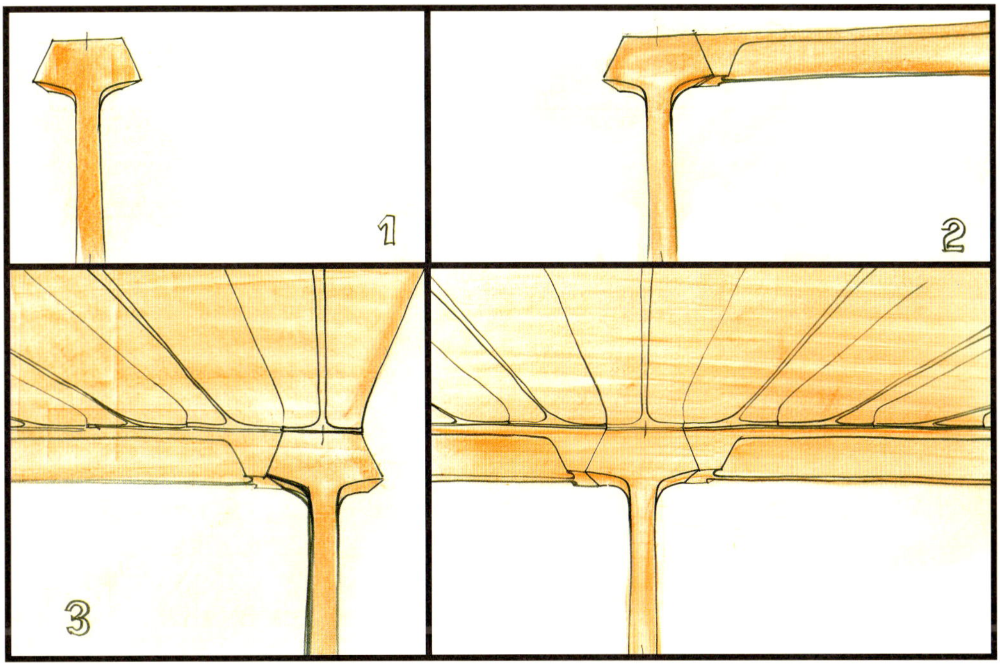
1
2
3

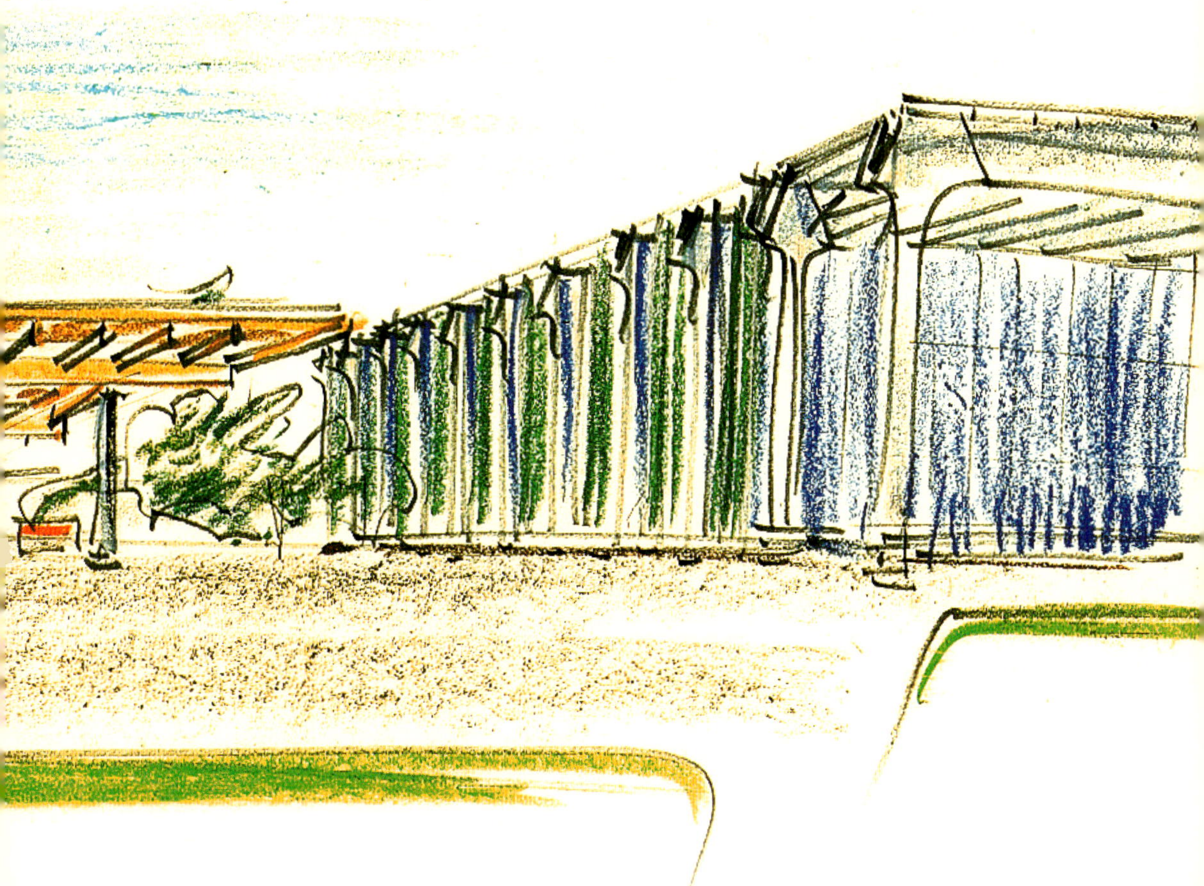

STABILIMENTO ARMITALIA
A CINISELLO BALSAMO (MILANO), 1968

チニゼッロ・バルサーモのアルミタリア社屋／ミラノ，1968年

ミラノ郊外の高速道路インターチェンジ近くに建つこの工場は、建設後約35年を経過した現在もなお人々を驚嘆させ続けている。角の丸いサッシフレームで軽快にデザインされ、かつ曲面を有する外装パネルで構築された建物は、あたかも鉄道の客車を連想させ、この地のランドマークとなっている。建物の各ブロックは、現場打ち鉄筋コンクリートの柱と屋根スラブ、さらにプレファブリケートされた鉄筋コンクリートの外装パネル（着色された採石で仕上げられている）で構成されている。作業場は正方形のグリッド、オフィスと倉庫は長方形のグリッドで計画されている。外観は伝統的な軒・庇のラインを消し去り、丸みのある表情になっている。外装パネルは、地表面から離れて陰のラインをつくり、建物全体が浮き上がって見えるように設計されている。各屋根ユニットの中央部には、自然光を取り入れるトップライトが配置され、各ユニットのまわりには人工照明と、空調設備が納められている。

(N.M)

ARMITALIA PLANT, CINISELLO BALSAMO, (MILAN), 1968. Near a highway interchange on the outskirts of Milan, an industrial building that continues to amaze, almost thirty-five years after its construction. A horizontal signal whose overall image – determined by facing elements with a curved profile, lightened by frames with rounded corners – seems to be a reminder of that of rail cars. Each volume has the same structure (with a square grid in the workshop and a rectangular grid for the offices and warehouse) in pilasters and roofing slabs poured in box-moulds, then filled with panels in prefabricated reinforced concrete (with an external finish in colored crushed stone), whose profile cancels out the traditional eaves line. The lower part of the panels is detached from the ground, causing a shadow that underscores and seems to raise the entire complex. The roofing slabs contain the skylights for zenithal lighting at their center, with the artificial lighting and air conditional plant elements housed at the ends.

長辺方向断面図／Longitudinal section

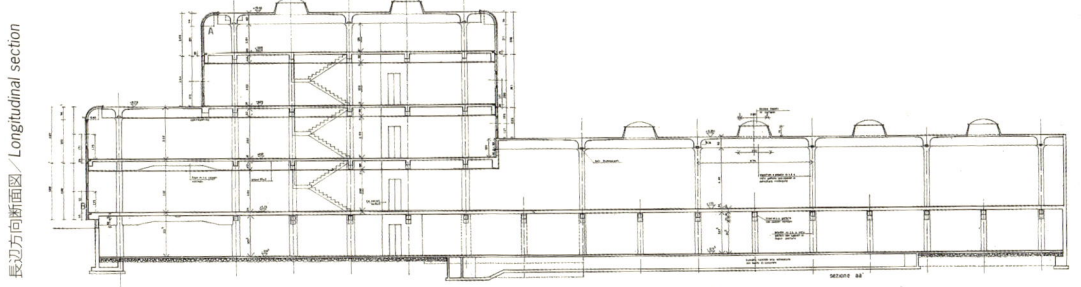

構造設計：ジュリオ・バッリオ，ジョバンニ・コロンボ，アルベルト・ヴィンターニ／Structures Giulio Ballio, Giovanni Colombo, Alberto Vintani

平面図 / General Plan

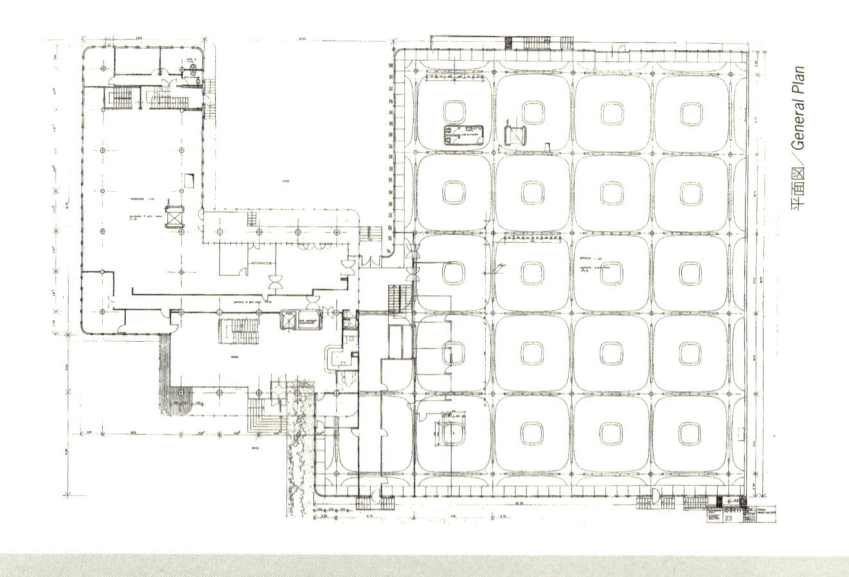

屋根スラブ施工図／Executive drawing of the roofing

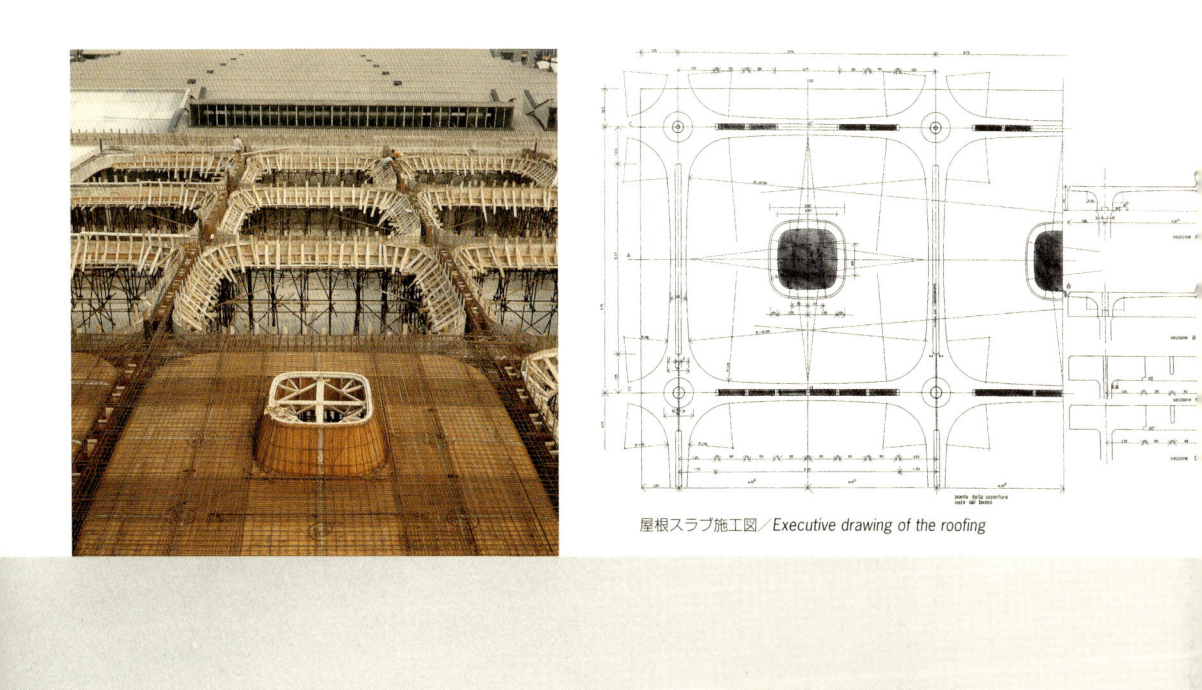

SISTEMA COSTRUTTIVO U70 ISOCELL 1969

構造システム U70 ISOCELL, 1969年

特許を有するこの構造システムは、従来のものを改良し、発展させたシステムである。前作同様3エレメント構成で、これまでより梁部材の長さが短く、梁せいも小さくなっている。しかし、屋根部材の長さは大きくなり、厚さも増している。それにより梁せいと屋根部材の高さが同一になり、梁型が出ない連続的な同一面を形成し、内部間仕切のレイアウトや設備配管の自由度が増している。トップライトは梁部材にも屋根部材にも設置が可能で、屋根排水の雨水管は柱に内蔵されている。このシステムは、新しい道路交通法に対応するため改良され、特に屋根部材の柱間隔が18〜21mになり、各パネル（伝統的な鉄筋コンクリートの壁パネルや、金属フレームとガラスで構成された透明のユニット）は、アルミ押出成形を使った精巧で洗練されたユニットに改善されている。

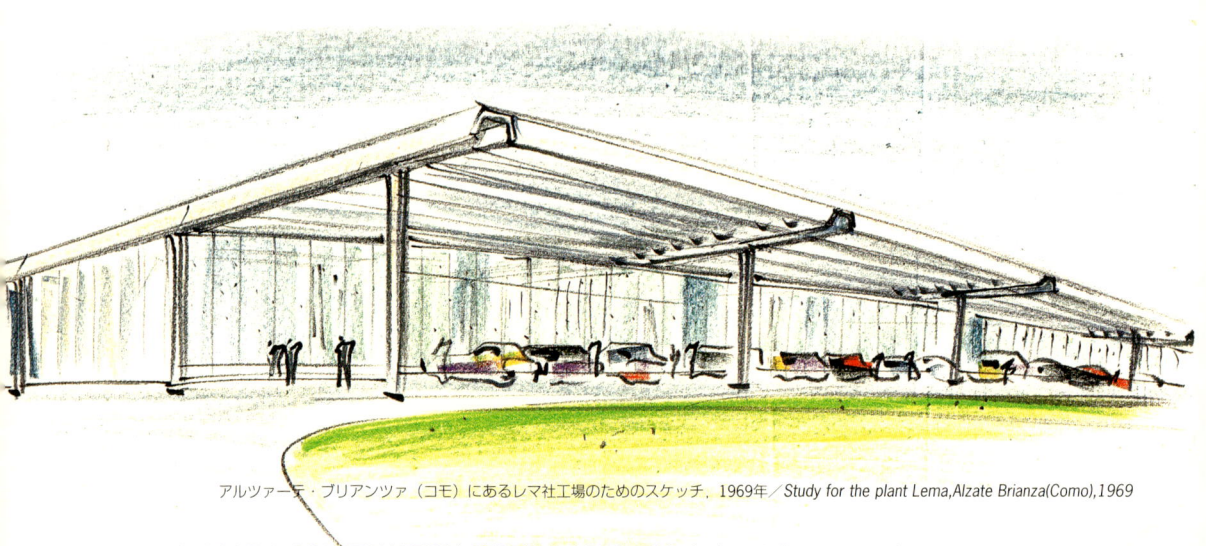

(I.M)

アルツァーテ・ブリアンツァ（コモ）にあるレマ社工場のためのスケッチ，1969年／Study for the plant Lema, Alzate Brianza(Como), 1969

U70 ISOCELL CONSTRUCTION SYSTEM, 1969. This industrially patented construction system is the mature evolution of its predecessors. Once again there is a trilith, but in this case the beam reduced in length (with respect to the usual design) and therefore in height, while the roofing segment increases in length, and therefore in thickness. Thus the beam and the roofing segment can coincide in terms of height, forming a continuous intrados line to permit extreme freedom in the installation of plant elements and facings. The skylights are placed both in the beams and the roofing parts, while the drainpipes run inside the pilasters. Over the years the system has been updated (to comply with new transport regulations), increasing the span of the roofing segments from 18 to 21 meters and perfecting the panels (traditional closed panels in reinforced concrete and transparent units in metal and glass), defined by use of a sophisticated extruded aluminium section.

トゥラーテ（コモ）にあるウニフォール社工場, 1982年／*Plant Unifor, Turate(Como), 1982*

構造設計：ジュリオ・バッリオ，ジョバンニ・コロンボ，アルベルト・ヴィンターニ／*Structures Giulio Ballio, Giovanni Colombo, Alberto Vintani*

アルツァーテ・ブリアンツァ（コモ）にあるレマ社工場，1969年／Plant Lema, Alzate Brianza(Como), 1969

構造システムのエレメント / Structural element chart

97

SISTEMA COSTRUTTIVO BRIONA 1972

構造システム BRIONA，1972年

「U70 ISOCELL」と同様に、プレキャスト・プレストレストコンクリートによる3エレメント構成で、梁ユニットと屋根ユニットの組合せは相方向性を有する。このシステムも特許を取得し、特にこの構造システムの汎用性は際立っている。このシステムは、一辺7.2mの正方形グリッドと、プレファブリケートされた鉄筋コンクリートの9エレメント（柱、3タイプの梁、3タイプの屋根版、2タイプの破風板／平、出隅）で構成されている。柱エレメントは円柱の上に一辺1.2mの正方形の平板をもち、平板と屋根版を支える梁エレメントがかみ合って柱・梁が構成されている。構造体の外周部は、将来の拡張が可能であるとともに、意匠的にも洗練されたコーニスのエレメントになっている。隣接する各スパンの屋根版は、梁エレメントへの荷重を有利に分散させるために、方向を変えて配置されている。また、設備配管もあらかじめ屋根エレメントの補強リブに沿って配置するように想定されている。このシステムは平面計画を拡張することが可能で、各柱はほかの柱と常に連結することができる。外装は構造の自立性と平面計画の自由さを強調して、外周の柱よりセットバックして取り付けられる。

(O.H)

構造設計：ジュリオ・バッリオ，ジョバンニ・コロンボ，アルベルト・ヴィンターニ／
Structures Giulio Ballio, Giovanni Colombo, Alberto Vintani

ジュッサーノ（ミラノ）にあるフェッグ社施設．1977年／Plant Feg, Giussano(Milano), 1977

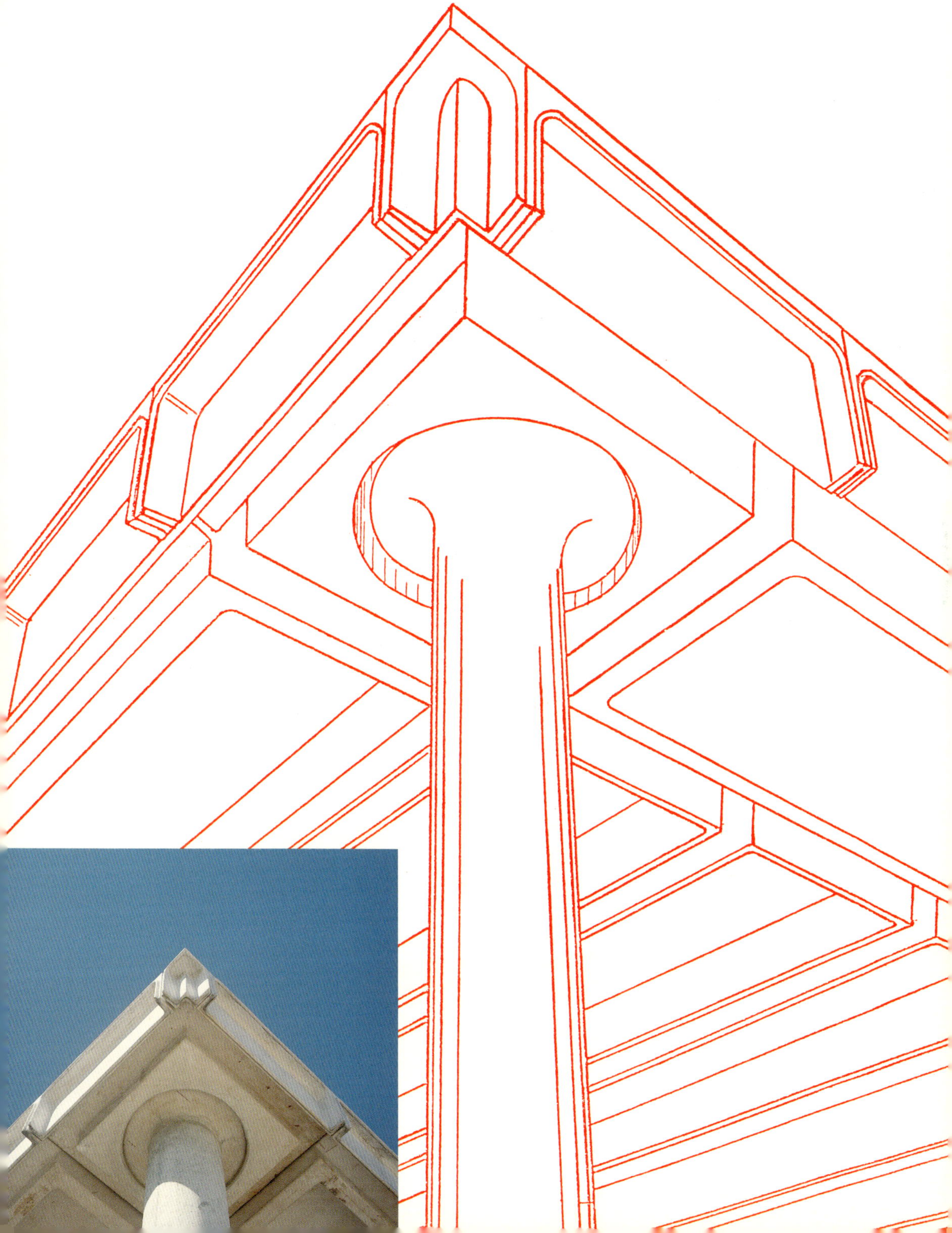

BRIONA 1972 CONSTRUCTION SYSTEM. As in the case of the earlier U 70 Isocell, another patent to certify the quality of a particularly flexible construction system. Once again this is a trilithic system in prestressed reinforced concrete, again with a beam and roof panel solution for complanar assembly. Briona 1972: a construction system based on square modules (7.2 meters per side) and composed of nine prefabricated elements in reinforced concrete (a pilaster, three beams, three roofing panels, a linear wing and a corner wing). The pilasters have a circular section and terminate in square slab capitals (1.2 meters per side), whose faces are attached to the support beams for the roofing. The perimeter of the construction is defined by the wings of the cornice, adding a further, original refinement to the construction scheme. The positioning of the roof segments between the adjacent spans is alternated to improve the distribution of the load on the beams; the housing of the plant elements is placed between the ribbing of the intrados of the roof. The system provides for the possibility of multi-level construction; therefore the pilasters can be stacked. The facing panels (in different materials) can be recessed with respect to the external pilasters to free and highlight the structure.

17327 22629 B/77

FIG.8

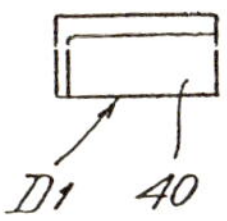

FIG.9

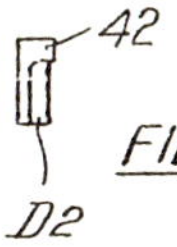

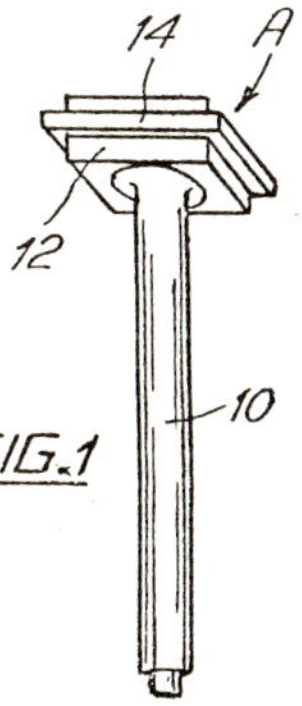

FIG.1

FIG.5

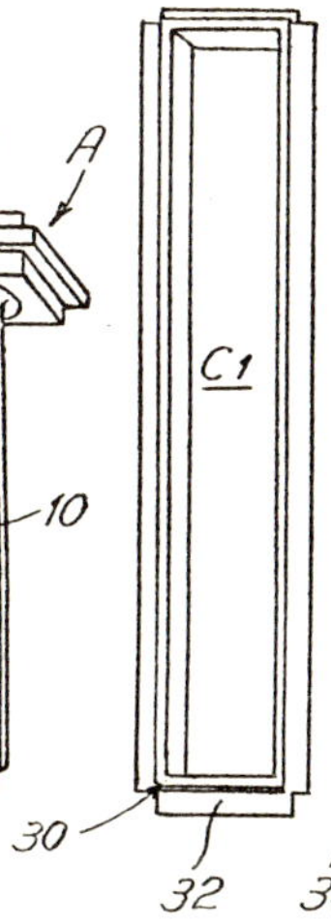

FIG.6

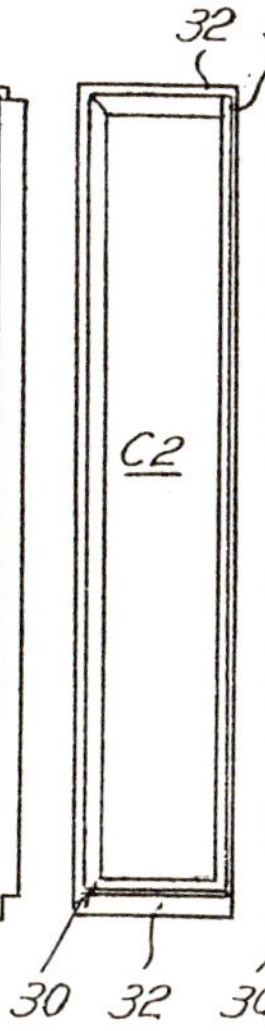

FIG.7

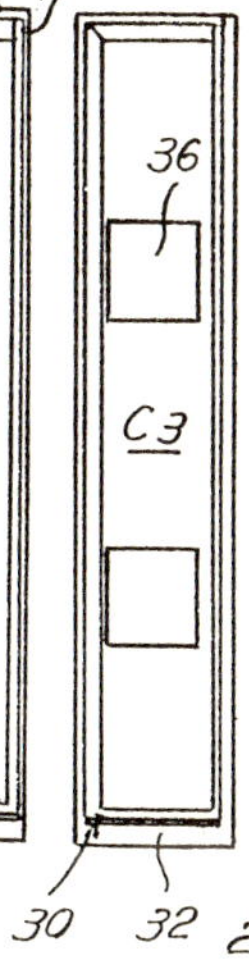

FIG.2

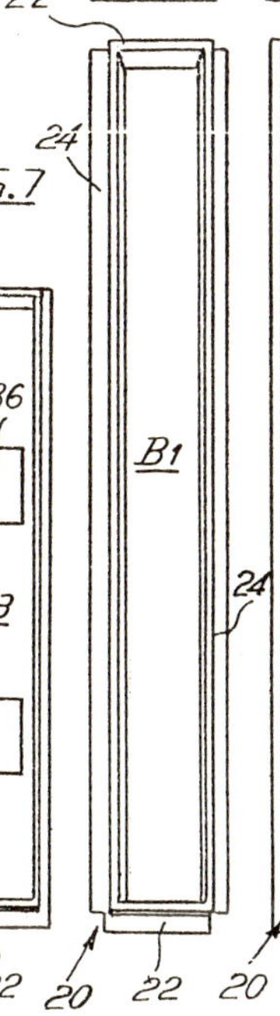

FIG.3

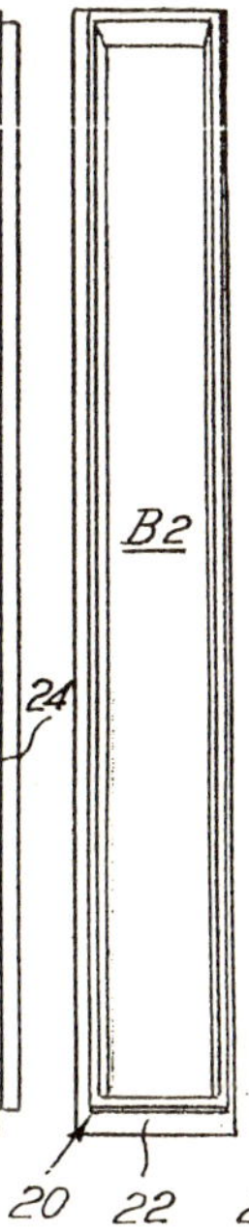

FIG.4

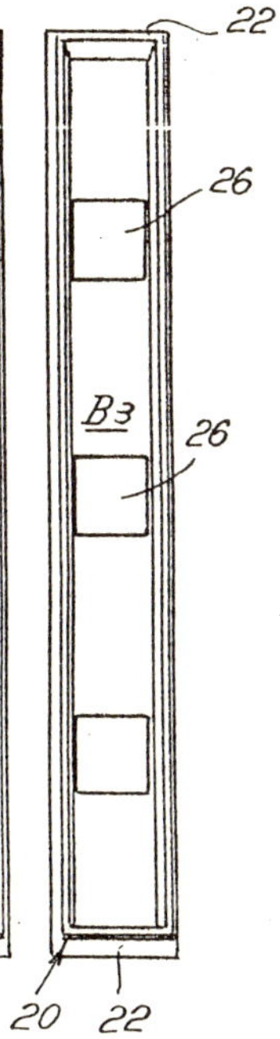

FIG.11

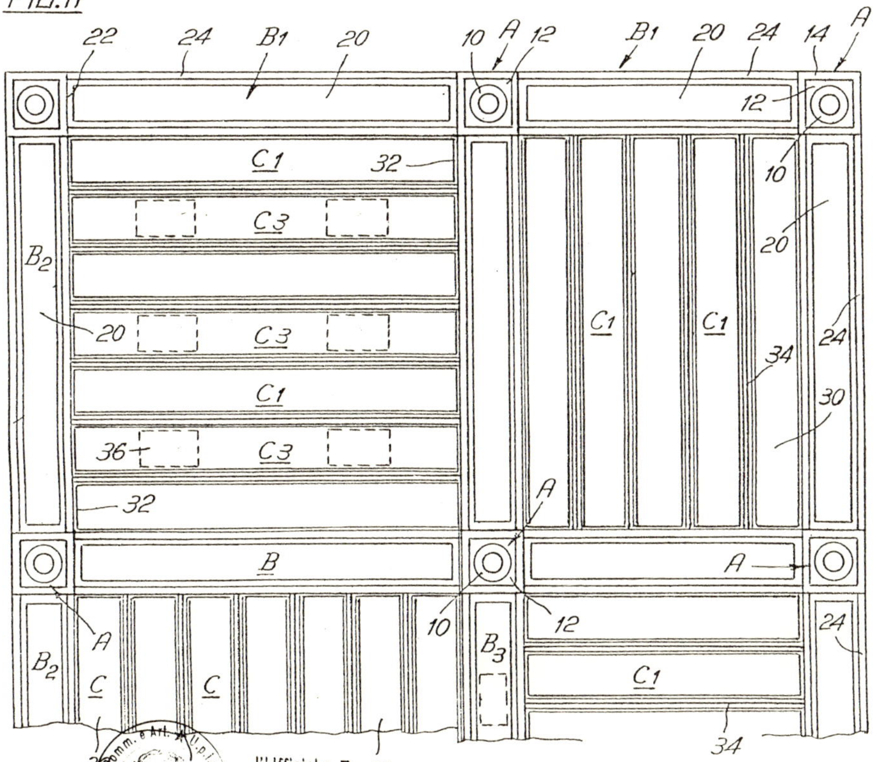

PROGETTO DI UNA MEGASTRUTTURA A MAGLIA QUADRATA, 1975

グリッド状の巨大架構計画, 1975年

この計画は、1辺40mの正方形屋根を1ユニットとするプレストレストコンクリートで立案されている。この巨大架構は、パドバ国際見本市の新しい主会場として計画されている。すべてのエレメントが建築および構造上の問題の優れた解決策であると同時に、その形態は機能を表現する設計になっている。例えば、屋根を支える柱は、基部において軸力や曲げ応力に耐えるように膨らみをもっており、また、梁は自重を軽減するために梁断面の中央部をくり抜いて軽量化している。さらに梁の接合部には、建築設備と照明を内蔵する楕円状の球体が設置されているというように。巨大で堂々としているが、同時に繊細で洗練された架構体である。相反する概念が成立している建築。

(M.T)

構造設計:ジュリオ・バッリオ, ジョバンニ・コロンボ, アルベルト・ヴィンターニ/Structures Giulio Ballio, Giovanni Colombo, Alberto Vintani

PROJECT FOR A SQUARE-GRID MEGASTRUCTURE, 1975. A square roof, 40 meters on each side, forms the module for this prestressed reinforced concrete structure designed to house the new headquarters of the International Fair of Padua. Every element is designed to achieve both constructive-structural results and to possess a high level of formal identity. Thus the pilasters supporting the roofing are strengthened at the base to better support the combined compressive and bending stress, the beams are lighter at the center of their section to diminish their weight, the joining of the beams is emptied where possible to house an ellipsoid space for the technical plant and lighting elements. A imposing but very refined megastructure: almost an architectural oxymoron.

屋根構造フレーム構成図／*The structual framework of the roofing*

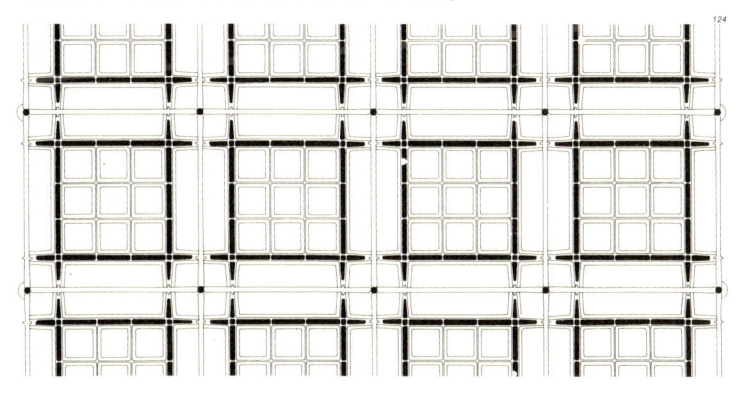

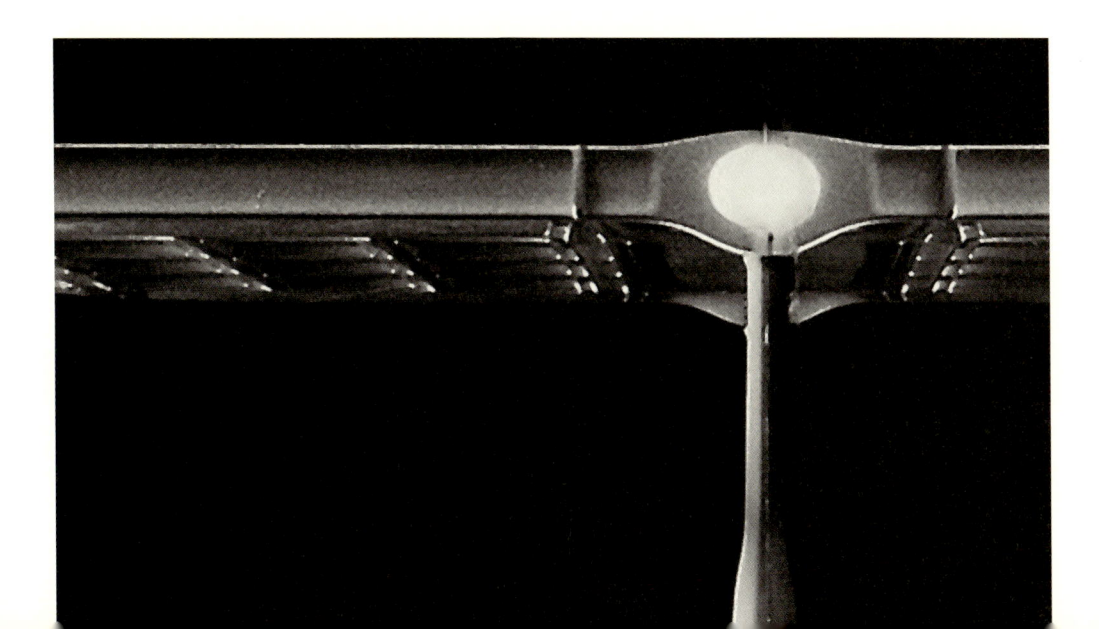

SISTEMA COSTRUTTIVO FACEP 1976

ファチェプ社による構造システム，1976年

逆Y字の梁デザインは、この構造システムの特徴をよく表現している。これは1964年の「ファチェプ社の構造システム」の最初のテーマである、屋根裏をフラットにする条件を外し、梁型が下に突出するシステムを再び採用したことである。構造グリッドは10.6×20m（梁長と一致する）の長方形である。幅2.5mの屋根パネルは、トップライトを有する部材と取り替えることができる。柱と梁の関係は、屋根部材の張出し部とも形態的に一体化している。屋根パネルは、素材の耐力特性を最大限に発揮させて、厚さを最小にしている。このシステムはほかのシステムと同様に、外装パネルは金属やガラスなど種々の選択が可能である。

(M.O)

FACEP CONSTRUCTION SYSTEM 1976. The upside-down Y profile of the beams creates the characteristic image of this construction system that returns to the original theme of the Facep 1964 structure, in which the lowered beam negates the complanar character of the intrados. The structural grid is a rectangle measuring 10.60 x 20 meters (corresponding to the length of the beam), while the roofing is composed of 2.5 meter panels alternated with skylights. The relationship of the beam to the pilaster simplifies the formation of overhanging roofing elements. The resistance characteristics of the material are "stretched" to the limit, and therefore the thickness of the roofing panels is truly minimal. As always, different options are offered for the facing panels, in sheet metal or glass.

ブッソレンゴ（ヴェローナ）にある展示施設，1976年／Building for expositions in Bussolengo(Verona),1976

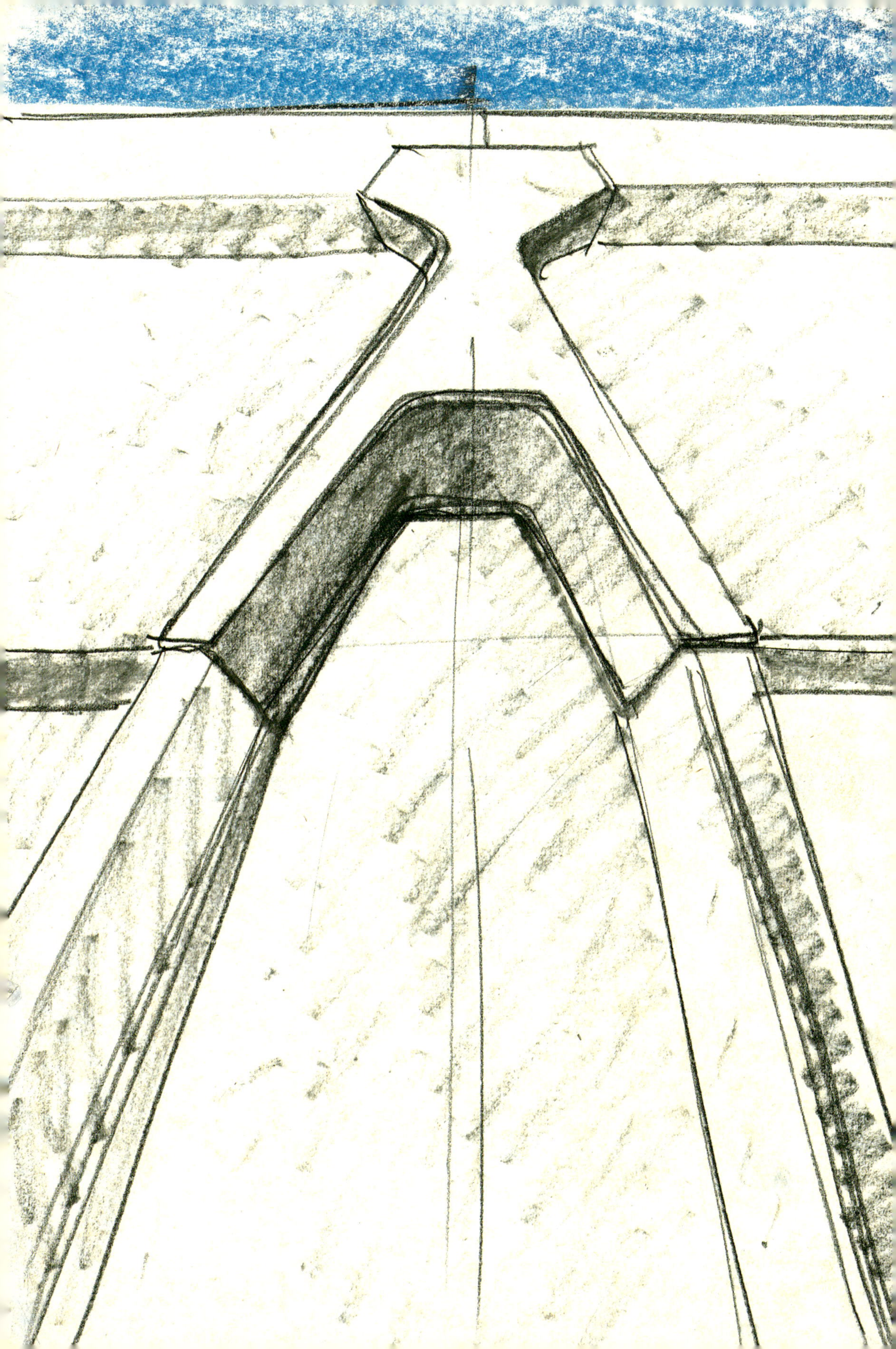

106

構造設計：ジュリオ・バッリオ，ジョバンニ・コロンボ，アルベルト・ヴィンターニ／Structures Giulio Ballio, Giovanni Colombo, Alberto Vintani

長辺方向断面図／*Cross section*

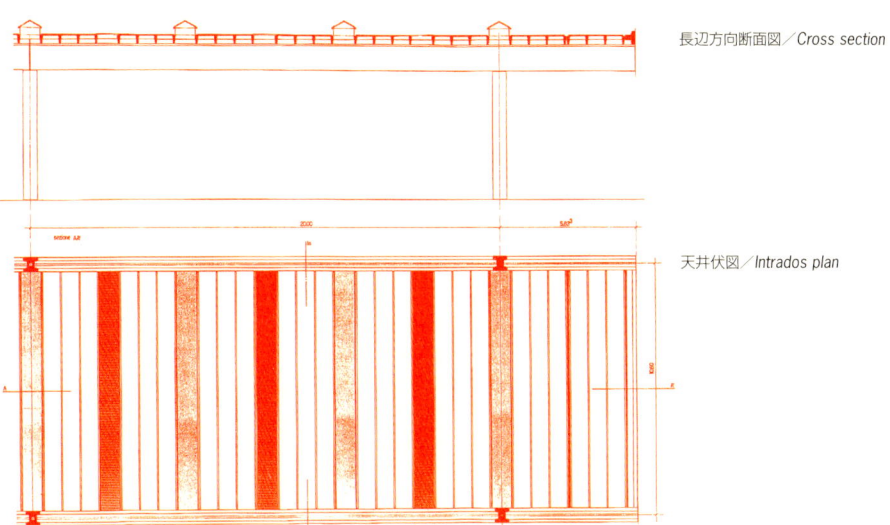

天井伏図／*Intrados plan*

UFFICI SNAIDERO
A MAIANO DEL FRIULI (UDINE), 1978

マイアーノ・デル・フリウリのズナイデロ社オフィス／ウディネ，1978年

3棟の建物で構成された複合工場施設。各建物は、展示ホール、サービススペース（食堂、医務室、会議室、更衣室）、オフィスで構成されている。展示ホールは連続する鉄骨門型トラスの架構に特徴があり、グリッド状の屋根が門型トラスの架構に支えられている。外部の仕上げはアルミ押出成形材の支柱にガラスが嵌められている。サービススペースは、地震で倒壊した以前の建物の基礎と同一のモデュールで、逆ピラミッド形の柱頭をもつ鉄骨柱がトラス構造の屋根を支えている。オフィスは、4本の鉄筋コンクリートの円柱と屋根の交差梁から各階の床版が吊り下げられている。楕円形の舷窓によって、軽快にデザインされたFRPの外装パネルは、この建物に独特の存在感を与えている。「チニゼッロ・バルサーモのアルミタリア社屋」の発展形である。

(C.I)

SNAIDERO OFFICES, MAIANO DEL FRIULI (UDINE), 1978. Three separate buildings for a single industrial complex. One for showroom space, one for services (dining areas, infirmaries, meeting rooms, locker rooms), and one for offices. The showroom hall is characterized by a series of reticular portals in steel that support a roof with a square grid; the filler panels are in glass with uprights in extruded aluminium. The adjacent building for the service facilities has a structure in steel with a square grid (reflecting the modular design of the first, and built over the existing foundation of a building destroyed by an earthquake) with pilasters that terminate in a "capital" in the form of an upside-down pyramid, whose sides are connected to the triangular roofbeams. The office building is perched on four reinforced concrete pylons with a circular section bearing the crossed beams of the roofing, which support the floor slabs with a series of tie-rods. The facing panels of the facade (in polyester reinforced with fiberglass), lightened by elliptical portholes, give an unmistakable image to this showcase building, which can be seen as the natural evolution of the previous project for Cinisello Balsamo.

サービス棟／Services building

オフィス棟／Office building

構造設計：ジュリオ・バッリオ，ジョバンニ・コロンボ，アルベルト・ヴィンターニ／Structures Giulio Ballio, Giovanni Colombo, Alberto Vintani

外装パネル／Facing panels

展示場棟／*Showroom building*

UFFICI IMM A CARRARA, 1991

カラーラのIMM社オフィス、1991年

インターナショナル・マルミ・エ・マッキナ社の中核施設としての建築的イメージは、同社の業務内容を建築的に表現することである。当初のアイディアは、構造も屋根も間仕切壁も、建物をすべて大理石でつくることだった。しかし、下部構造に過度の荷重をかけないために、レストランと厨房を内包する基壇を設け、その上に鉄骨造のオフィスがつくられている。外装にはアルミパネルとガラス、屋根にはカラーラ・ビアンコの大理石が採用されている。ヴォールト屋根のユニットは、わずか厚さ6cmで、幅1m、長さ（スパン）が5mである。各ユニットは同一の石の塊からコンピュータ制御で連続的に局面切断されている。この素材の特性を追求する中で、大理石に内在する力を構造材として使用に耐えることを平然とさりげなく実現している。アンジェロ・マンジャロッティが大理石の特性を追求し、大理石を構造材＝圧縮材としてはじめて使用した記念碑的な建物である。

(O.H)

MANAGERIAL HEADQUARTERS OF INTERNAZIONALE MARMI E MACCHINE, CARRARA, 1991. The architectural image of the headquarters is conceived to underline the character and quality of the company. The initial idea was to create a building entirely built in marble (structure, roofing and facings). The solution finally utilized features a base with restaurants and kitchens, an office building with a metal structure (to avoid excessive weight born by the lower parts), facings in aluminium and glass and roofing in white Carrara marble. The vaults – only 6 centimeters in thickness, by 5 meters in length and 1 meter in width – are obtained by means of successive cutting of the same block of marble with numerically controlled machines. Utilized here for the first time, this solution investigates rarely exploited resistance characteristics of the material (such as that of compression), placing the accent on possibilities normally overlooked in its structural applications. Another record for Angelo Mangiarotti.

構造設計：ジャンカルロ・バローディ、アルベルト・ヴィンターニ／Structures Giancarlo Parodi, Alberto Vintani

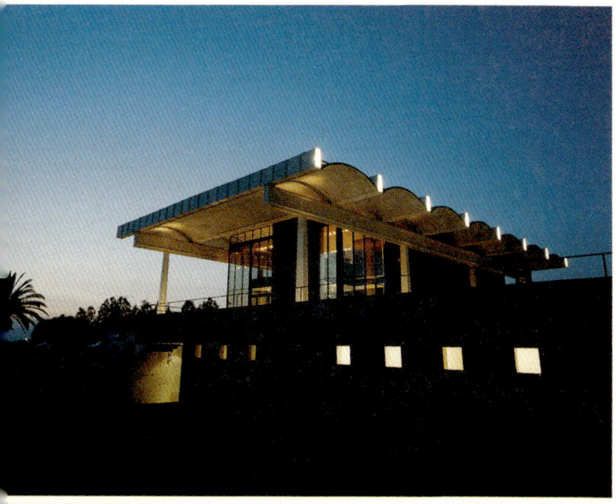

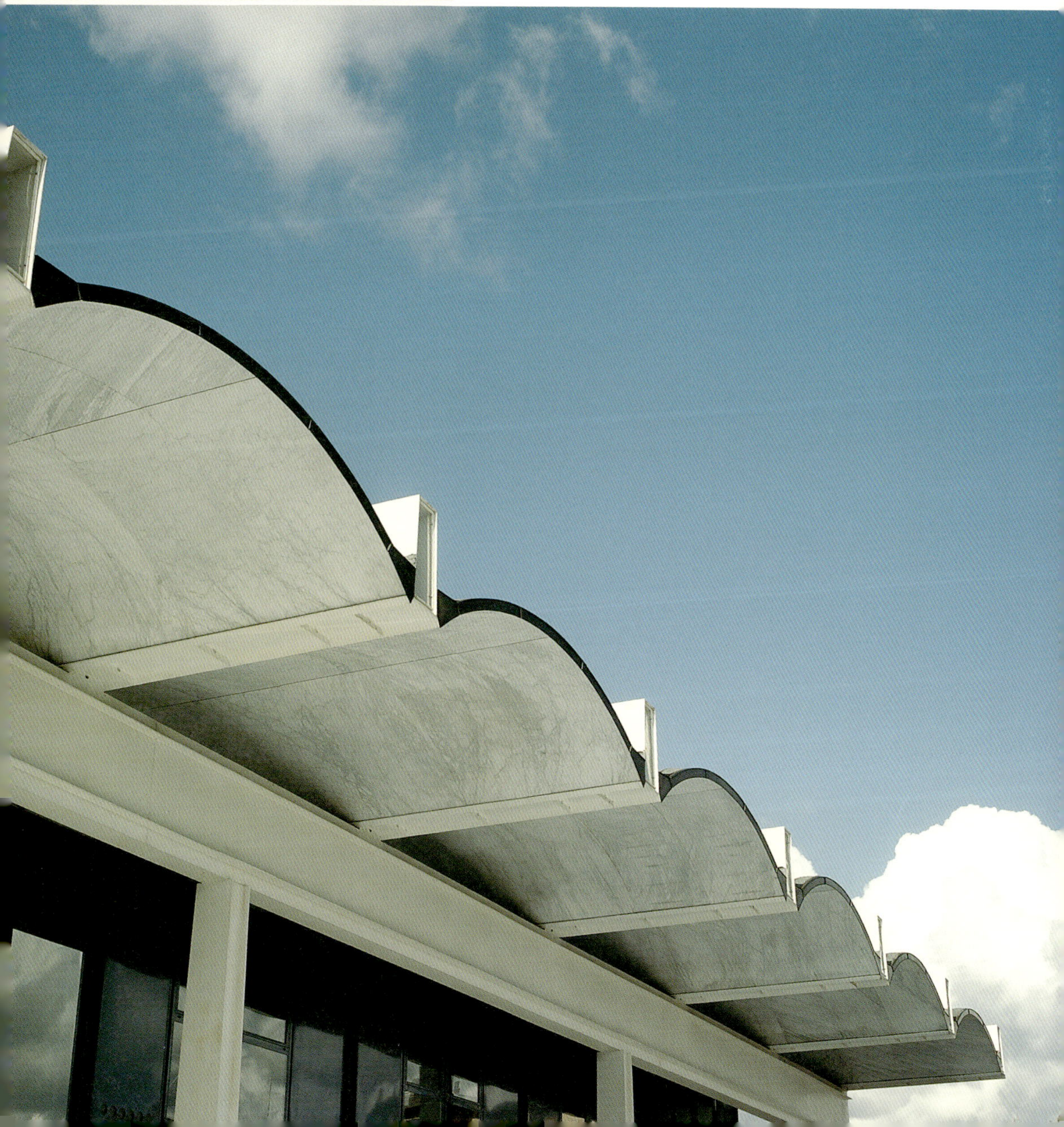

屋根ヴォールト詳細図／Detail drawing of the roofing vaults

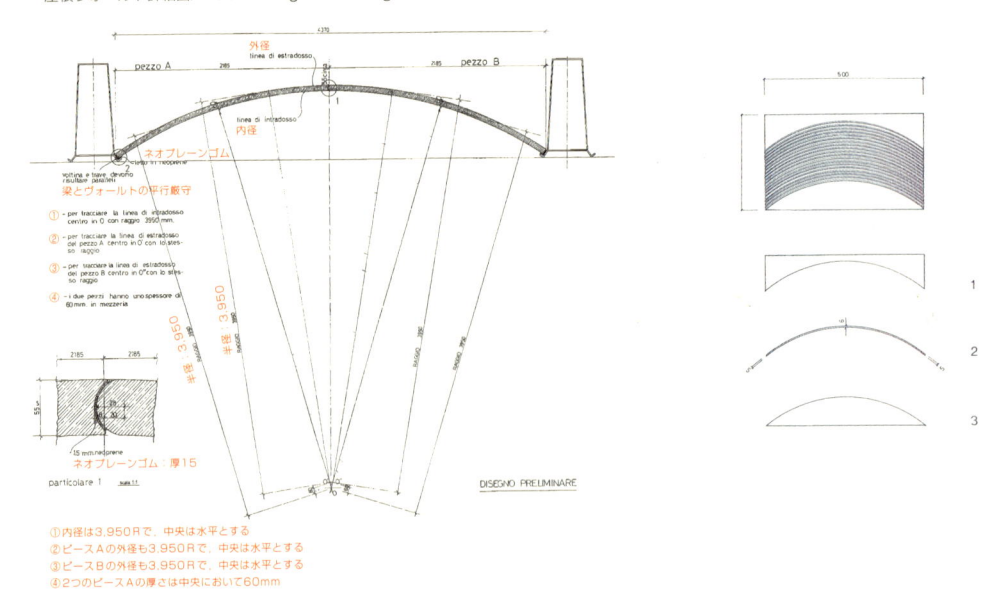

天井伏図／Intrados plan

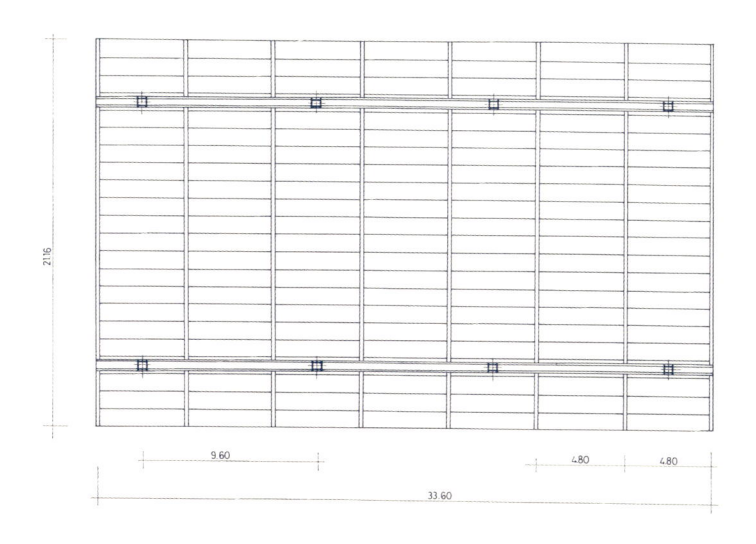

STUDIO DELLA STRUTTURA S99, 1999

構造体S99のためのスタディ，1999年

「構造体S99」は、ドイツの道路交通法の規制を順守する可能性を模索する中で生まれた。通常に運搬できる最大サイズは幅3m、長さ24mである。これらのサイズは、柱、梁、屋根という従来の3エレメント構成から〈2エレメント構成〉（利点はコスト削減と施工期間の短縮である）への転換である。つまり、梁と屋根を合体し、運搬可能な最大サイズがトップライトの配置計画において大きな自由度を与えている。法的な制約を順守し、経済性に配慮した、千年来の伝統を越える構造システムである。

(Ka.M)

構造設計：アルベルト・ヴィンターニ／Structures Alberto Vintani

STUDY FOR THE S99 STRUCTURE, 1999. A project stimulated by the possibilities offered by German regulations permitting transport by truck, without particular difficulties (and without special police escorts) of prefabricated components up to 3 meters in width and 24 meters in length. Sizes that make it possible for the tradition trilith (composed of pillar, beam and roofing) to be transformed into a veritable "bilith" – advantageous in terms of costs and assembly time – where the beam is no longer necessary as it is substantially "incorporated" in the roofing, whose measurements correspond to maximum transportable size and permit great freedom in the positioning of skylights. To go beyond (venerable) traditions by paying attention to standards and economics.

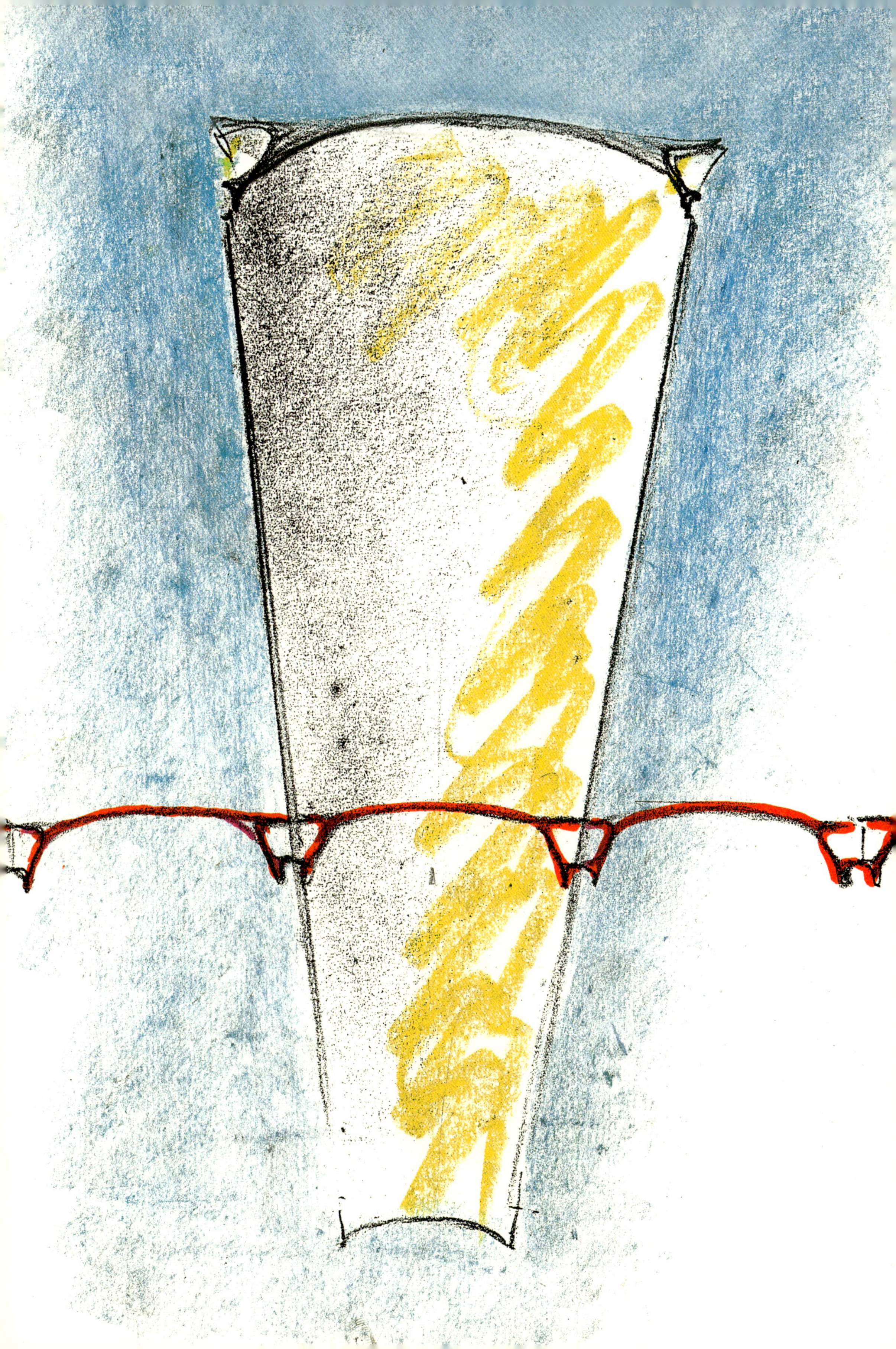

STAZIONI FERROVIARIE
CERTOSA E ROGOREDO A MILANO, 1982

チェルトーザおよびロゴレードの鉄道駅／ミラノ，1982年

この屋根構造体は、駅舎のプラットフォームにおける個々の要求に対応して設計されている。鉄骨のY型柱が三角形の断面をもつ大梁を支持し、その大梁に2本のタイロッドを用いて吊り下げられたアルミパネルとガラスの庇が取り付けられている。この庇は高さを変えて連結することができ、乗降客が通る駅の入口から列車までの通路を覆うことができる。また、構造体の大きさを変えて、通常の柱間よりスパンを大きくすることで、プラットフォームにおける動線の自由度がさらに増すことも可能である。駅につながるビルの外観は、全体がアルミニウムパネルで覆われたとてもテクノロジカルな様相を漂わせている。この建物は、マンジャロッティが続けていた「チニゼッロ・バルサーモのアルミタリア社屋」や「マイアーノ・デル・フリウリのズナイデロ社オフィス」と同様に、企業施設のデザインにつながるものである。

(Ke.M)

ロゴレード駅スケッチ／*Rail station Rogoredo*

構造設計：ジュリオ・バッリオ，カルメロ・ラッファ，アルベルト・ヴィンターニ／*Structures Giulio Ballio, Carmelo Raffa, Alberto Vintani*

ロゴレード駅／Rail station Rogoredo

CERTOSA AND ROGOREDO RAIL STATIONS, MILAN, 1982. A roofing structure for the rail platforms to adapt to the different needs of each individual station. Steel Y pilasters support a triangular-section beam to which the canopies in sheet aluminium and glass are attached with tie-rods. The profile of the canopy can vary in keeping with the need to connect spaces of different heights, offering shelter for travelers in every passage from the entrance to the station to the trains. The sizing of the structure has made it possible to increase the traditional distance between the pilasters, for greater freedom of movement on the platform. A highly characteristic feature – fully linked to Mangiarotti's research for industrial buildings, such as the Armitalia plant and the Snaidero offices – is the image of the buildings connected to the station, completely clad in aluminium panel with a very technical look.

チェルトーザ駅スケッチ／*Rail station Certosa*

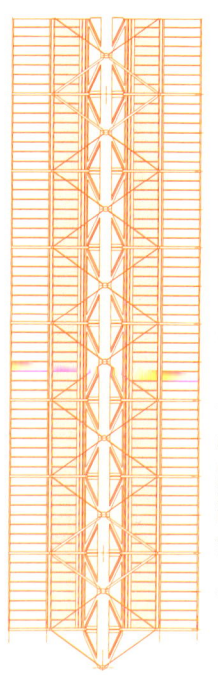

キャノピー屋根伏図／*Extrados plan of the canopy*

キャノピートラス梁断面図／Cross-section of the canopy

チェルトーザ駅／Rail station Certosa

STAZIONI FERROVIARIE SOTTERRANEE VENEZIA E REPUBBLICA A MILANO, 1982-98

地下鉄ヴェネツィア駅とレ・プッブリカ駅／ミラノ，1982-98年

カルロ・ベルテッリは、言っている。
「ヴェネツィア駅とレ・プッブリカ駅は、地下にあるためにこのように美しいのだろう。マンジャロッティは、地上に建設するための制約を受けなかったために現代建築における最もすばらしいデザインを表現することができた」
ミラノの鉄道と地下鉄の交差点にあるこれら2つの地下駅舎は、とても重要な公的再開発事業の一環として、計画的にも技術的にも錯綜した問題を抱えながらも、非常に洗練された施工計画をもとに実現した。ヴェネツィア駅では街路レベルからほんの数メートル下に計画されるため、分節アーチ工法が採用され、地上での交通を妨げることなくトンネル工事が完成

レプッブリカ駅（ミラノ地下鉄）スケッチ／*Repubblica Station*

した。地上面は、まず駅舎の構造体を建設するための支持盤として利用され、その後は掘削して埋設し、それを繰り返して工事を進めた。この構造体はアーチ形状でヴォールト部に中2階を設け、さらにプラットフォームのスペースを確保している。レ・プッブリカ駅は街路レベルより20m下にあり、その行程に現れる美しいプロポーションをもつ鉄筋コンクリートの構造体が目を奪う。近くには超高層ビルや巨大構築物があるため、施工は露天の穴を掘削することと、地盤の補強をすることから始められた。マンジャロッティは、建築的仕上げに関わるヴォールトのデザインから入口のキャノピーに至るまで、細心の注意を払って上品に仕上げたが、施工管理が困難なため、完成までに多くの年月を費やしている。 (Ke.M)

レプッブリカ駅（ミラノ地下鉄）／*Repubblica Station*　　　共同者：ミラノ地下鉄／*With Metropolitana Milanese*

地下鉄駅入口スケッチ／Studies for the entrance canopy

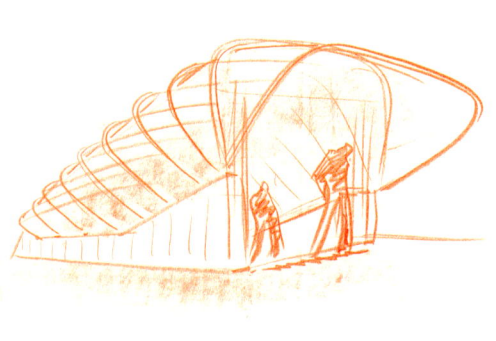

レプッブリカ駅（ミラノ地下鉄）／Repubblica Station

VENEZIA & REPUBBLICA UNDERGROUND STATIONS, RAIL BYPASS, MILAN, 1982-1998. "Perhaps they are so beautiful because they are underground. [Mangiarotti] has been able to express the best of contemporary architecture without the interference ground-level taste" (Carlo Bertelli). Two stations of the Milan Rail Bypass, renewing a period of very important public works, created in very complex phases of design and engineering, and constructed with very sophisticated methods. For the Venezia station, just a few meters below street level, cellular arch technology has been utilized, permitting construction of tunnels without interrupting traffic at ground level: the terrain is initially utilized as a support surface for the construction of the structure itself, and then excavated. The arch form of the resulting structure makes it possible to attach a mezzanine to the vault, leaving the platform spaces open. The Repubblica station is characterized by a structure in reinforced concrete

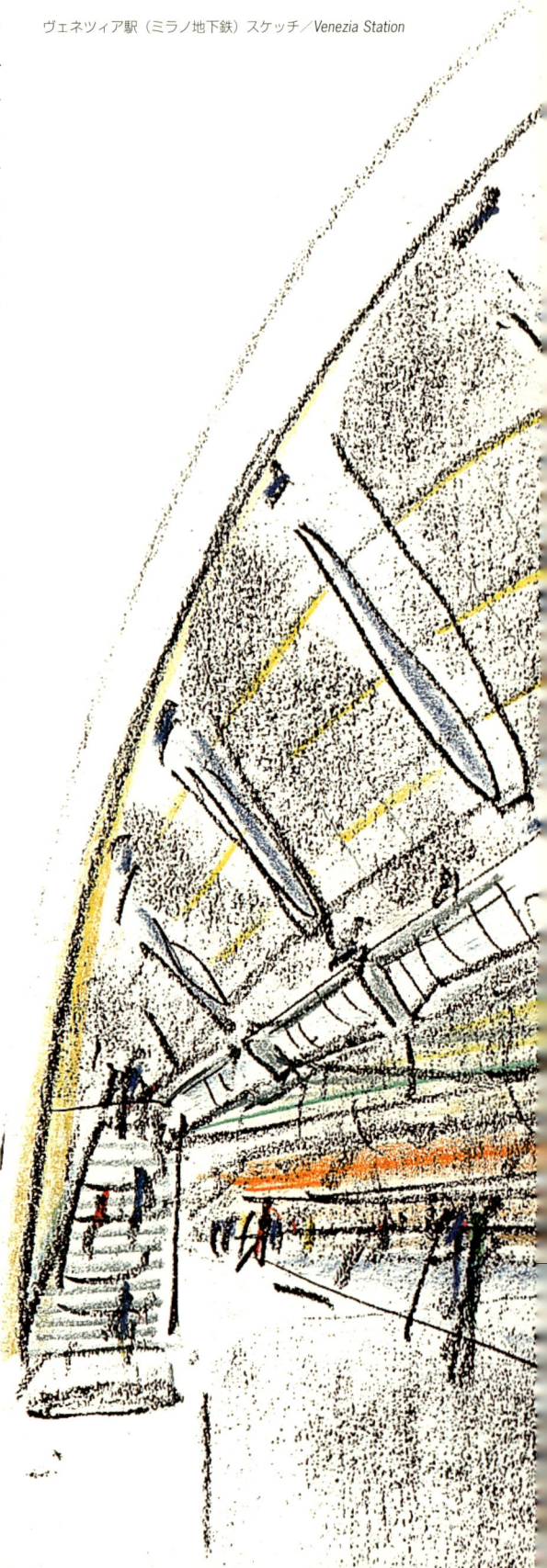

ヴェネツィア駅（ミラノ地下鉄）スケッチ／Venezia Station

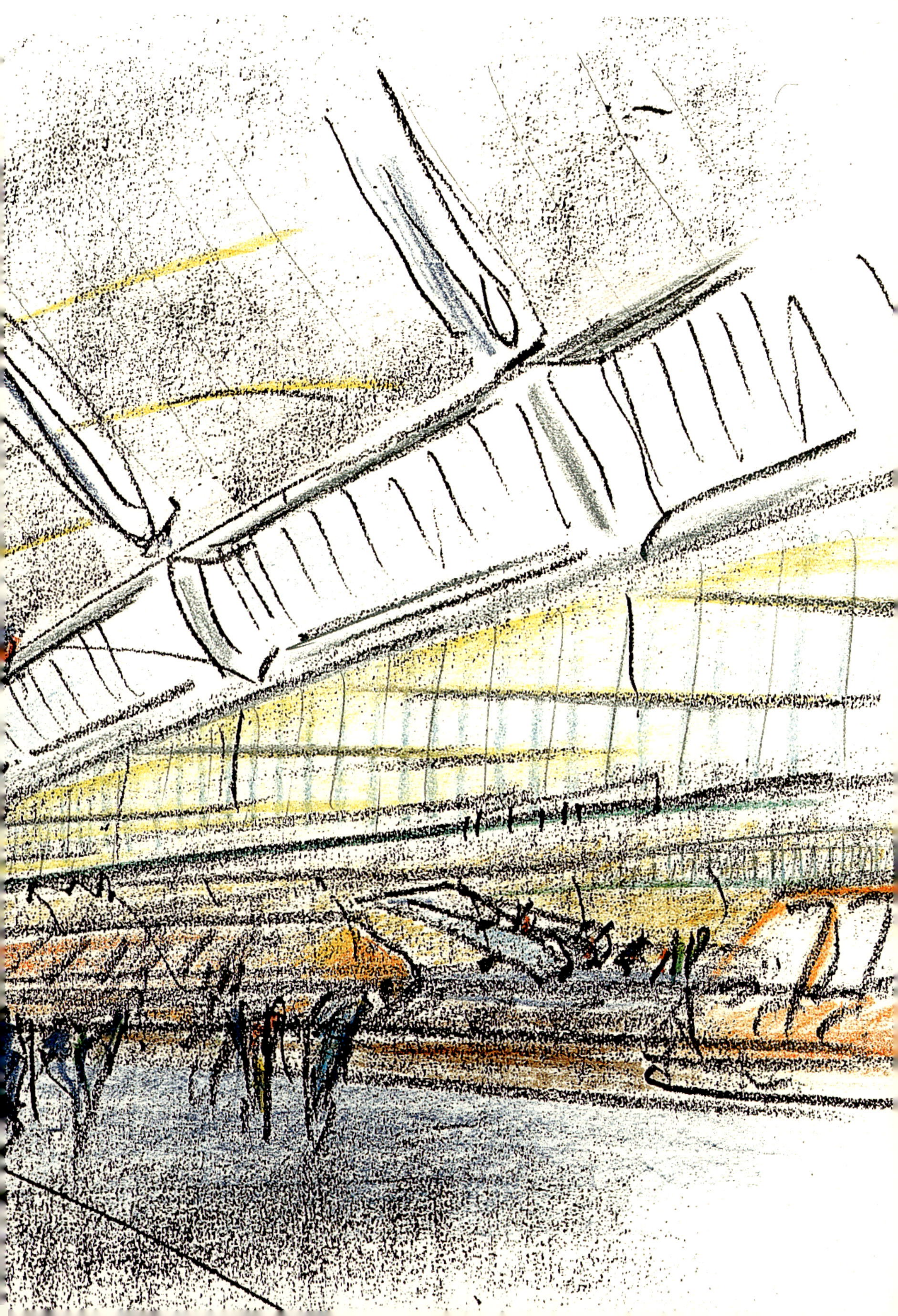

スタディのためのスケッチ／Working sketch

of noteworthy proportions, descending to a depth of twenty meters below street level. Due to the vicinity of skyscrapers and other large constructions, the worksite was organized in terms of initial excavation and reinforcement of the terrain. In every aspect of the architectural finishings – from the design of the vaults to that of the entrance canopy – Mangiarotti has been particularly attentive and refined, in spite of the difficulties in monitoring a construction project that took many years to complete.

ヴェネツィア駅（ミラノ地下鉄）／Venezia Station

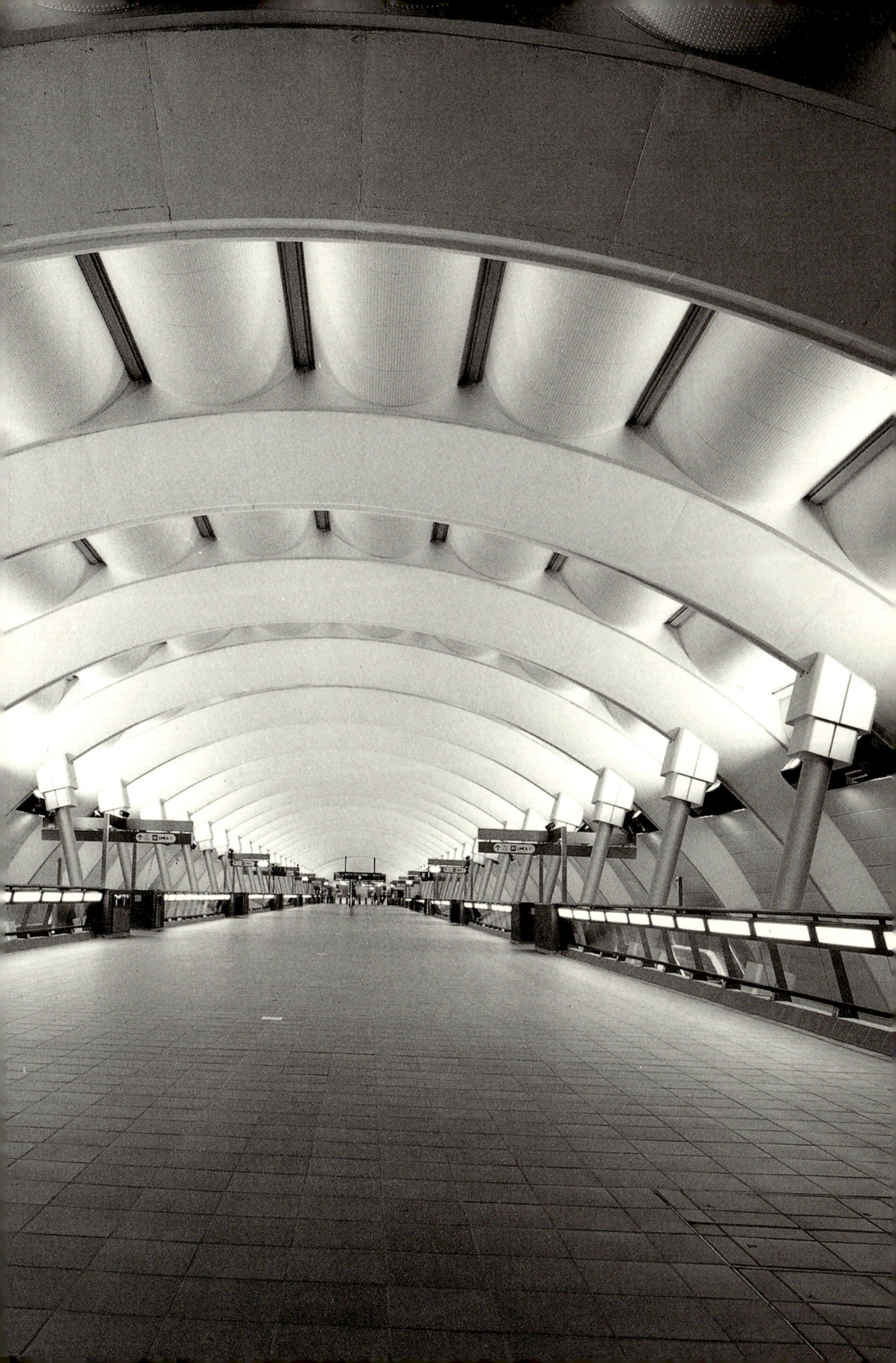

PROGETTO DI UNO STADIO A PALERMO, 1987

パレルモのサッカー競技場計画，1987年

この計画は，1990年のサッカー・ワールドカップのために企画され、特に周辺環境との関係に注意が払われている。スタジアムは、傾斜した地面に直接支えられているプレファブリケートされた鉄筋コンクリートの階段席と、地面とわずか4点でつながり、あたかも宙に浮かぶような大屋根にデザインされた2つの大きな金属の帆で構成されている。さらに、階段座席からは周囲の景色を楽しむこともできる。

(Y.T)

DESIGN FOR A STADIUM, PALERMO, 1987. For the soccer World Cup of 1990, a project that pays particular attention to the relationship with the site. A stadium in which the prefabricated reinforced concrete stands rest directly on the sloping terrain, while the roofing, with its two large metal sails, seems to take flight, attached to the ground at four points only to offer a view of the surrounding landscape for the spectators.

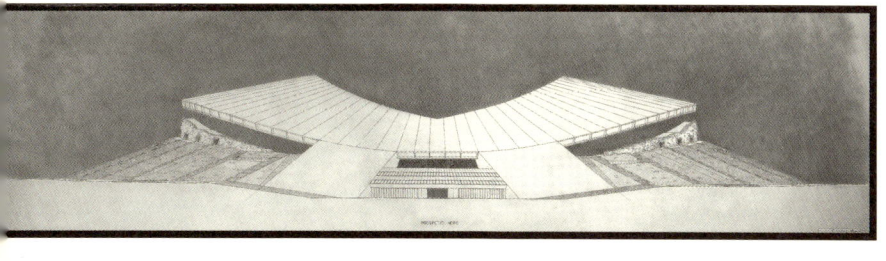

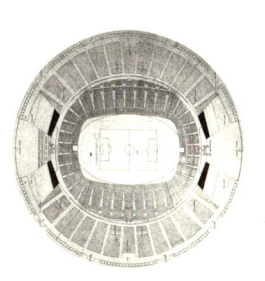

構造設計；ジュリオ・バッリオ，アルベルト・ヴィンターニ／*Structures Giulio Ballio, Alberto Vintani*

PROGETTO DI UNO STADIO A CATANIA, 1987
カターニアのサッカー競技場計画，1987年

この計画は，1990年のサッカー・ワールドカップのために、パレルモと同時期に計画されたもう1つの競技場である。マンジャロッティは言っている。
「私は魚取りの網籠のようにすべての要素を構造的に1つにしたかった………。支えつつ覆う、構造と意匠の一体化が私の常なる関心事である！」
スタジアムは網状の金属構造で構築され、目立った地勢のない平坦な土地のランドマークになっている。

(N.M)

DESIGN FOR A STADIUM, CATANIA, 1987. Created at the same time as the design for Palermo, another stadium for the World Cup of soccer in 1990. "I wanted it to all function structurally together, like a fish trap… To support and cover at the same time, my usual obsession!" A reticular metal structure incorporates, in a single volume, all the parts of the stadium, becoming a landmark in a flat zone without striking features.

構造設計：ジュリオ・バッリオ，アルベルト・ヴィンターニ／Structures Giulio Ballio, Alberto Vintani

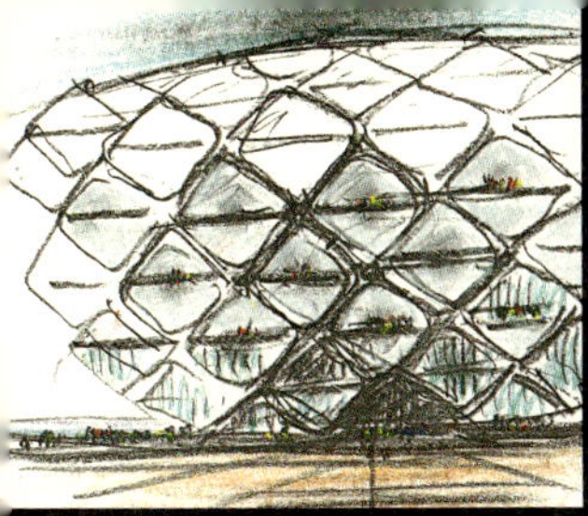
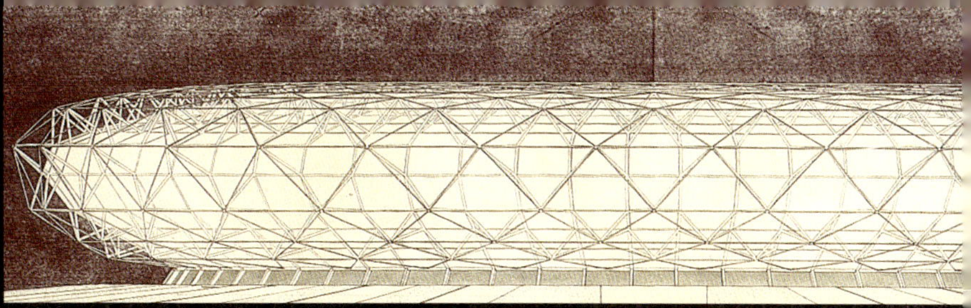
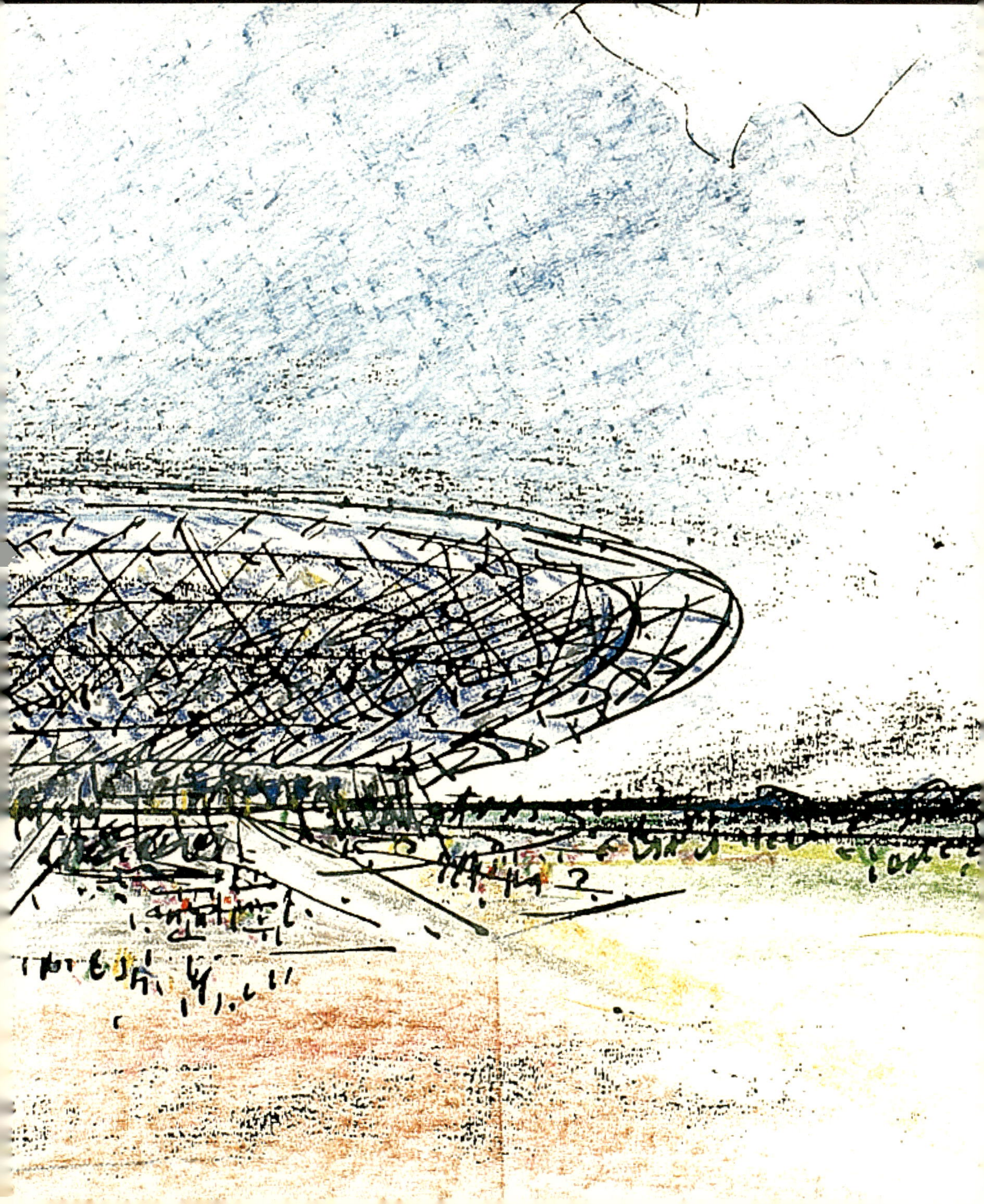

PROGETTO DI UN PONTE PEDONALE A RIOMAGGIORE (LA SPEZIA), 1997

リオ・マッジォーレの歩道橋計画，1997年

「提案された計画は、素材の特性を詳細に観察し、かつ的確な構造分析を基に、使用される部材を最小限のボリュームに抑え、最適なフォルムを導き出す。多様な状況をシステム化する研究過程の到達点である」と、アンドレア・カンピオーリは評している。

繊細な歩行者専用の2連アーチの橋は、35mスパンで架けられ、ワイヤーケーブルで圧着接合した大理石ブロックで構成されている。この橋は構造的には2つのアーチによる3ヒンジ構法で、類型的に前例のない構造の橋であり、現代建築の成果を土木工学に応用している。これは、一流の技術者であるアンジェロ・マンジャロッティに最も相応しいテーマである。

(I.M)

DESIGN FOR A FOOTBRIDGE, RIOMAGGIORE (LA SPEZIA), 1997. *"The proposed solution is the point of arrival of a path of research in which many different aspects have been perfected based on meticulous observation of the characteristics of the material and careful structural analysis, aimed at the definition of the optimal form in relation to the minimum quantity of material utilized"* (Andrea Campioli). *Two spans of 35 meters covered by two slender walkways (in a structure with two arches and three joints) made completely with blocks of marble prestressed with steel cables. An absolutely unprecedented choice for a typology, that of the bridge, which by its nature has brought great modern architecture closer to civil engineering: an ideal theme for the honoris causa engineer Angelo Mangiarotti.*

モンタージュ写真／Photo montage

構造設計：アルベルト・ヴィンターニ／*Structures Alberto Vintani*

SULL'ARCHITETTURA

建築について／グィド・ナルディ

アンジェロ・マンジャロッティの多岐にわたる活動を子細に観察すると、その創造の歩みの最大の特徴が研究と模索の姿勢にあることが明らかになる。建築デザイン、プロダクトデザイン、そして最近の実験的彫刻でも、常に最も先進的なテーマに取り組んでいる。その彼の姿勢は、現代建築の世界においてまったく独自の地位を獲得している。彼が設計した建築は、実用品や実験的彫刻と同様に、常にオリジナルな解決策を提示している。それと同時に、現実の解釈を具体的に表現する力をもっており、堅実で厳格な理念に貫かれている。

マンジャロッティの作品からは、芸術表現の客観性への関心が感じられる。この目標を追求するデザインワークの原点は、素材の特性と生産技術の可能性であり、特に工業的技術には大きな関心をもっている。このことからマンジャロッティのデザインは、理論的にも重要性を帯びてくる。建築とデザインに関する現在の議論に関して、1つの基準点となるであろう。

本来のデザインの意味において、今日のデザイン活動がすべてのレベルで示しているあいまいさに対し、マンジャロッティは毅然とした姿勢で臨んでいる。問題の表層しか把握できず、部分的な解決や、自己矛盾した解答しか見出せないデザインのアプローチに対して、彼は強烈な批判を浴びせている。一方、彼自身が選んだアプローチは、デザインのより幅広い解釈をもとに構想から具現化に至るまでの全工程で出てくるあらゆるニーズに応える、唯一の必要不可欠な解決策を探るものである。

構造的真実と最適なデザインの融合を追求する姿勢は、彼の仕事に表れている。1つの人格に両方が共存していることは稀であり、だからこそマンジャロッティは真の巨匠と言えるのである。

自己と社会の両方に対して直截さと風刺精神を込めて、彼は建築家の職能について独特な観点と愛情を示している。つまり、生産技術と建築構成に対する挑発的な実験的探求を行うこと、各部位のデザインと全体の意匠がそれを物語っている。

1950年代後半、ミラノで初めて住宅のプロジェクトを手がけたとき、マンジャロッティは建築の設計を始めるにあたって、同時代の技術的可能性を積極的に活用する考え方を表明している。虚偽のない架構、使われる素材や技術に対して客観性をもつ建築的表現、技術革新を活用した表現上および空間上の革新性、ユーザーが享受し得る豊かな自由度を内包した設計、これらがマンジャロッティの理論の根幹を構成している。これらが目指すところは、設計における倫理を形成することにある。この倫理が占める位置は、往々にしてアカデミックな権威とは反対の立場、つまり建築の現場と建築の利用のされ方が主役となる場である。

(M.K)

ファサードのためのスタディ／Study for a facade

ON THE ARCHITECTURE

Careful observation of the multifaceted activity of Angelo Mangiarotti enables us to identify the characteristic motif of his path of research. His need to constantly come to grips with the most highly evolved scenarios of architectural design, industrial product design and, more recently, sculptural experimentation has given him an utterly original role on the contemporary architecture scene. The buildings he has designed, like the useful objects and the experimentation with sculpture, always offer original solutions, but at the same time they are capable of giving concrete expression to a line of interpretation of reality marked by great consistency and conceptual rigor. What emerges from Mangiarotti's works is an interest in the objectivity of artistic expression, pursued through a design practice that starts with the characteristics of the material and the potential of production technologies, with particular reference to those of a distinctly industrial character. In this way Mangiarotti's design practice also assumes theoretical relevance, becoming a point of reference in the present debate on architecture and design. Taking a clear position with respect to the ambiguity with which design activity today, on all levels, presents itself in relation to its original meaning, Mangiarotti radically criticizes the most reductive approaches, those capable of grasping only the surface of problems, achieving partial, contradictory solutions. He opts instead for a more extensive view of the design process, seen as a unique, necessary area in which to channel all the factors of the entire process of conception and realization of an artifact. His work demonstrates a pursuit of synthesis, of "architectonic" truth and design suitability rarely found simultaneously in a single personality, making Mangiarotti a true Master. With simplicity and irony regarding both the world and himself he manages to communicate a very special way of viewing and loving the profession, through his often provocative explorations between production technologies and architectural composition, design of the single parts and the language of the whole. Already in his first residential projects in Milan, in the second part of the 1950s, Mangiarotti fully expressed his thinking on architecture, an approach always ready to take advantage of the potential of contemporary technologies. Truth in building, objectivity of architectural expression in terms of the materials and techniques utilized, formal and spatial innovation never separated from technical innovation, the central nature of the relationship between what is designed and freedom of utilization for users: these are the cornerstones of Mangiarotti's theoretical reflection, all aimed at the configuration of an ethics of design that is often in contrast with the positions of the academic establishment, in which the dimensions of construction and utilization of architecture play a leading role.
■*Guido Nardi*

OROLOGI SECTICON, 1956

時計：セクティコン，1956年

壁掛け、据置き、および卓上時計のシリーズのデザインでは、ベース部・中央部・文字盤をプラスチック製のカバーで一体化することを意図している。最も普及した代表的なモデルはキノコ型のフォルムで、安定感のある末広がりのベース部、電池を内蔵し、握りこぶしのように理想的に絞り込まれた中央部、そして判読しやすさを何よりも重視した広くすっきりした文字盤で構成されている。

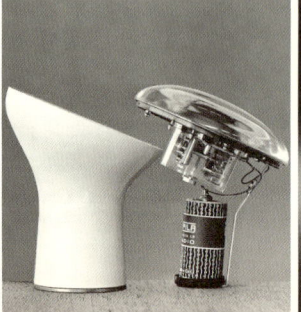

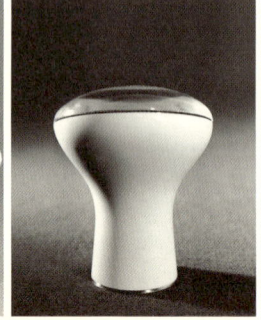

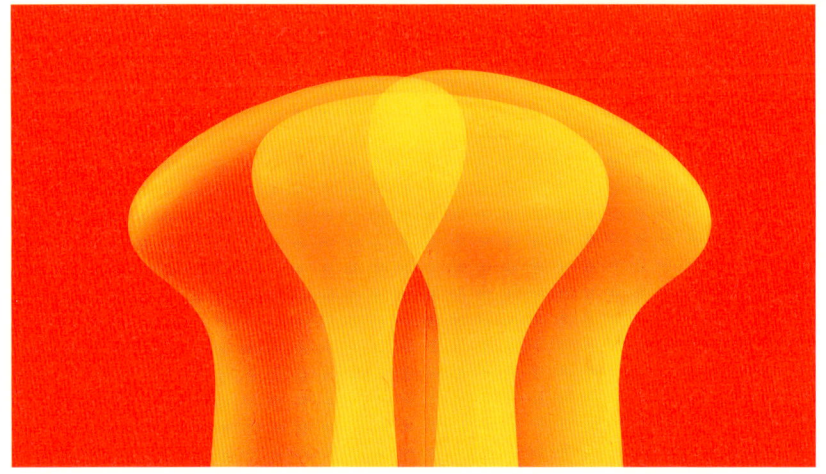

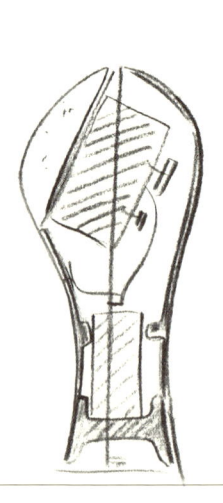

(O.H)

共同者：ブルーノ・モラスッティ／With Bruno Morassutti
製造：ユニバーサル・エスケイプメント社／Produced by The Universal Escapement ltd

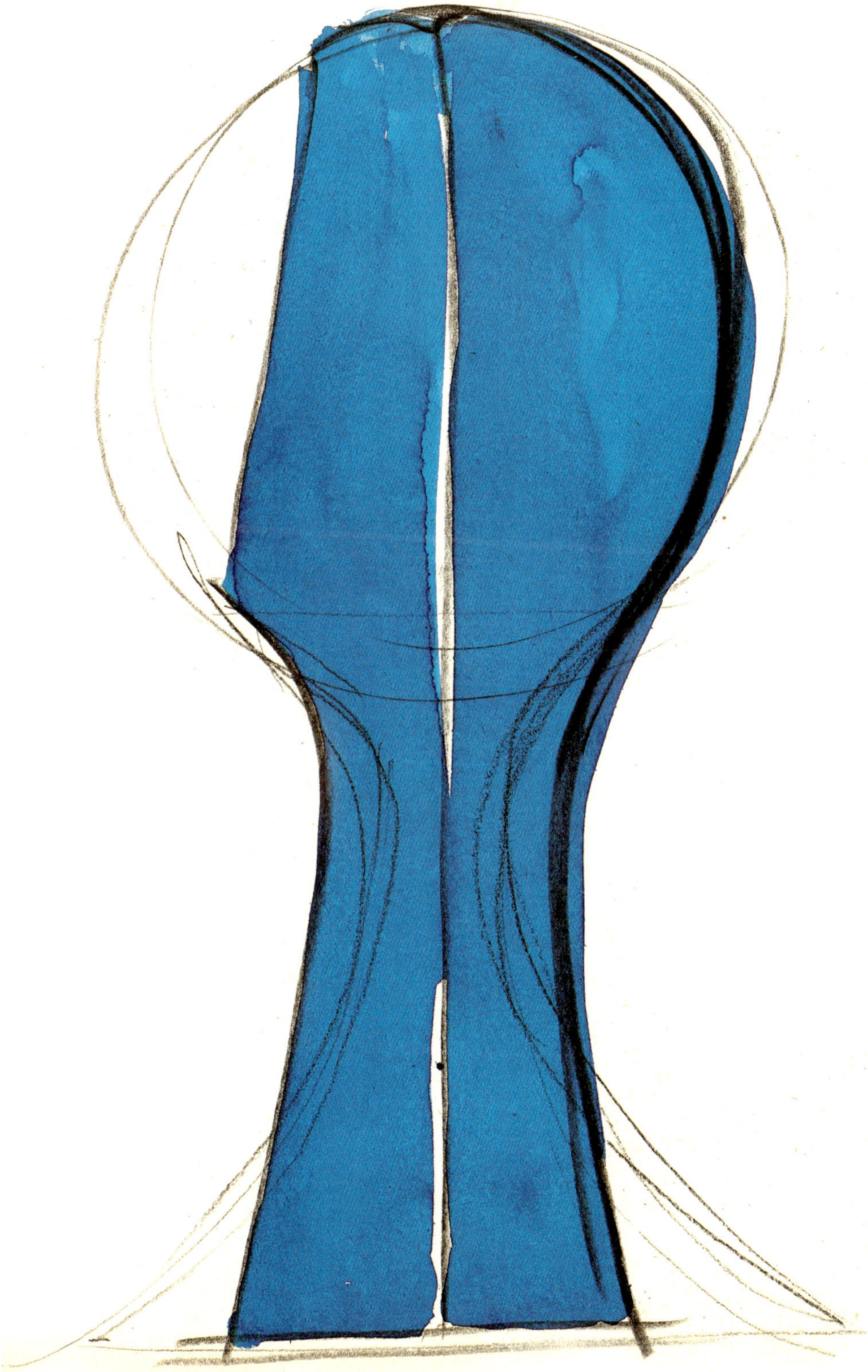

SECTICON CLOCKS, 1956. A single volume in plastic comprises the base, the support and the face in the design of this collection of table and wall clocks. In the most representative and widespread model the "mushroom" form features a wider base for greater stability, a smaller central section – an ideal grip – for the batteries, and a large face for clear legibility.

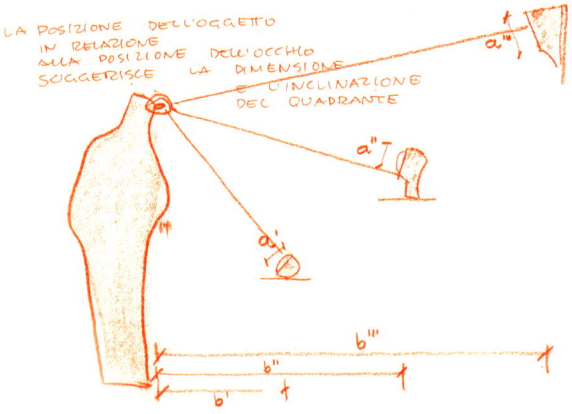

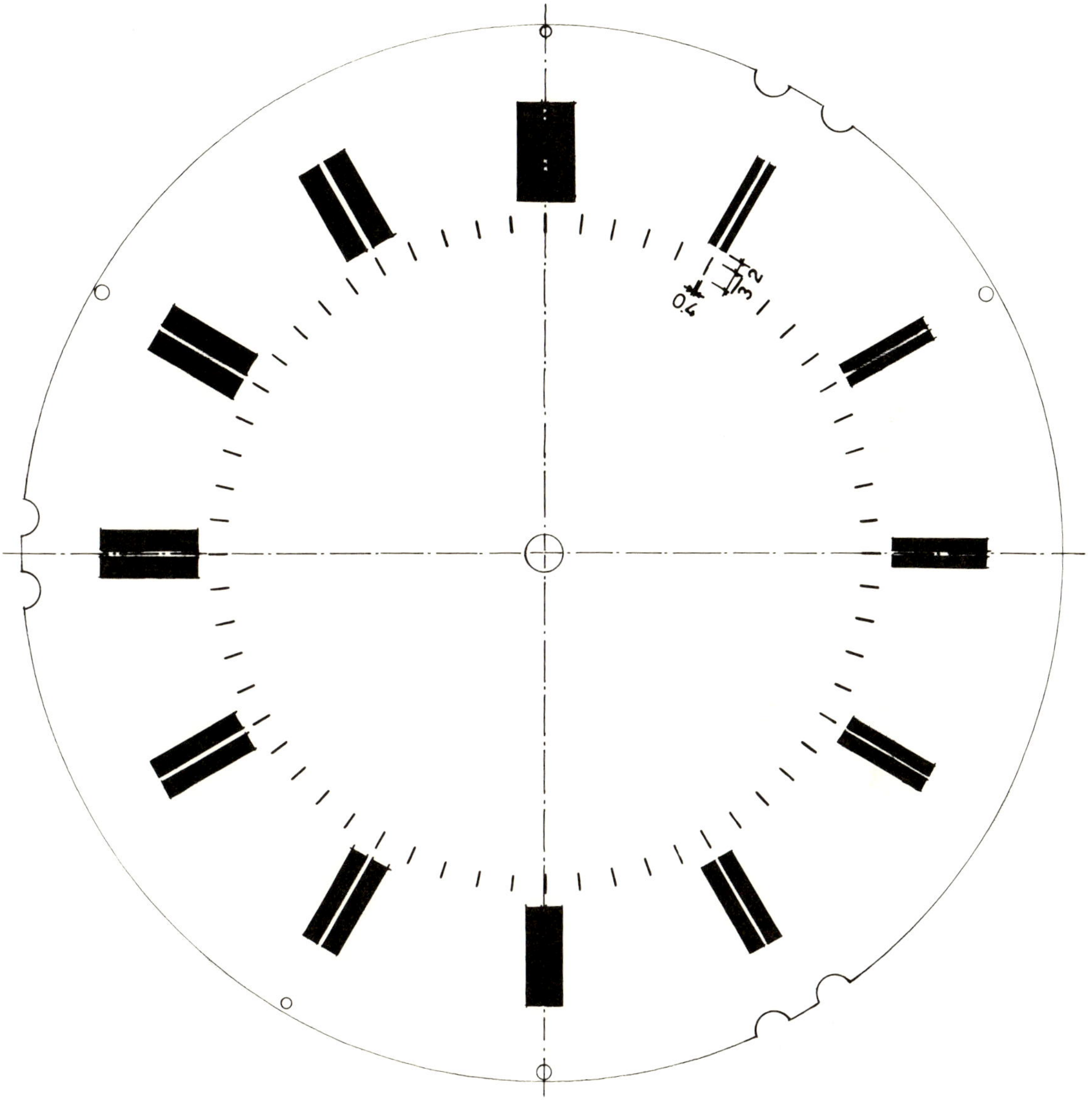
0.4
3
2

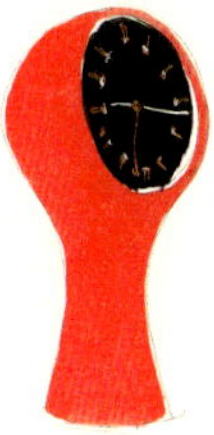

STUDI PER AUTOMOBILI, 1961

自動車のスタディ，1961年

アルファロメオのコンサルタントを務めた数年間で、マンジャロッティはワンボックスカーやスポーツカーのいろいろなデザインスタディを試みている。特に彼の直感（後に多くの自動車メーカーが採用する生産方法）に興味が引かれる。マンジャロッティのアイディアは、標準化された構造体および駆動装置と、セダン・スポーツカー・ステーションワゴンなどのいろいろなボディの2つに大別して合理的に生産できることである。

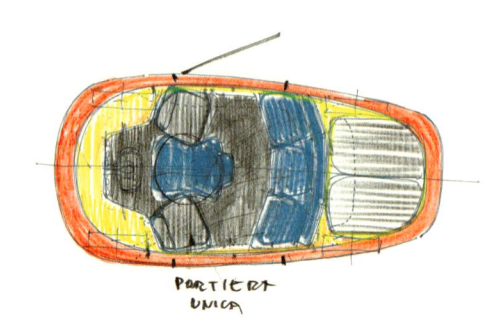

(M.T)

STUDIES FOR AUTOMOBILES, 1961. In his work as a consultant for several years at Alfa Romeo, Mangiarotti developed a number of designs for single-volume cars and sports cars. One particularly interesting intuition – later utilized by many automakers – is the idea of optimizing production by breaking the vehicle down into two parts: a standard structural and mechanical base, and variable bodywork for sedans, sports cars or station wagons.

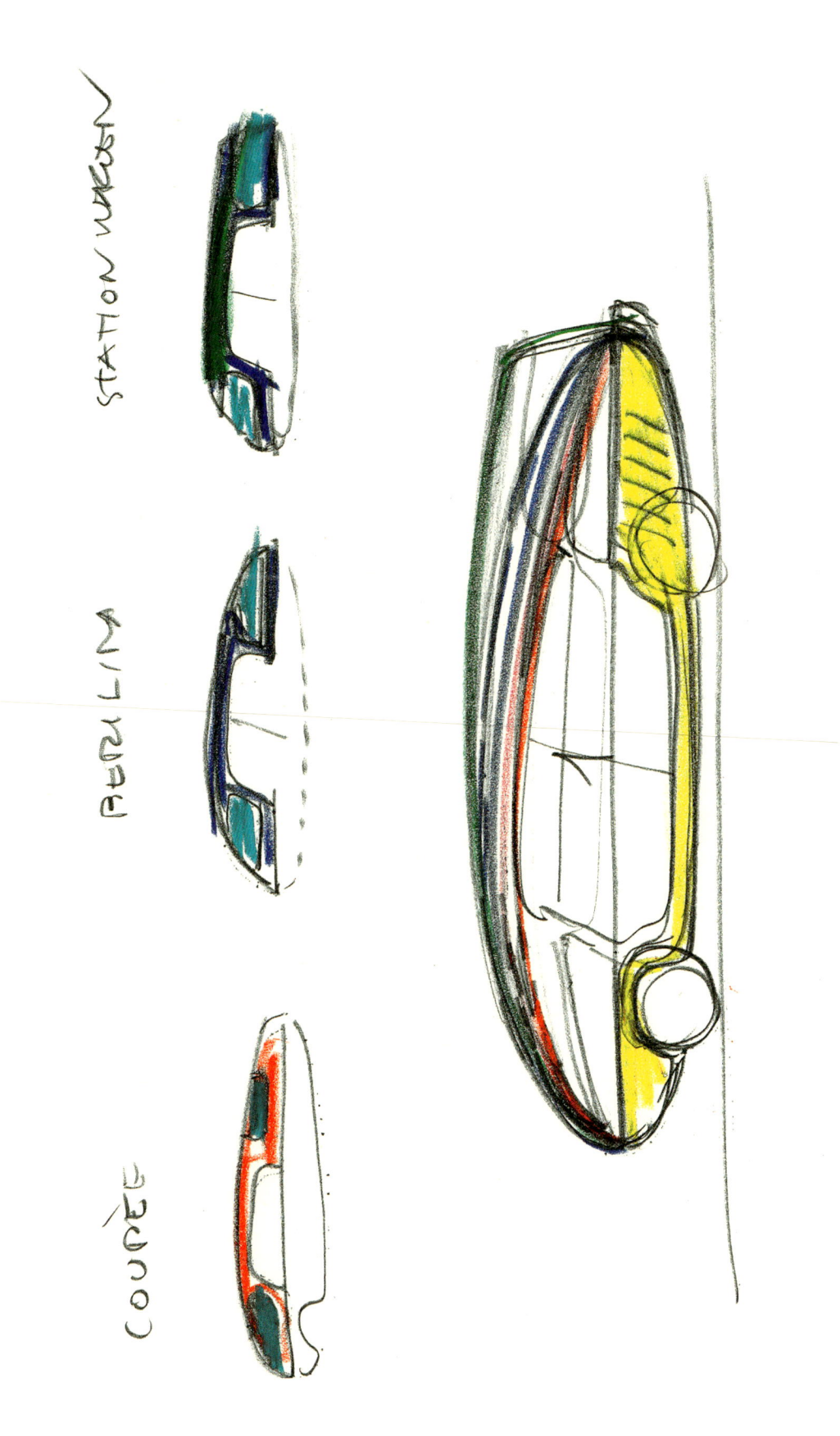

STATION WAGON

BERLIM

COUPÉ

PROGETTI DI APPARECCHI RADIO, 1966

ラジオのプロジェクト，1966年

楽しく使うことができる2つの提案。手で聞きたい向きに動かせる2タイプのラジオ。このようなアイディアだけで十分である。

(M.O)

DESIGNS FOR RADIOS, 1966. Two hypotheses to get some pleasure out of use. Two radios to rotate (by hand) toward the listening zone. It's the thought that counts.

ラディオマレッリ社のためのプロジェクト / *Designed for Radiomarelli*

PROGETTO DI UN TELEVISORE PORTATILE, 1966

ポータブル・テレビのプロジェクト，1966年

断面・バランス・重心が合理的に処理された、かつ見る人の位置に合わせて向きが上下に変えられるデザイン。

(C.I)

PORTABLE TELEVISION, 1966. Through study of the section/equilibrium/barycenter, a dual position option permits adjustment of the orientation of the set with respect to the position of the viewer.

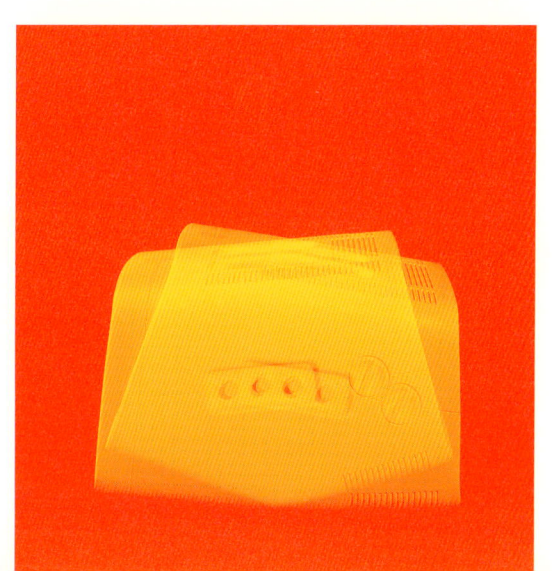

ラディオマレッリ社のためのプロジェクト／*Designed for Radiomarelli*

VASI IN BRONZO FUSO E TORNITO, 1962

鋳型成型と旋盤加工によるブロンズ製花器シリーズ，1962年

一連のブロンズ製花器は土の鋳型で成型し、旋盤加工後に艶出しして製作されたもの。このコレクションがミラノのアルフォルム店で紹介されたとき、ジッロ・ドルフレスは言った。「おそらく、はかなさに対する美、すべての芸術的産物が有する固定化された瞬時性への無意識（あるいは過剰に意識的）な反応が、鋼鉄より硬く耐久性に富み、極めて純度と強度の高いブロンズを使って、これらの興味深い一連のブロンズ製花器の製作に、マンジャロッティを駆り立てたのであろう」

それぞれの花器は土の鋳型を用いることとブロンズの特性から、まったく同一の花器をつくることはできない。しかし、それらの花器は容易に繰返しのできる形と、それらの仕上げとの対比の中に、この一連のブロンズ製花器がもつ美的特性を見出すことができる（土の鋳型による決して同一にならない不規則でざらざらした仕上げと、後工程の旋盤加工による常に完全で艶のある仕上げとの対比の中に）。

(O.H)

製造：フォンデリーヤ・バッタリヤ社からカッペリーニ社に移行／*Produced by Fonderia Battaglia, later Cappellini*

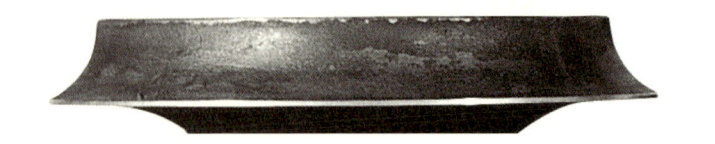

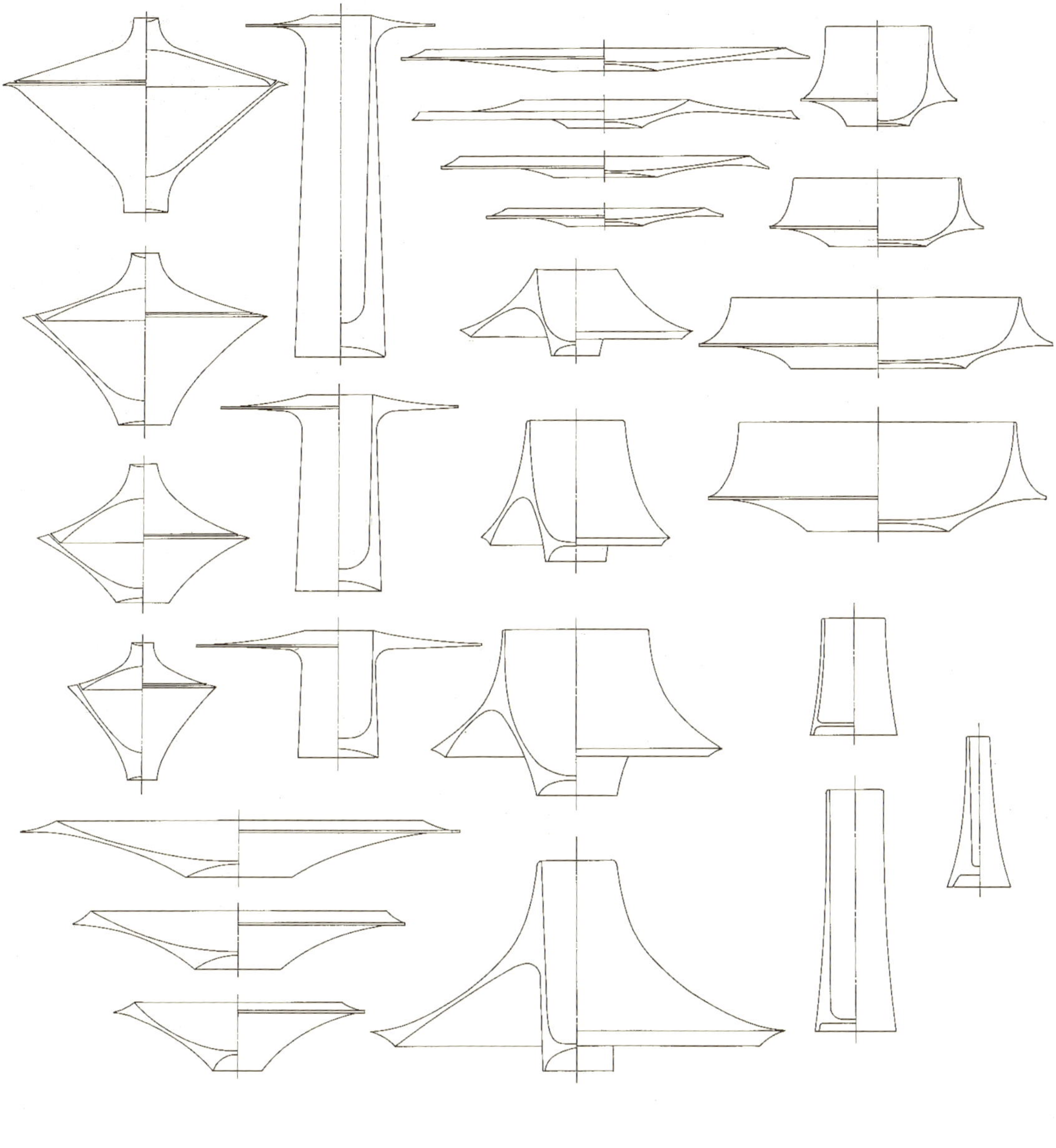

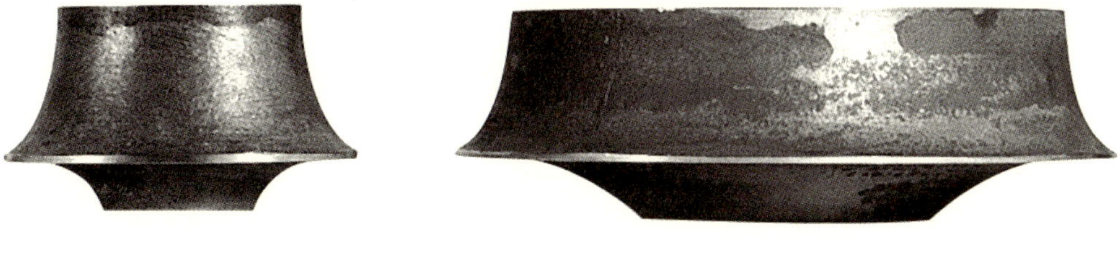

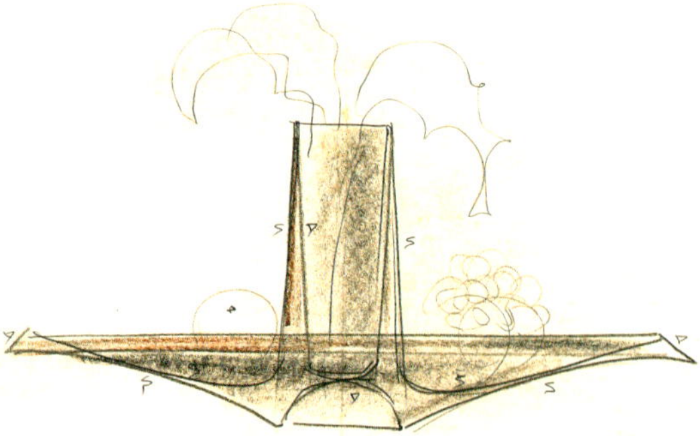

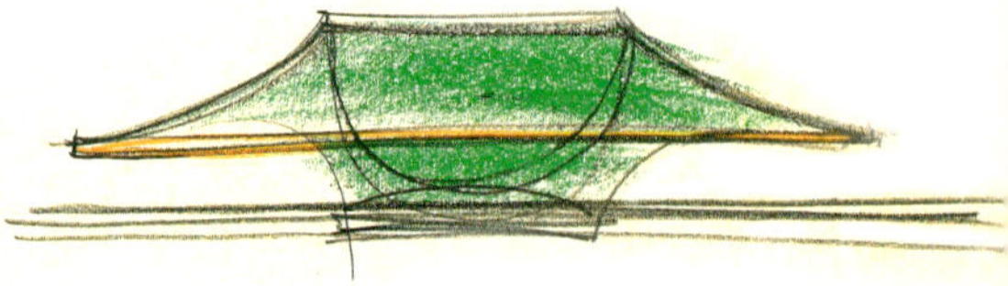

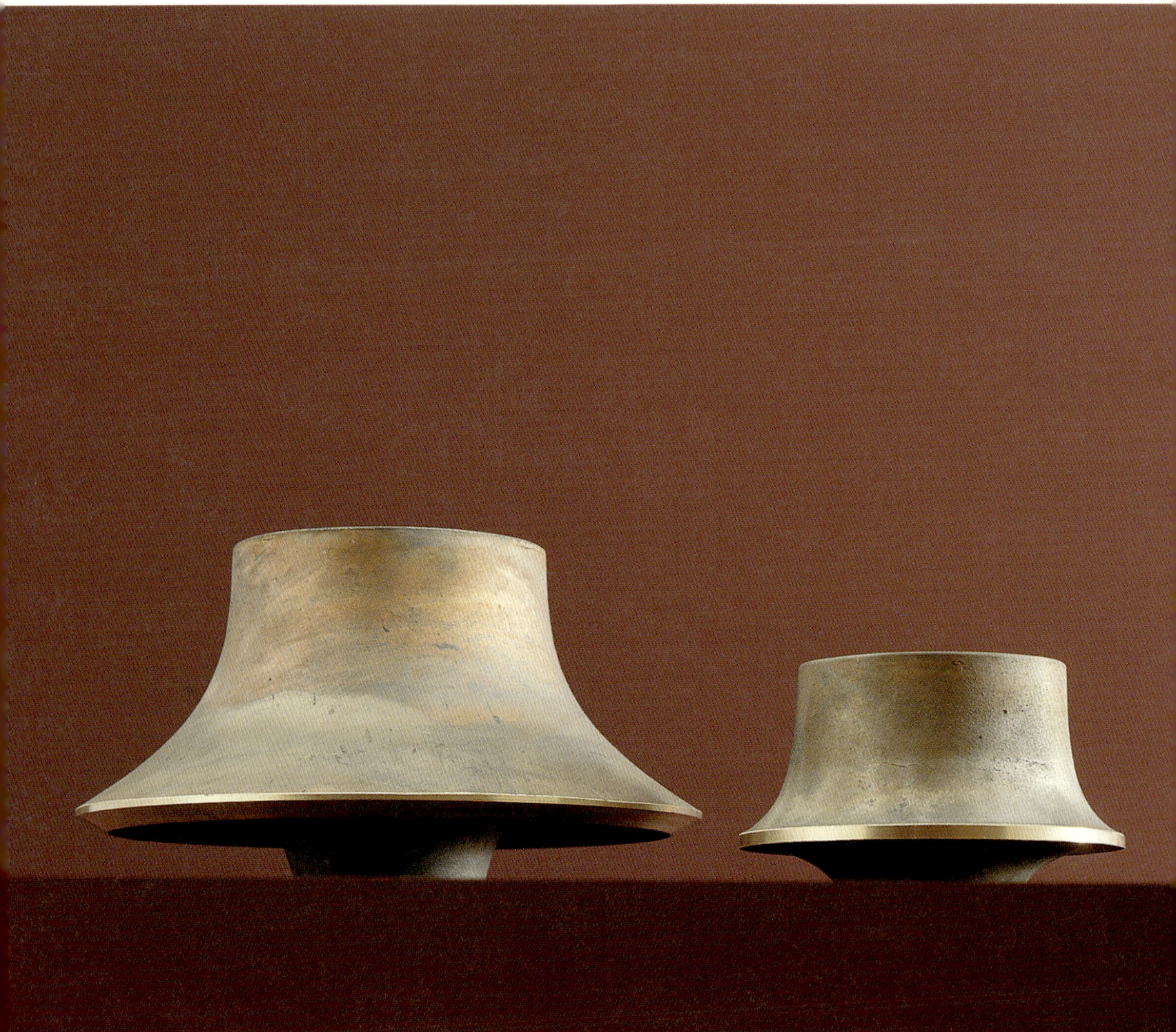

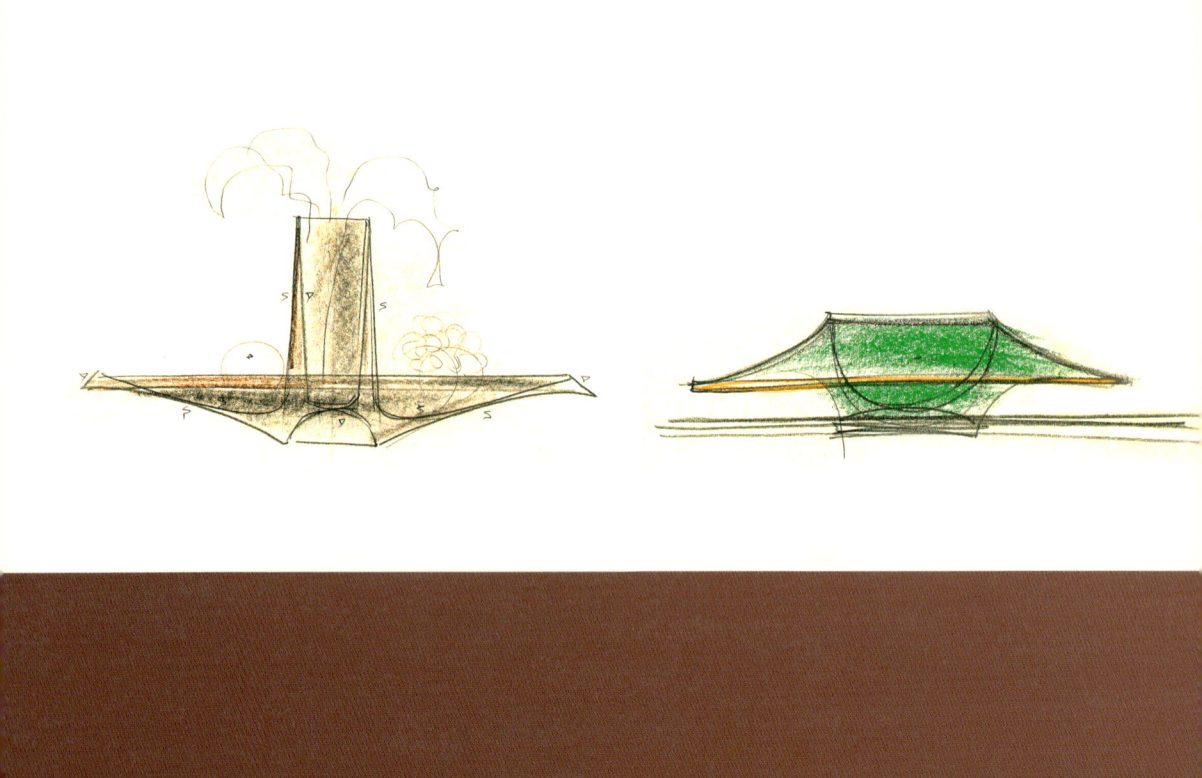

VASES IN CAST TURNED BRONZE, 1962. Bronze vases produced as sand castings which are then turned and polished. At the presentation of the collection at the Arform shop in Milan Gillo Dorfles remarked that "Perhaps an unconscious (or all too conscious?) reaction to the ephemeral aesthetic, to the present transient nature of artistic products, has led Mangiarotti to construct these curious metal objects, cast in very pure, very resistant bronze, more solid and eternal than steel". One-of-a-kind pieces (the sand casting procedure and the characteristics of the bronze prevent the production of identical vases) but also serial objects (their design makes them easy to repeat) that use the contrast between the finishings – irregular, rough surfaces from the casting, perfect, shiny surfaces from the subsequent turning – to achieve their characteristic beauty.

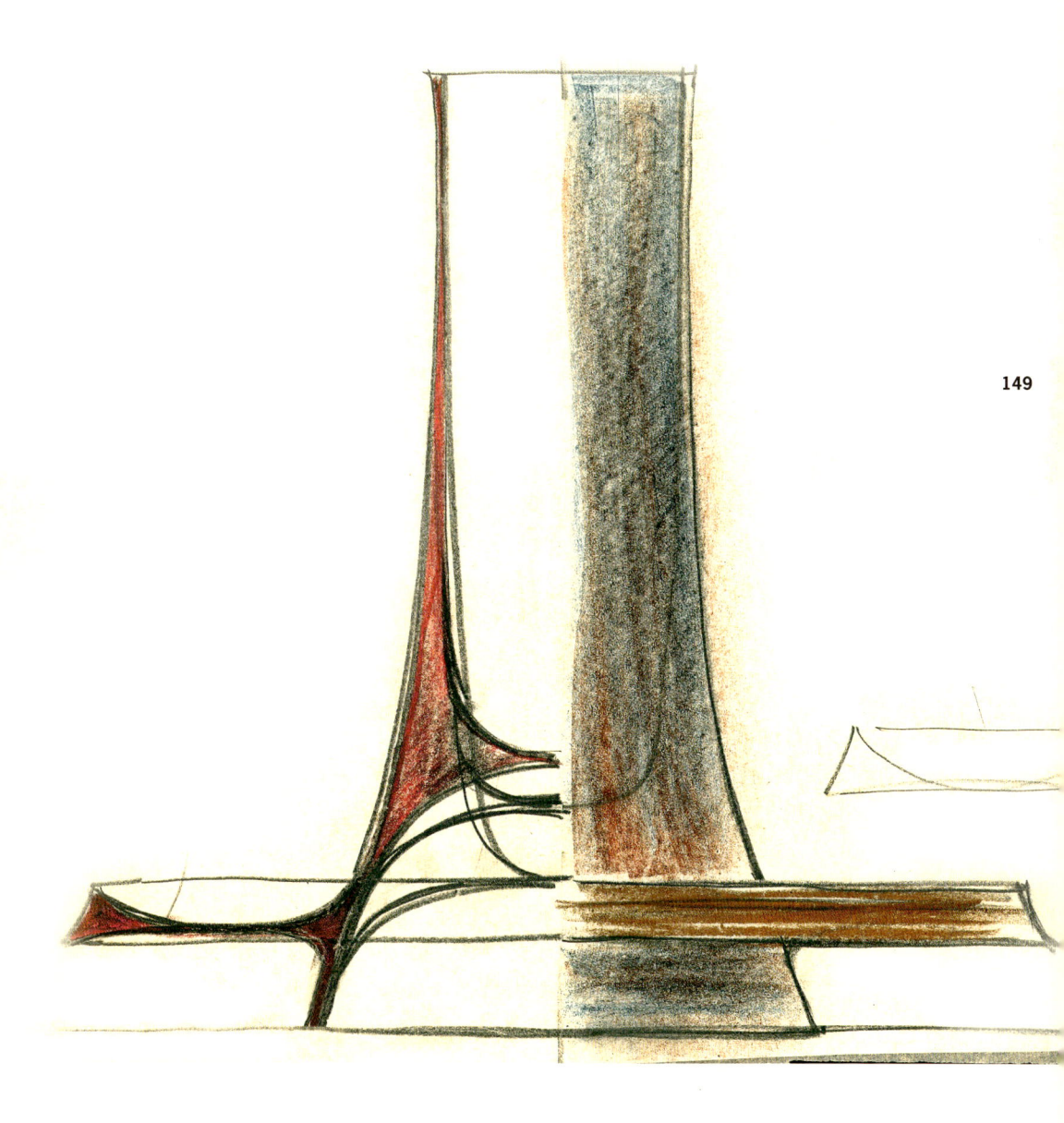

VASI TREMITI, 1964

躍動する花器，1964年

変わったフォルムで、多彩な色付けが施されたヴィチェンツァの陶器は、ダネーゼ社のために製作された花器シリーズ。ほかの花器では見られない曲がりくねったフォルムは、素材の特性と制作技術の高さに裏付られた無限の可能性を秘めている。そして洗練された色使いとの融合が、この有機的で珠玉のシリーズの価値をさらに高めている。

(Ka.M)

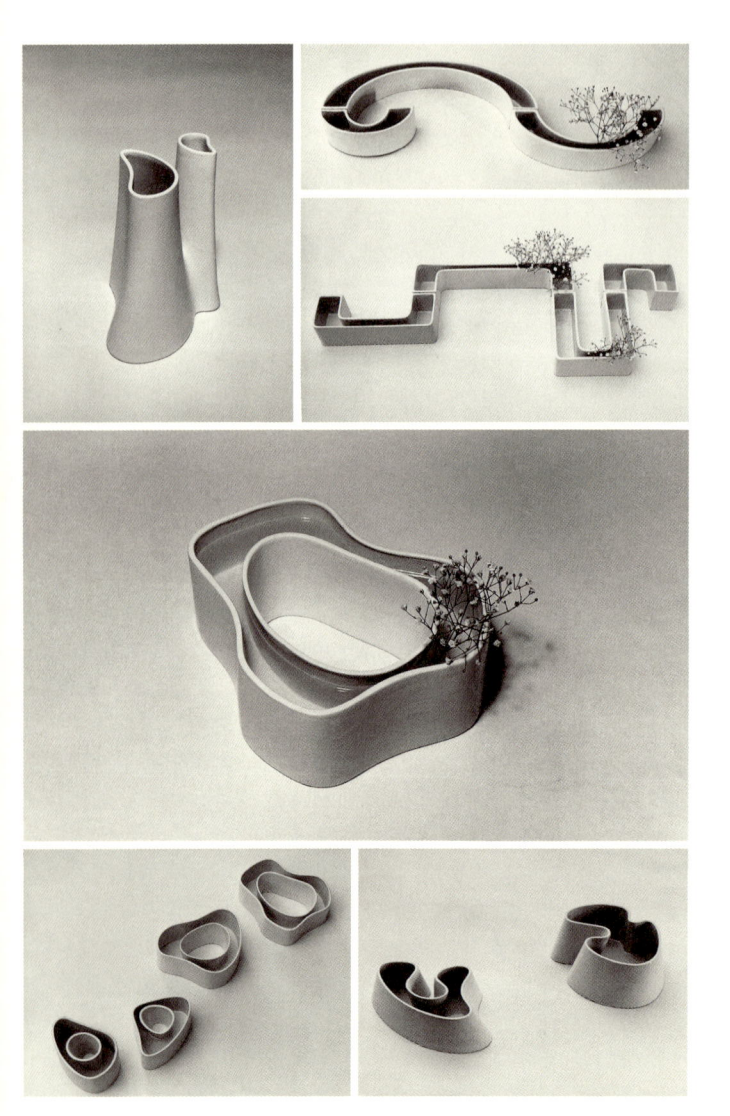

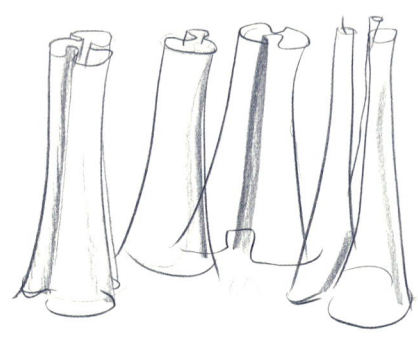

製造：ダネーゼ社 Produced by Danese

TREMITI VASES, 1964. The earthenware of Vicenza is the material utilized for this unusual, variegated series of vases created for Danese. The working techniques and characteristics of the material permits use of sinuous forms that would otherwise be unthinkable, even allowing for unprecedented undercuts. The use of refined color combinations enhances the results in this collection of organic jewels.

PORTACENERE BARBADOS, 1964

灰皿：バルバドス，1964年

「灰皿：バルバドス」は、イタリアンデザインの古典の1つ。従来の灰皿と異なり、いつまでも新鮮な感覚のこの灰皿は、2つの組合せでできている。1つは、ベースが2つの異なるゾーンに分かれており、外側は吸殻と灰を集めるゾーン、内側はタバコの火を消すために高くなっている。もう1つはベースの上部に取り付けるリング状のフォルムで、簡単に取り外すことができるとともに、吸殻を覆い隠し、火のついたタバコを載せることもできる。この灰皿は簡便にして清潔な作品。

(Y.T)

製造：ダネーゼ社／*Produced by Danese*

BARBADOS ASHTRAY, 1964. An Italian design classic. A timeless ashtray where the far-from-banal breakdown of the object into two pieces (a base with two different zones: a recessed outer zone to contain ashes and cigarette butts, a higher central area for putting out the cigarette, and an upper ring to conceal the refuse and to permit positioning of a lit cigarette) facilitates production and cleaning.

OGGETTI IN VITREOUS-CHINA, 1968

ガラス質磁器による小品，1968年

高い強度と水をまったく浸透させない素材の特性が、20種以上の家庭用の小品シリーズ（花瓶、トレイ、ボール、灰皿、卓上小物入）を誕生させた。自由で独特のフォルムは、花やほかのものを入れるのに理想的で、特に何も入っていないときでも実に美しい。　(N.M)

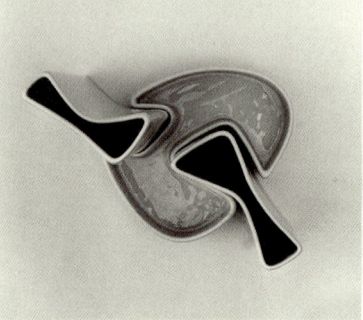

製造 ブランビッラ社/ Produced by Brambilla

OBJECTS IN VITREOUS CHINA, 1968. The strength and total impermeability of the material make a series of over twenty objects for the home (vases, trays, bowls, ashtrays and other small containers for the table) possible, with free, unusual forms, ideal to contain flowers or other things, and strikingly beautiful even when empty.

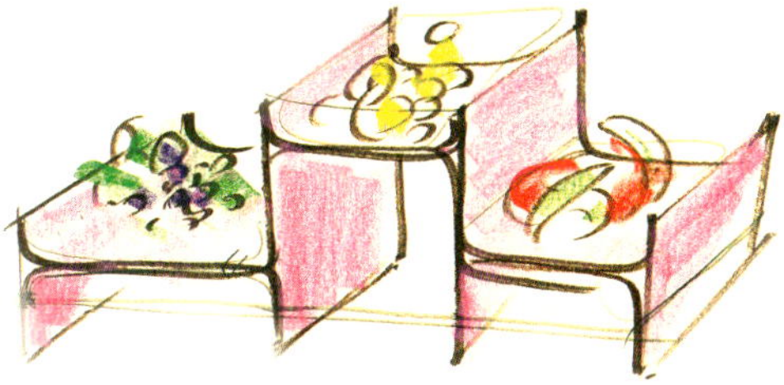

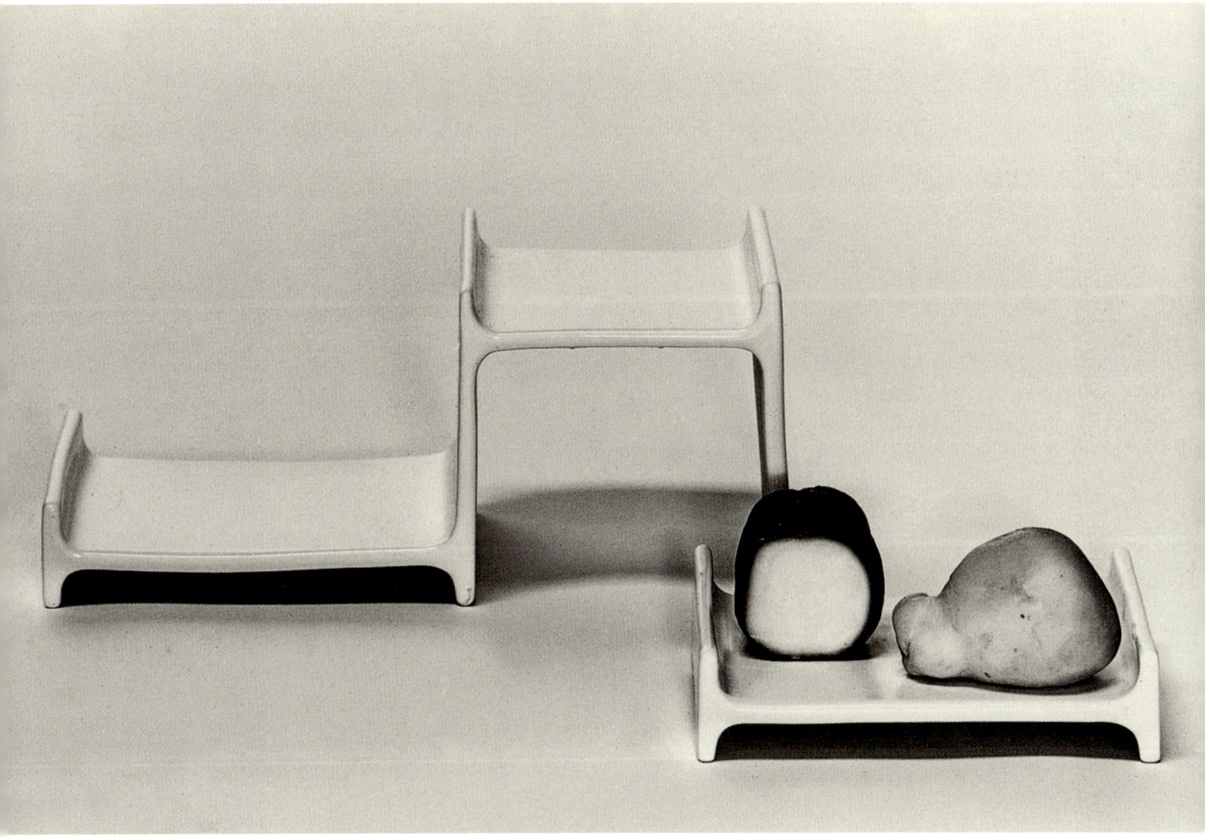

VASI COMPONIBILI IN TERRACOTTA, 1968

テラコッタ製組合せ植木鉢，1968年

この植木鉢は、わずか3要素で構成されている。1段目は、内側に水を入れておくために全体が釉薬され、掴みやすいように縁がついている。2段目は、水が通るための穴があいた土壌用の鉢である。そして3段目は、積み重ねることができるリング状の鉢で、移植しなくても植物の成長に合わせて鉢の大きさ（高さ）を変えることができる。完璧な植木鉢。 (I.M)

COMPONENT FLOWERPOTS IN TERRACOTTA, 1968. Just three elements. A base with internal glazing to hold water, with border to facilitate grip. A pot for the soil with a hole for the water. A stackable ring to increase the size of the pot as the plant grows, to avoid transplanting. That's all.

製造 ブランビッラ社／Produced by Brambilla

terra 土 a
ghiaia 小石 b
acqua 水 c

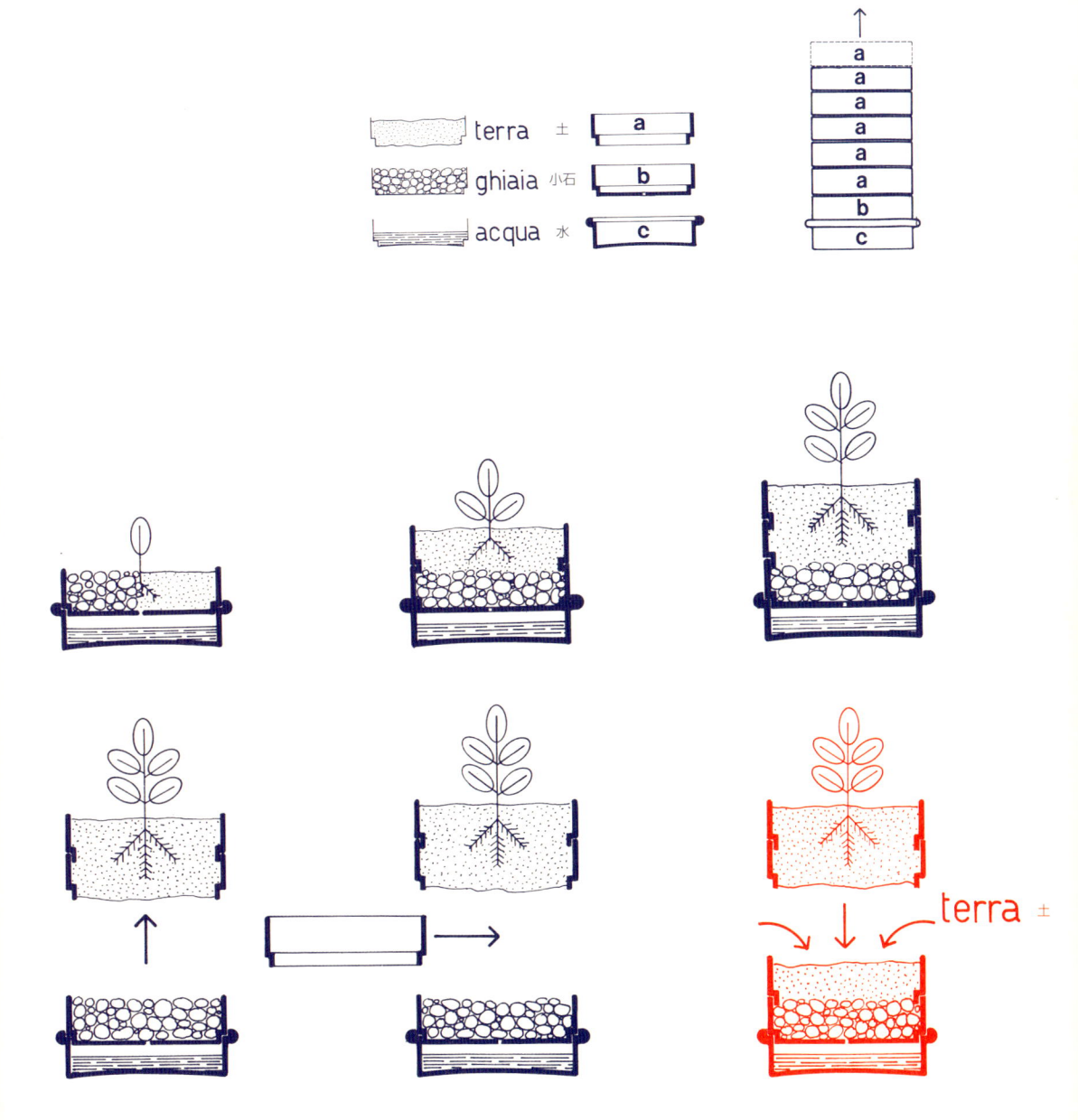

terra

VASI IN MARMO FRESATO, 1971

切削加工による大理石の花器，1971年

切削加工の造形的可能性を模索したもの。この多様な花器シリーズは、設計者の簡単な平面スケッチをもとに、職人の手仕事でつくられたもの。できあがったフォルムはすべて異なり、その切削加工の表面仕上げのみが共通している。

線の溝をもつ花器シリーズ「カヴァエドロ」においては、切削加工は刃が通過した跡を残すだけで、軽快さと光の効果を引き出すために活用されている。

(O.H)

156　VASES IN MILLED MARBLE, 1971. Milling as an expressive possibility. In the Variations Vases the free plan of the vases, simply "sketched" by the designer, is "interpreted" by the craftsman during manual production, leading to constantly different forms; the milling remains a surface treatment. In the striped Cavaedro Vases the milling penetrates to produce effects of light and lightness.

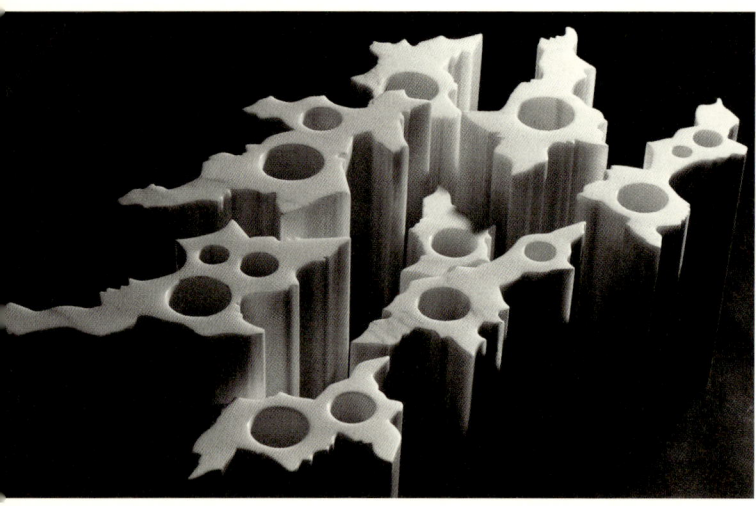

花器「カヴァエドロ」，製造：イテル社／
Vasi Cavaedro, Produced by Iter

花器のヴァリエーション，製造：アンロー社／
Produced by Henraux

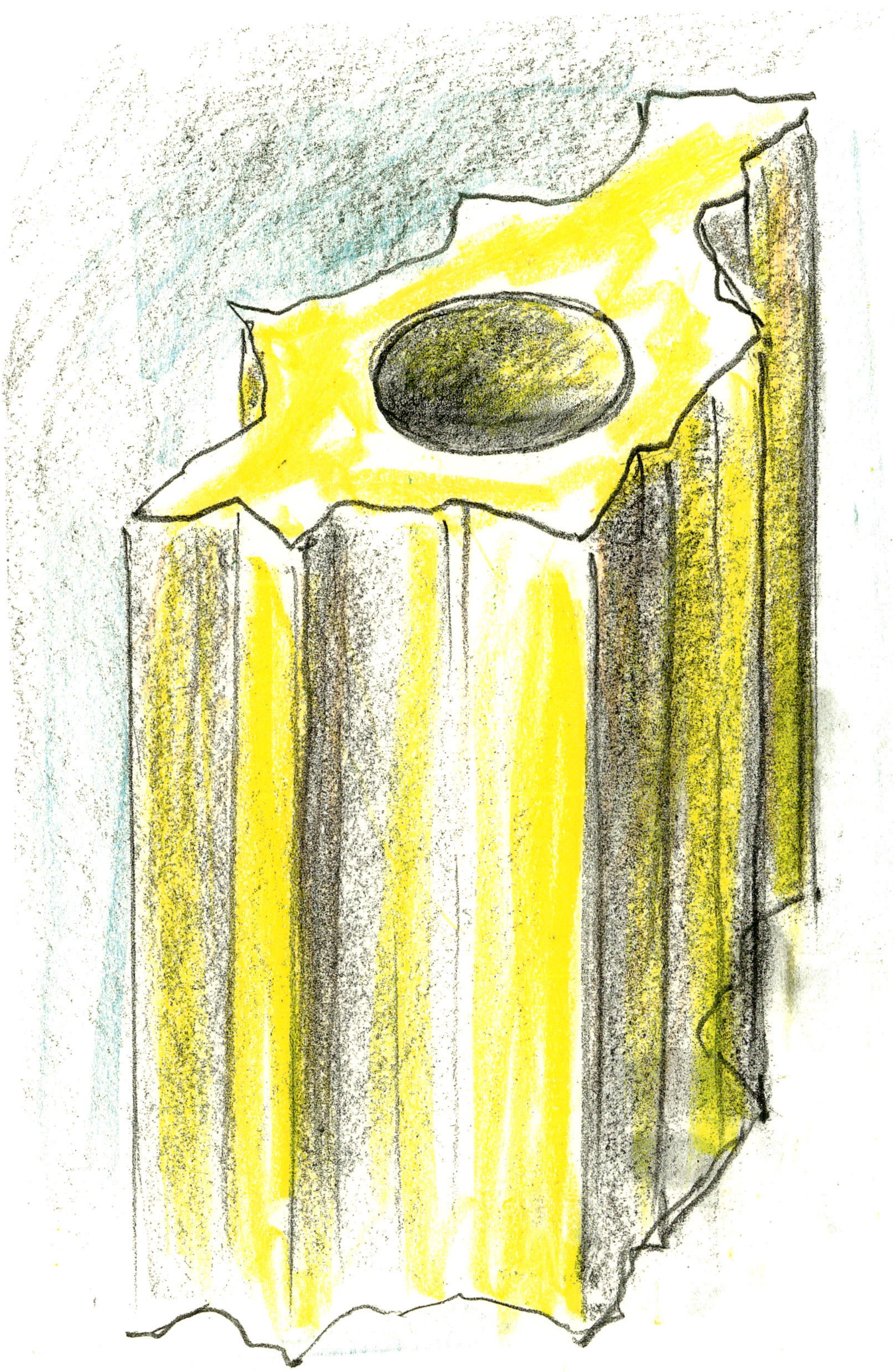

LAMPADA CONDUTTORE DI LUCE, 1962

照明器具：コンドットーレ・ディ・ルーチェ（光の伝導体），1962年

コロンボ兄弟（ジャンニとジョエ）がつくった「アクリリカ」と機能的によく似たランプである。この照明器具コンドットーレ・ディ・ルーチェは、その後広く普及するシステムとなる。光のチューブの照明システムで、端から端へ光が伝わるパースペックス（アクリル樹脂）チューブの特性を上手に活用している。

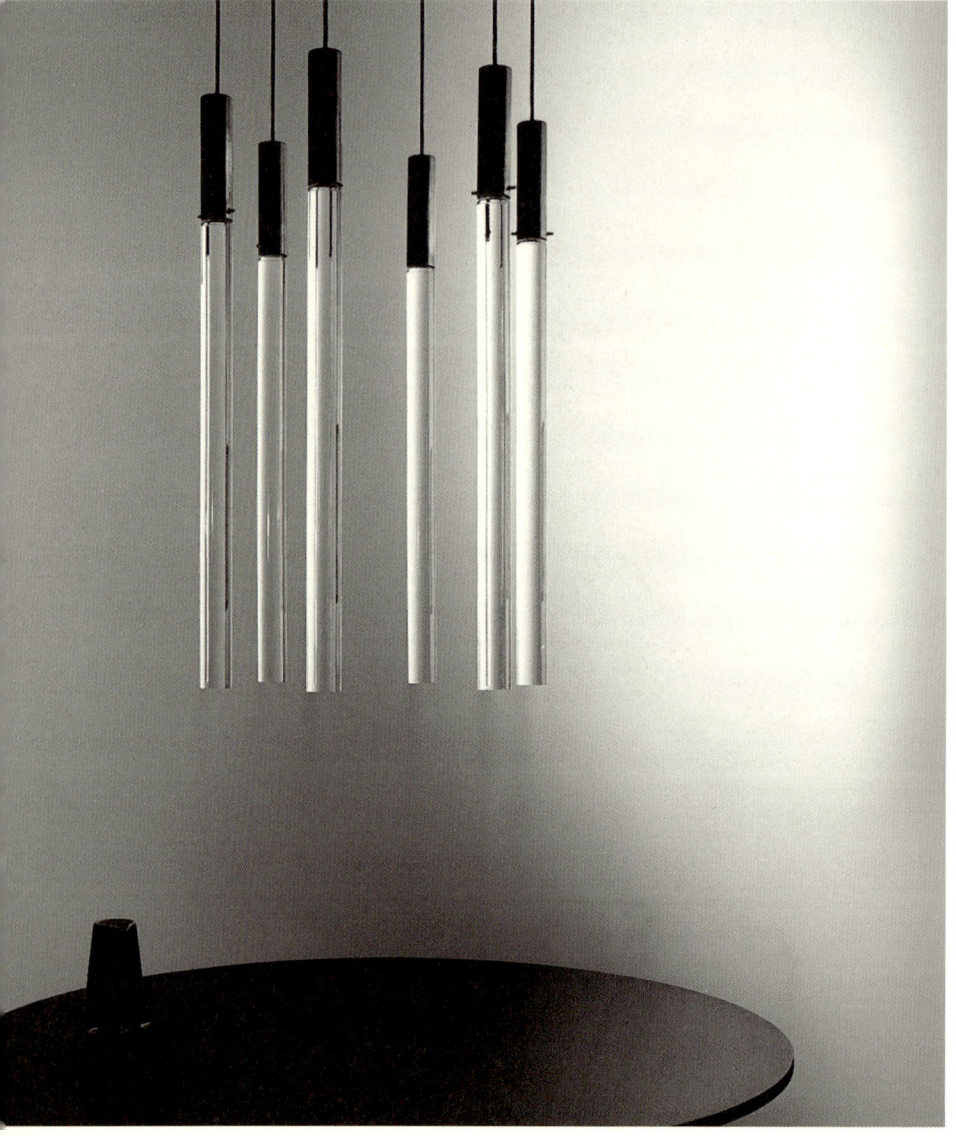

(M.T)

製造：カッペリーニ社（2000年） / Produced by Cappellini(2000)

CONDUTTORE DI LUCE LAMP, 1962. *The functional twin of its contemporary the Acrilica lamp by the brothers Gianni and Joe Colombo, the Conduttore di luce lamp exploits the capacity of a tube of perspex to conduct light from one end to the other, as in the fiber optic lighting systems in widespread use today.*

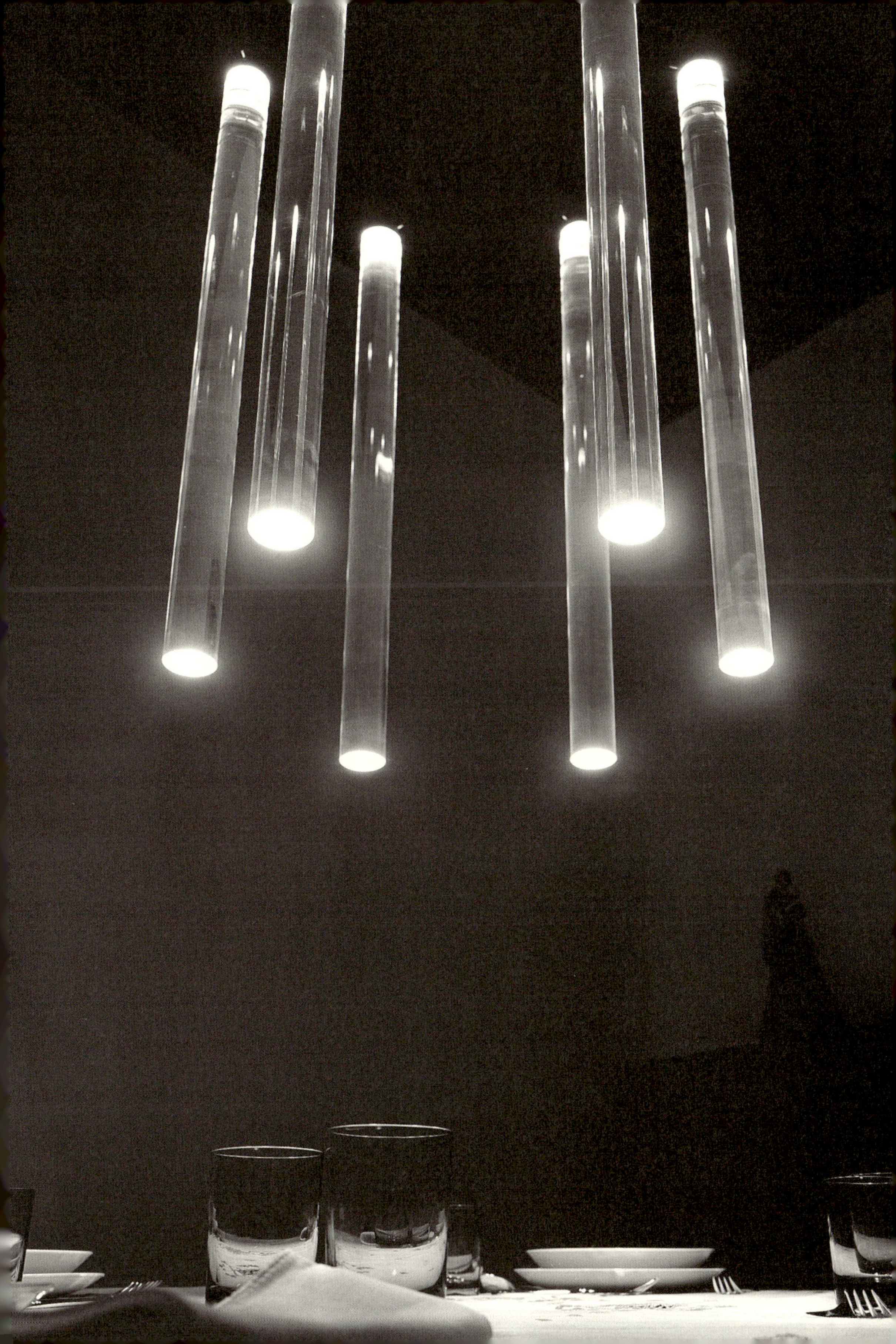

LAMPADA LESBO, 1966

照明器具:レスボ,1966年

曇りガラスを用いた吹きガラスによる照明器具。下部の不透明部は光源を隠し、上部のそれは明かりの一部が支持面へ反射する。曇りのない中心部は、光を拡散する働きをする。この照明器具は、マンジャロッティが繰り返し用いている特徴的な〈キノコ〉型フォルムの代表的な応用例である。

(M.O)

製造:アルテミデ社/Produced by Artemide

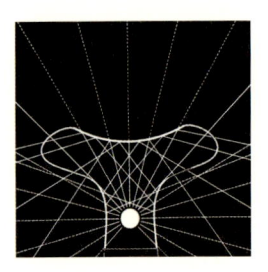

LAMPADA SAFFO, 1966

照明器具：サッフォ，1966年

LESBO AND SAFFO LAMPS, 1966. Lamps in shaded blown glass. The shading of the base permits concealment of the light source, while the upper shading reflects a part of the light toward the support surface. The central part, without shading, ensures diffused lighting. The characteristic "mushroom" form, a recurring feature in Mangiarotti's work, can be seen here in one of its most pertinent applications.

製造：アルテミデ社／*Produced by Artemide*

LAMPADA A SOSPENSIONE V+V, 1967

吊り構造の照明：V+V，1967年

「ある日、ヴェニーニの工房で、職人たちがカルロ・スカルパがデザインしたプリズムの大きな照明を組み立てている現場に遭遇した。その照明はガラスの部分を支えるために視界を妨げる金属の構造部材を必要としていた。そこで、私は金属の構造部材が不要で、同様の結果が得られることができないものかと考えた」

ひも状のガラスを切り、手作業で押しつぶしてリング状に閉じてから、2つの蹄鉄状の形にし、それを手前に折り曲げると1つのエレメントができあがる。そのエレメントを集合させると、複雑なフォルムが生まれる。1つのガラスの鉤は（房状のもの・カーテン状のもの・パネル状のものなど、タイプ分けされた形態上のバリエーションを可能にするために、何種類かのデザインに発展した）、単純な重力だけで極めて自由自在にほかのエレメントと組み合わせることができる。光源は本体から独立し、どこからでも一様に光を発散させることができる。つまり、ガラスの滝（各モデュールは25〜30個のガラスの鉤に耐えられる）の上にきらめく光の屈折と分散は、〈ガラスのマエストロ〉マンジャロッティの数え切れない発明の中でも格別な賞賛に値する。

(O.H)

製造：ヴィストーシ社からスキッパー社、カッペリーニ社へ移行　Produced by Vistosi, later Skipper, later Cappellini

9120B/67

FIG.1 FIG.2

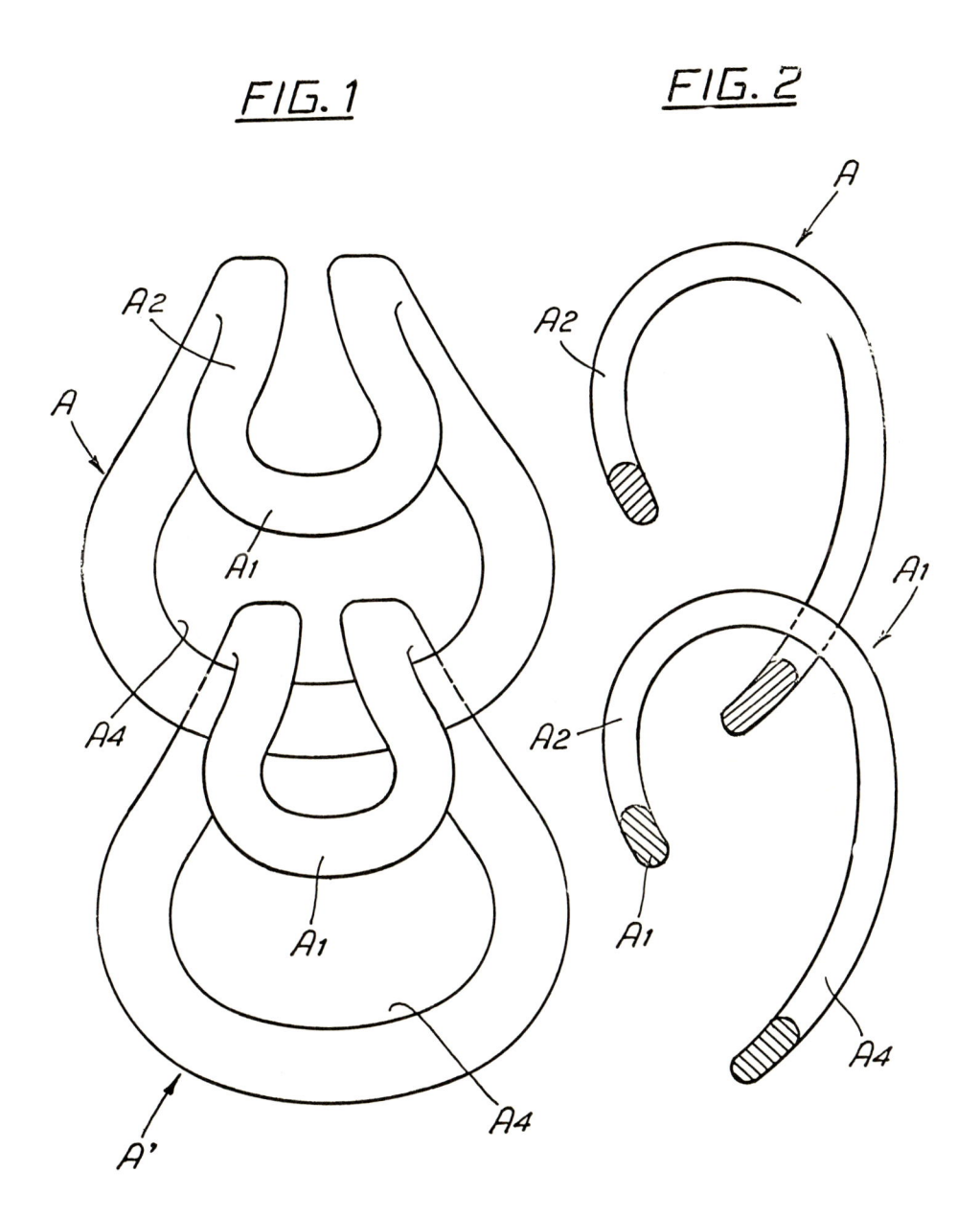

A2, A, A1, A4, A', A2, A, A1, A4

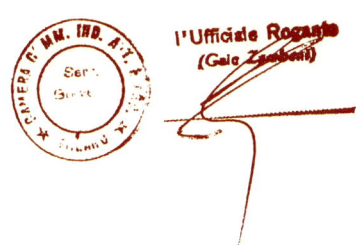

UFFICIO BREVETTI
Ing. C. GREGORI

V+V HANGING LAMP, 1967. "One day I was at Venini and they were assembling a large prismatic chandelier by Carlo Scarpa that required a cumbersome metal structure to support the glass parts. So I thought about achieving a similar result, without the need for a metal structure...". A "ribbon" of glass, cut and pressed by hand to form a double horseshoe ring, and then folded back. An element that when assembled generates complex forms, a glassy hook (later developed in different designs to permit variable, more or less orderly configurations: clusters, curtains, panels, etc.) that can be joined with others with great freedom, using only the force of gravity. The lighting is independent of the resulting structure, and can come either from above or from the sides: the refraction and destructuring of the light on the "cascades" of glass (each module/hook can support up to 25-30 pieces) are the extra surprise in yet another invention by the "master glassmaker" Angelo Mangiarotti.

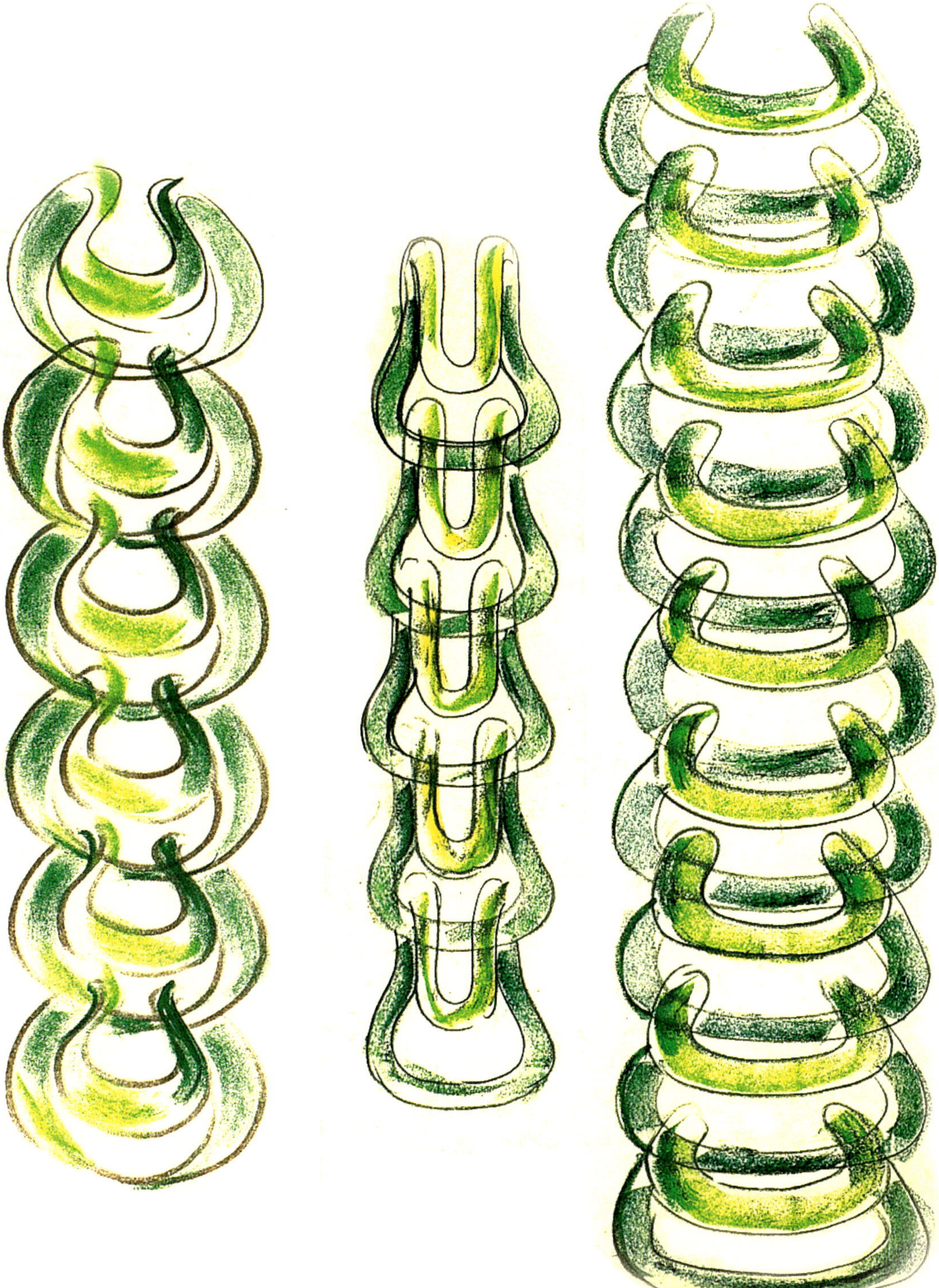

LAMPADA CEMENTA, 1971

屋外照明器具：チェメンタ，1971年

鉄筋コンクリートの外灯。光が目に直接入らないように、光源は下方に向けられている。形、大きさ、そして素材の選択によって座ることも可能にしている。

(Ka.M)

製造：キャンドル社からフォンターナ社、アルテ社に移行 / Produced by Candle, later Fontana, later Arte

CEMENTA LAMP, 1971. An outdoor lamp in reinforced concrete. The light is directed downward to prevent irritating glare. The form, sizing and choice of the material also permit utilization as seating.

LAMPADA EGINA, 1979

照明器具：エジーナ，1979年

型押しガラスによる逆円錐形の照明器具は、フロスト加工された鋸状の表面をもち、光源を隠しながら光を空間に放散している。同時に、透明なレンズ状の中央部は光を集光し、下部の空間を照らす。この小さな大発明は、アンジェロ・マンジャロッティがもつ30パテント中の1つ。

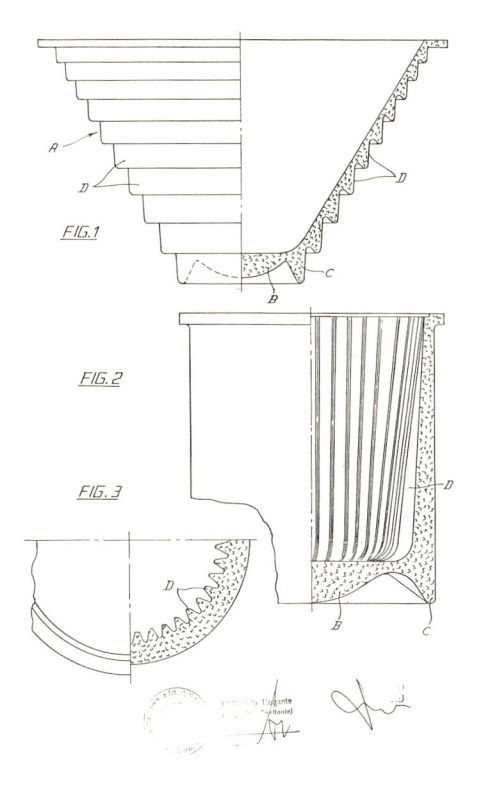

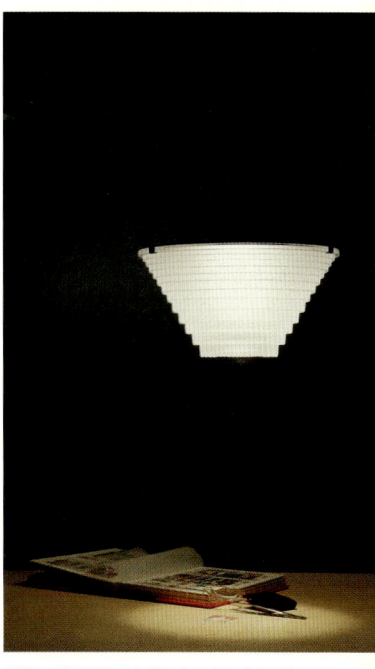

(Ke.M)

製造：アルテミデ社／*Produced by Artemide*

EGINA LAMP, 1979. A truncated cone in pressed glass with a serrated frosted surface diffuses light in space while concealing the light source, while the central transparent part is formed as a lens to concentrate a beam of direct light on the space below. A little big invention sealed by a patent, one of the many (thirty) held by Angelo Mangiarotti.

COLLEZIONE DI OGGETTI IN CRISTALLO
クリスタルガラスの小品のシリーズ

1986年から現在まで続いているクリスタルガラスシリーズは、デザイナーとメーカーのコラボレーションの模範的な例である。クリスタルガラスの特性と製造技術に細心の注意を払って、10種の斬新な小品が生まれた。

「この製品の造形には、新しいセンスに伝統的な技術と形態を融合させ、古のイタリアの巨匠たちの知恵を現代に活かす才能が表現されている」と、ヴィットリオ・ファゴーネは評している。これらのテーブル小物は、伝統的なフォルムを再生し、用途と機能性に対応した新しいフォルムを創造している。具体的には、アルコールグラスシリーズ「タッチ・グラス」では、クリスタルガラスと手の接触の仕方に注意が払われ、ワイングラスとデキャンタグラスシリーズ「ビブロ」では、下部とカップ部分が左右非対称であること、花器シリーズ「インベルノ（冬）」では、簡易なもので枯死した草花を再生させること、一番輝かしい成果をあげたクリスタル容器「エオロ」では、貯えること・注ぐこと・補充すること・飲むことのすべてを可能にしたこと、油さし「オルペ」では、蓋のデザインが伝統的な容器の〈ゴッチャ（雫）〉を想起させ、特に外周部に沿ってオイルが垂れることを防ぐフォルムにしたこと、ウィスキーグラスシリーズ「アイス・ストッパー」と「エッブロ」では、飲む動作に即して氷を止める働きをするフォルム（窪み）を握りの部分として表現したことなどである。(O.H)

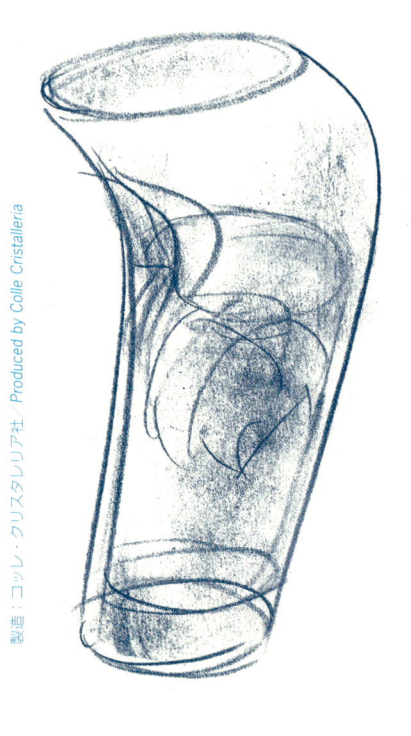

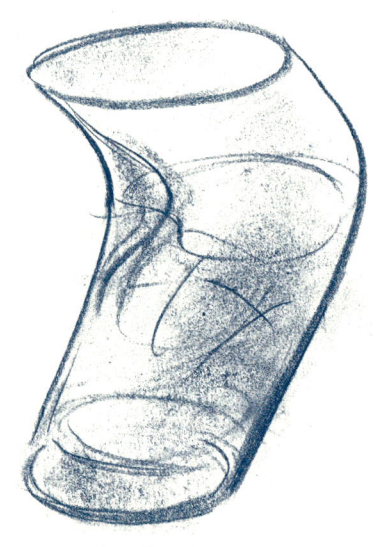

製造：コッレ・クリスタレリア社／Produced by Colle Cristalleria

ウイスキーグラス「エッブロ」, 1990／Whisky tumbler Ebbro, 1990

花器「インベルノ（冬）」シリーズ，1989年／Vases of the series Inverno, 1989

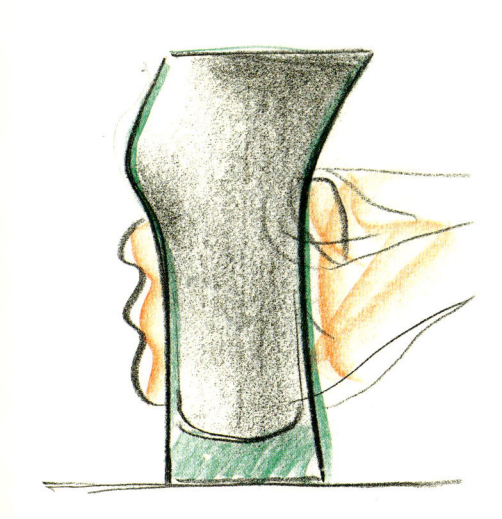

グラス「ハンド・ストッパー」，1993年／Glass Hand Stopper, 1993

テーブル小物「アスター」, 1986年／Centerpiece Aster, 1986

グラス「アイス・ストッパー」, 1986年／Glass Ice Stopper, 1986

COLLECTION OF OBJECTS IN CRYSTAL. *An exemplary collaboration between a company and a designer that has continued since 1986 and generated dozens of truly innovative objects created with extreme attention to the characteristics of crystal and its working techniques. "The overall image of this production reveals the capacity to link technical and formal tradition, to update the mastery of the Italian craftsmen of the past with a new awareness" (Vittorio Fagone). A collection of objects for the table with forms that encourage different uses and functions, revitalizing established typological traditions. Thus the Touch Glass series of glasses for alcoholic beverages focuses on the contact between the hand and the crystal; the Bibulo series of glasses and carafes revises the relationship between the cup and the base in the direction of asymmetry; the Inverno collection of vases permits dried flowers to live, almost concealing itself with its minimal design; the ascoidal Eolo vase sets a constructive record, brilliantly covering the function range of containing, pouring, filling, drinking; the Olpe oil cruet features a stopper design that leads the traditional "drip" back into the vessel rather than allowing it to slide down the external surface; the Ice Stopper and Ebbro whiskey glasses have a form that follows the gesture of drinking, while an imprint/grip retains the ice during the act of sipping. Amen.*

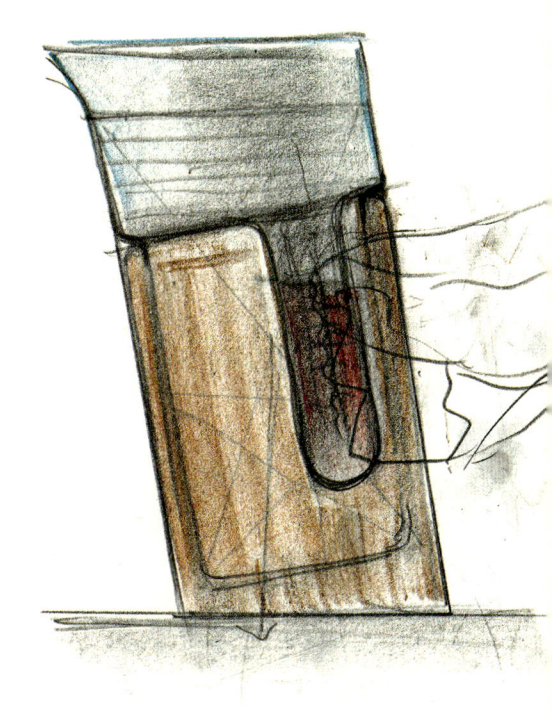

木とクリスタルガラスの小物のためのスケッチ，1989年／*Studies for glass and wood objects,1989*

油さし［オルペ］, 1990年／Olpe cruets,1990

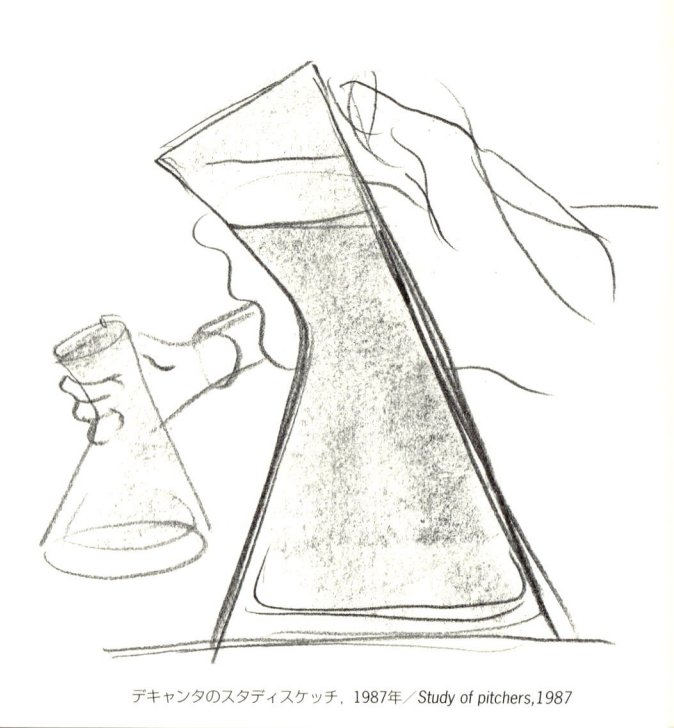

デキャンタのスタディスケッチ, 1987年／*Study of pitchers,1987*

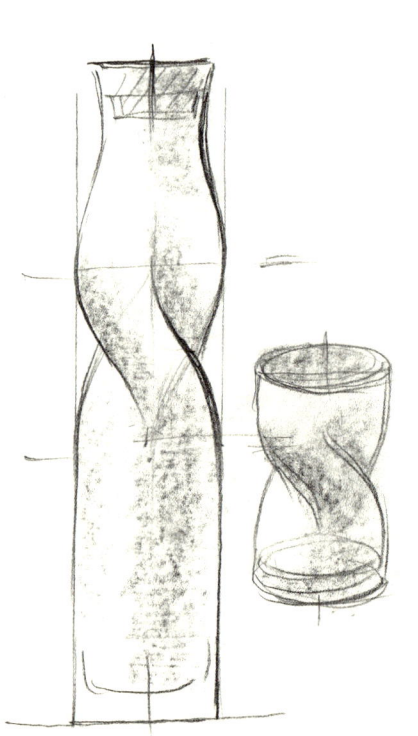

デキャンタとグラス「トルチェッロ」, 2001年／
Decanter and glasses Torcello,2001

ワイングラス「ビブロ」1991年／*Drinking cup Bibulo, 1991*

POSATE SERIE ERGONOMICA, 1990

テーブルウェアーシリーズ：エルゴノミカ，1990年

彼のデザインの中にある正確な人間工学に特に着目してほしい。このテーブルウエアーシリーズの握りの部分は、重さを軽減（薄板圧延スチールの採用）し、先端のエレメントは機能性を重視している。

(N.M)

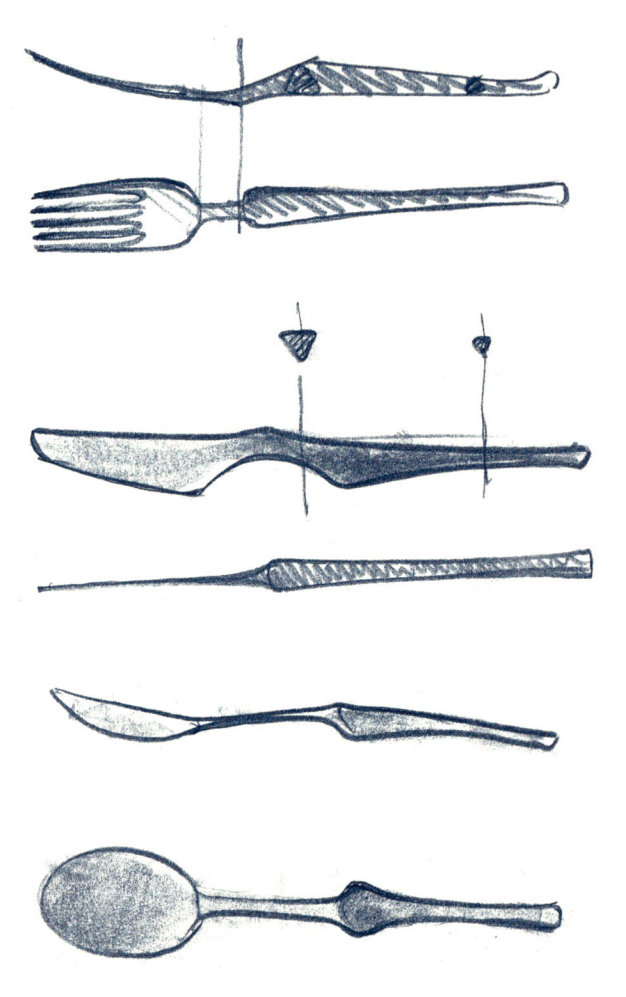

製造：メプラ社／Produced by Mepra

ERGONOMIC FLATWARE, 1990. With particular design focus on correct ergonomics, the grip of this flatware series is light in weight (thanks to the use of pressed sheet steel) for another functional plus.

CAFFETTIERA, 1991

コーヒーメーカー，1991年

ノウハウと繊細な配慮が凝縮されたスチール製のコーヒーメーカー。末広がりの底面は、コーヒーメーカー自体の安定性と、出来上がり時間を短縮するために火力を受ける面を大きくデザインしている。コーヒーメーカーは、コーヒーを注ぎやすくするために傾いたフォルムになっている。円形の平断面はジョイント部分（加圧部分と蒸留部分）の開閉を最もシンプルにしている。樹脂製の把手はできる限り金属部分から離して、加熱しないようにしている……。

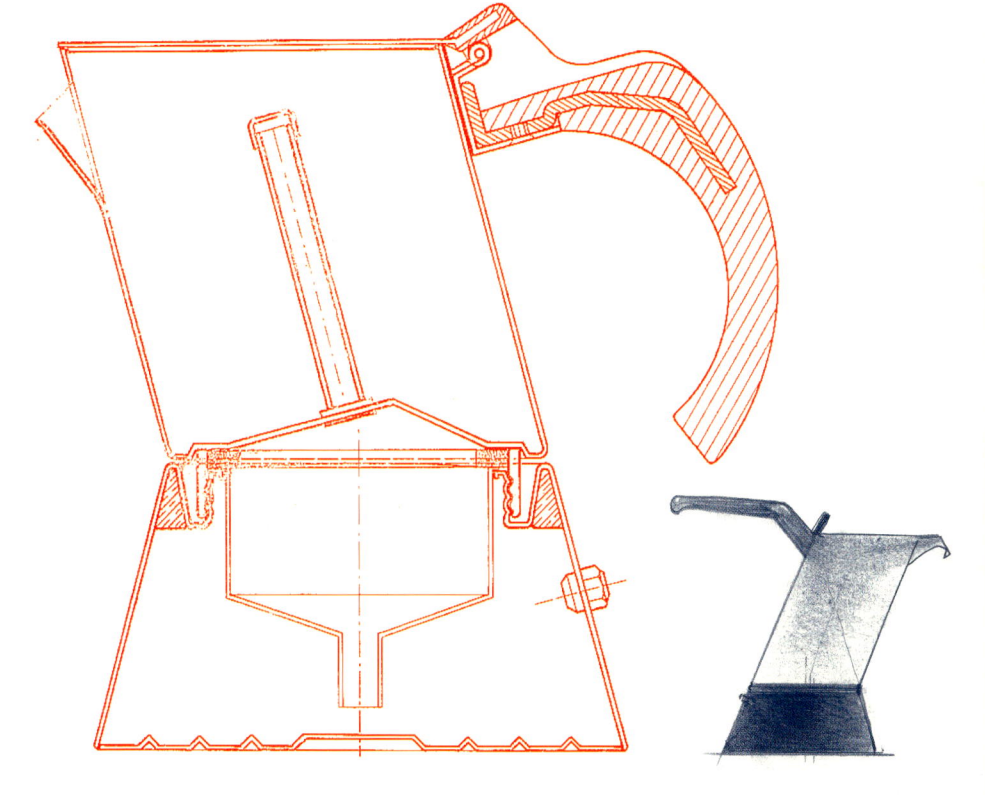

(I.M)

製造：メプラ社／Produced by Mepra

COFFEEMAKER, 1991. A steel coffeemaker as a concentrate of knowledge and attention to detail: the wider base increases both stability and the surface in contact with the flame (for rapid preparation of the coffee); the angle facilitates the gesture of pouring; the circular section makes opening and closing simpler; the handle in resin, as far as possible from the metal body, prevents overheating.

PROGETTI DI MANIGLIE

レバーハンドルのプロジェクト

最初のレバーハンドル「コモ」(オリヴァーリ社,1947年)から最新のモデルに至るまで、その開発目標は人間工学の観点から最良のフォルムを探求したことにある。オリヴァーリ社における新しいレバーハンドルプロジェクトの特徴は、掴むことを容易にしたレバーハンドルの角度にある。ヴァッリ・アンド・ヴァッリ社の「AM92シリーズ」では、曲りくねったフォルムが、手の平と指にフィットする理想的なフォルムをつくり出している。 (O.H)

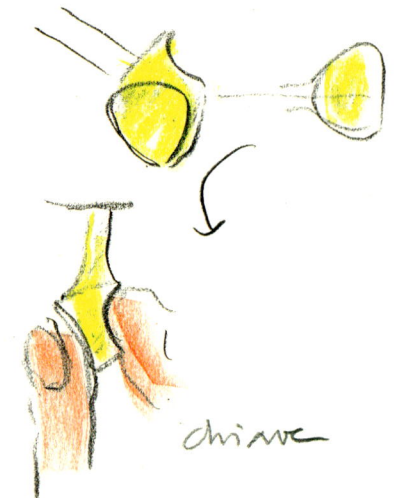

販売・製造：ヴァッリ・アンド・ヴァッリ社、フジタル社
Produced by Valli&Valli divisione Fusital

176

DESIGNS FOR HANDLES. From the first Como handle (Olivari, 1947) to the more recent models the objective remains that of finding the best form in relation to ergonomic requirements. In the design of a new handle for Olivari, an imprint and, above all, the particular angle of the handle facilitate grip. In the AM Novantadue series for Valli & Valli, the sinuous profile seems like the ideal counterpart for the form of the palm and the fingers.

オリヴァーリ社のためのレバーハンドル1991年／*Disigned for Olivari,1991*

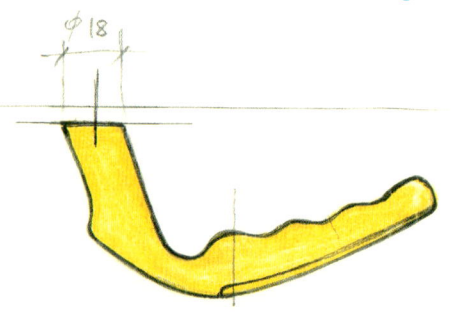

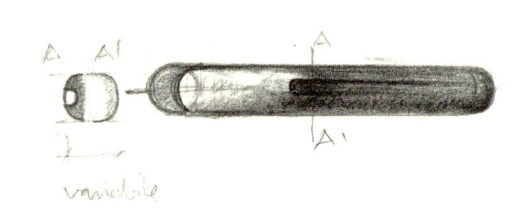

レバーハンドル「AM92」, 1992年／*Doorhandle AM Novantadue, 1992*

SEDIA CHICAGO, 1983

椅子：シカゴ，1983年

独立した構造で支えられた座部をもつ椅子の最初のイメージから発展して、グラスファイバーで補強されて一体化した椅子「シカゴ」が誕生した。この食事用の椅子は、有名な「パントンチェアー」と対極に位置する。つまり、「パントンチェアー」は、座る行為によってテーブルから遠ざかる方向に動くのに対して、「シカゴ」は会食者の座部にかかる重さによって食卓に近づくように動く。

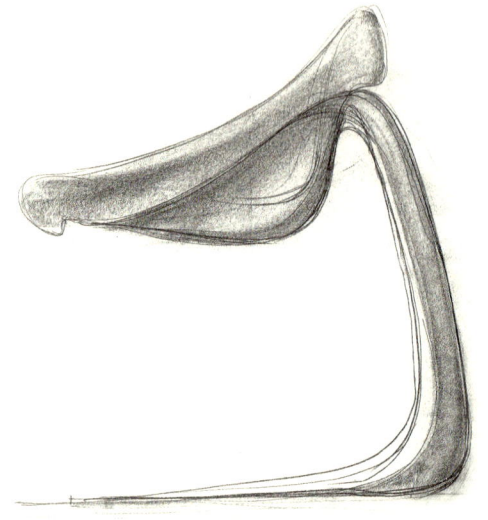

(O.H)

製造：スキッパー社からカッペリーニ社へ移行／
Produced by Skipper, later Cappellini

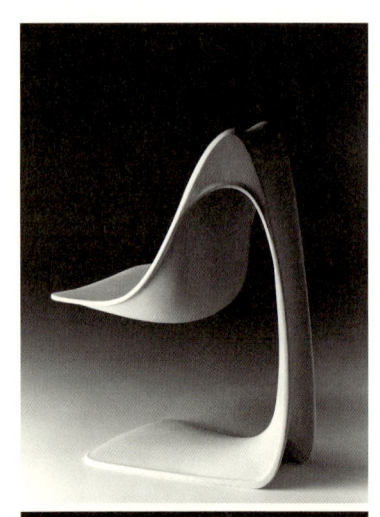

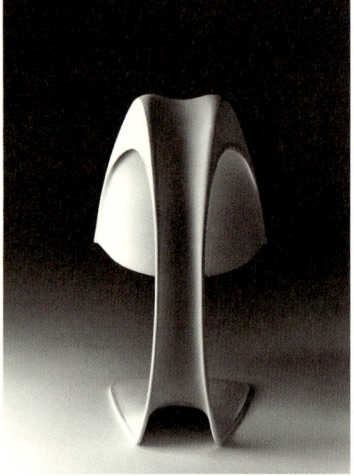

CHICAGO CHAIR, 1983. From the initial idea of a seat resting on an independent structure to the monoblock in reinforced fiberglass of the Chicago chair: a dining chair in which the structure permits the user to flex forward during use – unlike the famous Panton Chair, its declared counterpart – bringing the person dining closer to his meal rather than farther away from it.

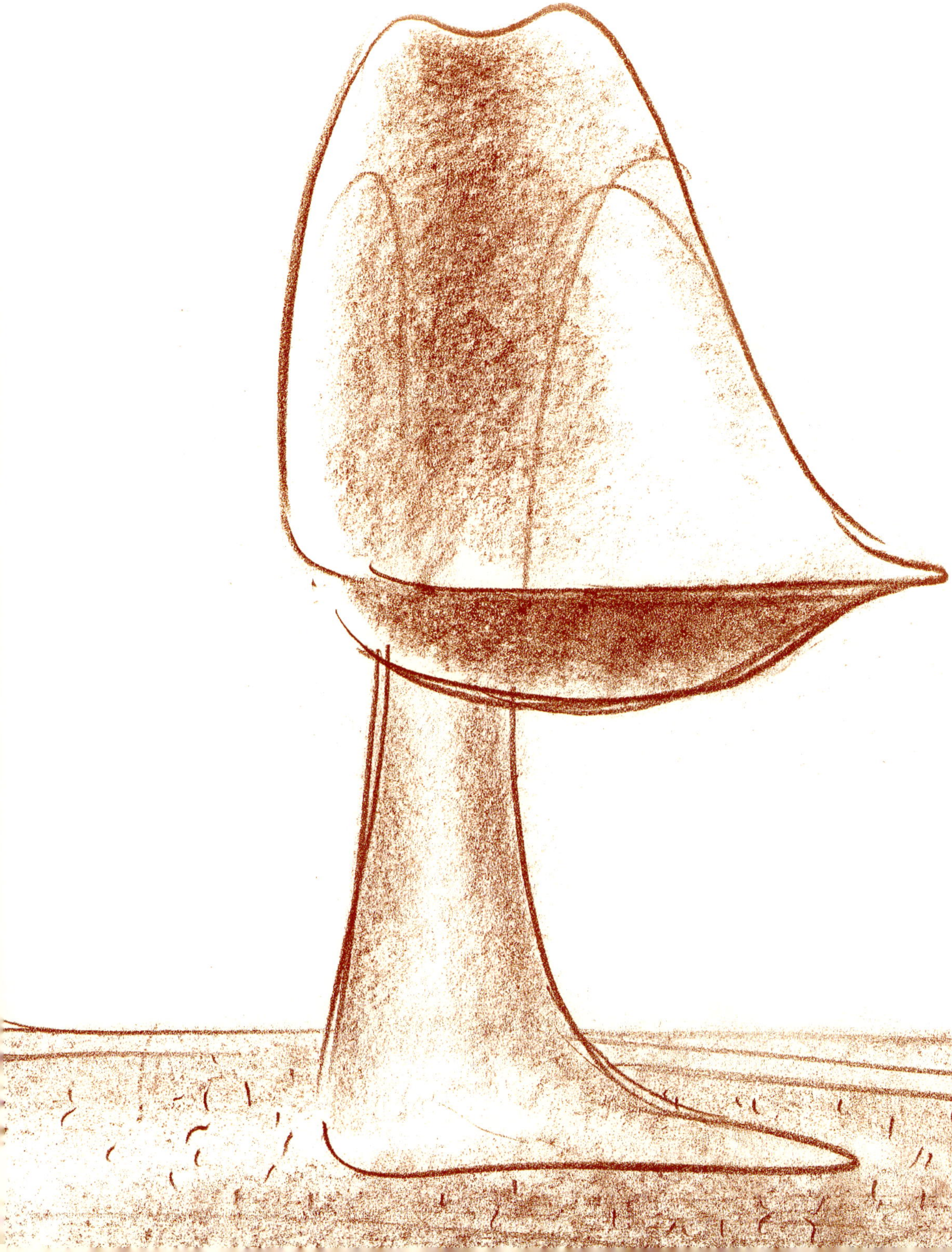

SEDUTA PER ESTERNI CLIZIA, 1990

屋外用椅子：クリーツィア，1990年

正確に、かつ複雑な切断が可能なNC制御の工作機械により、大理石の塊を簡単に切断するだけで椅子をつくることができる。材料ロスや製造コストが削減でき、まさに経済性も兼ね備えたアンジェロ〈エッシャー〉マンジャロッティ！

(M.T)

製造：スキッパー社からアンロウ社へ移行／Produced by Skipper, later Henraux

CLIZIA OUTDOOR SEATING, 1990. From the same block of marble, using numerically controlled machine tools that permit precise, complex cutting, it is possible to obtain seating elements in which the upper profile coincides with the lower, reducing scrap and costs. Angelo Escher Mangiarotti with a focus on economy.

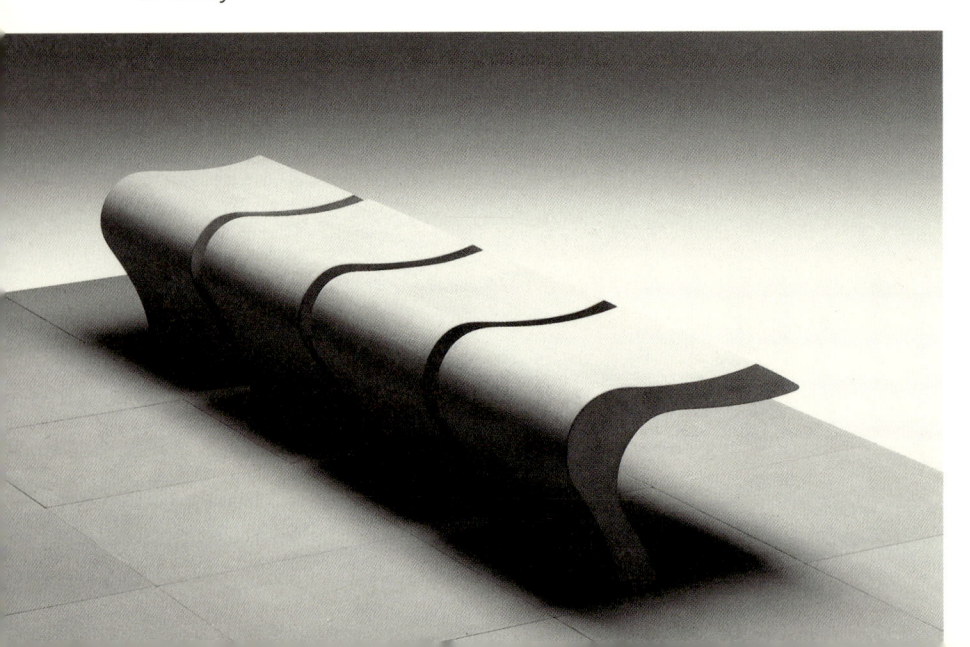

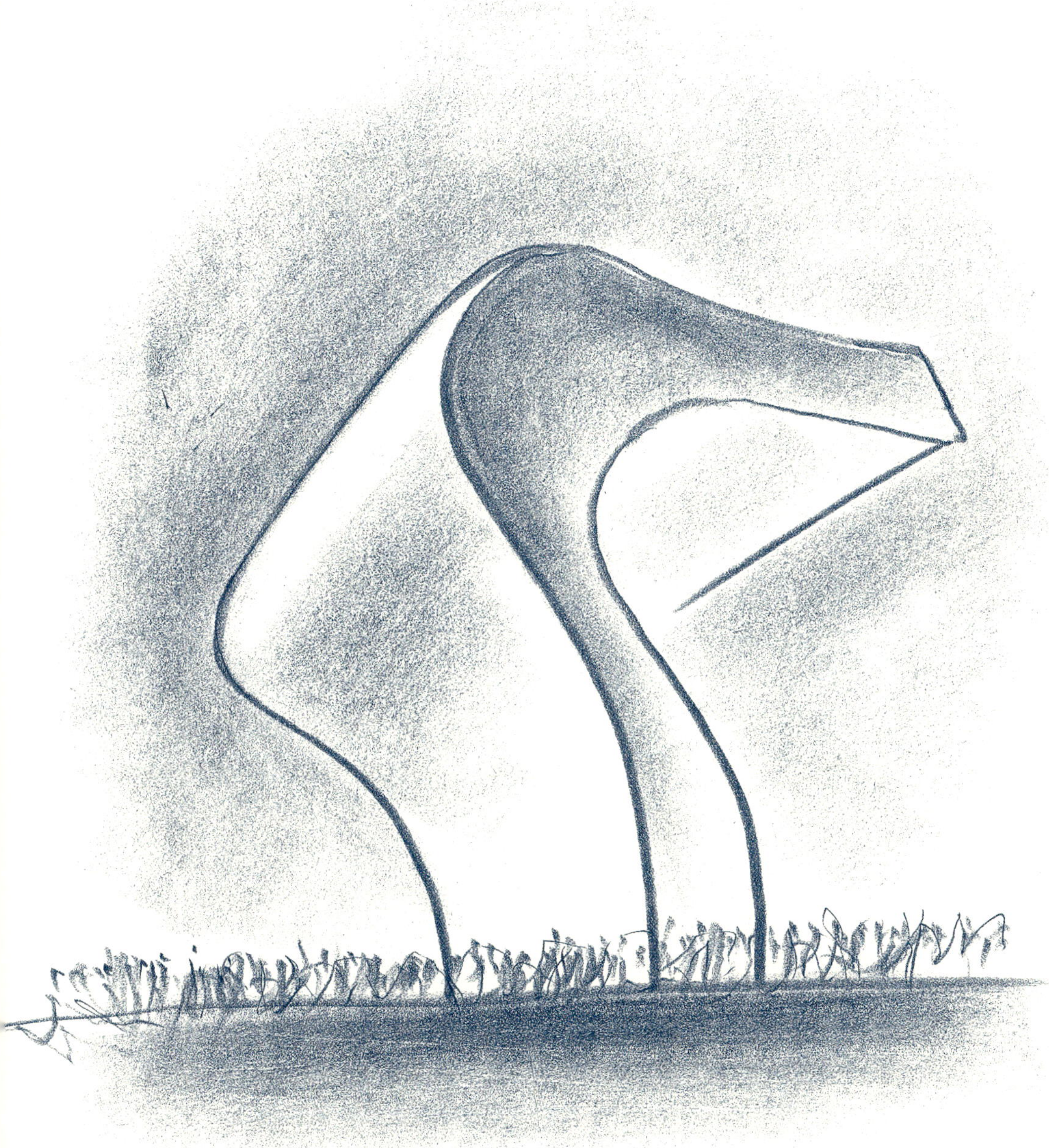

TAVOLI EROS, 1971

テーブルシリーズ：エロス，1971年

ジョイントのない家具を模索した結果、辿りついた最高傑作がこのテーブルである。大理石という素材を選んだことにより、素材の特性を完璧に活用した〈重力による嵌め込み固定〉が実現した。加工や仕上げも含めたこの特殊な解決策は、素材自体が示唆し定めたものである。「エロス」という名称は「幸いにもまだ機能する男性と女性の結合」を暗喩し、テーブルトップの重量を利用して「その硬度と重量があって初めて機能する」システムにより、安定性を確保しているテーブルシリーズ。天板（テーブルトップ）を受けて固定する旋盤加工された円錐形の脚は、その大きさと相まって最も安定性が高いものになっている。初期のテーブルトップは、クローズドホールを採用していたが、「連結の圧力に耐えることができなかった部分を除去」（ピエル・カルロ・サンティーニ）したオープンホールにデザインが手直しされている。

(M.O)

製造：ブランビッラ社からスキッパー社，カッペリーニ社へ移行／
Produced by Brambilla, later Skipper, later Cappellini

EROS TABLES, 1971. The high point in the research on furniture without joints, with the added touch of a gravity-based interlocking design perfectly matched with the choice of material: marble. A material that determines, requires and suggests particular solutions, working techniques and finishes. Eros – the name alludes to the "male-female coupling which fortunately still functions" – is a series of tables in which the tops, thanks to their weight, ensure the stability of a system that "won't work if it is not conceived as rigid and heavy"; where the truncated conical section of the turned leg that interfaces with and blocks the top is the most stable possible for its given volume; where the original gravity interlock is indicated by an opening in the top whose logical for is the result of "the elimination of those parts that would not have been able to bear the pressure of the interlock". (Pier Carlo Santini)

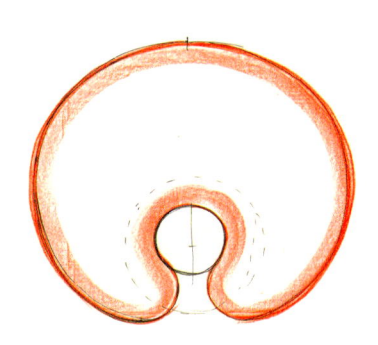

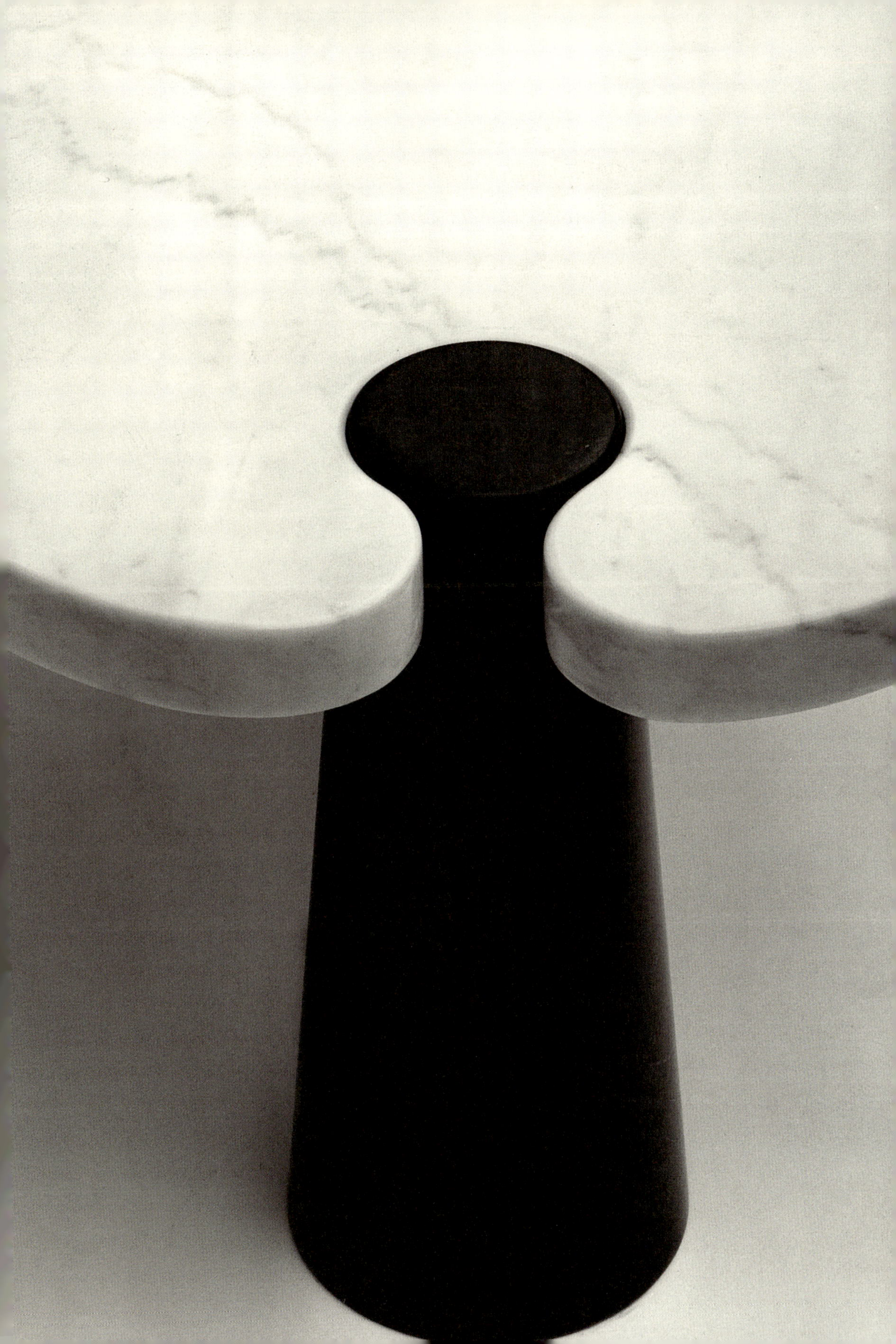

184

185

TAVOLI INCAS, 1978

テーブルシリーズ：インカス，1978年

「エロス」と対をなす「インカス」テーブルシリーズは、サンドブラスト仕上げのセレーナ石で製作されている。このテーブルは、屋外で使用するための理想的な素材と仕上げでつくられている。素材の「要求に従った」だけのジョイントデザインは、最も単純な直角の欠き込みをしただけの加工である。このシリーズの特徴はジョイントデザインにある。天板と支柱との取合いは、支柱の下方に向かって広がる傾斜した接合面だけで支えられ、ほかの垂直2面は構造的には働いていない。

(C.I)

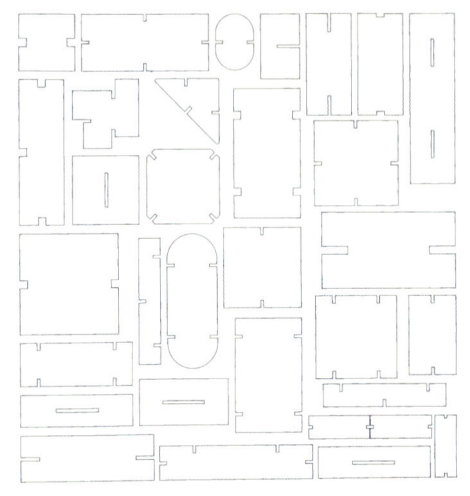

INCAS TABLES, 1978. The twin of the earlier Eros, the Incas table series is in sandblasted pietra serena, the ideal material and finish for outdoor use. The design of the joint "complies with the request" of the material for simpler working techniques, like the orthogonal cuts that characterize this collection. Assembly of the top with the support elements takes place along the inclined sides, while the vertical planes, obviously, do not contribute to the structural cohesion of the system.

製造：スキッパー社からカッペリーニ社へ移行
Produced by Skipper, later Cappellini

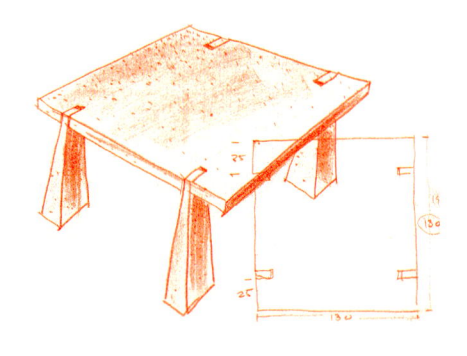

TAVOLI ASOLO, 1981

テーブルシリーズ：アゾロ，1981年

「アゾロ」テーブルシリーズの設計は、御影石の比類ない強靭さを知ることから始まる。御影石が有する物理的・力学的な特性の考察から、この素材の固有性を構造に活かしている。「アゾロ」は、2つのボタンホール（アゾロ）状の穴が開けられた天板に、天板の重量を支える2つの石板の脚を差し込むだけである。差し込まれる2枚の石板フォルムは台形で、それらが傾けられている。このフォルムが天板の上下動を止め、テーブルの安定性を確保している。この「アゾロ」は流行に沿った〈ミニマル〉ではなく、「エロス」と同様にスタイルを決める前に、まず素材の特性を知ることから導き出されたものである。

(O.H)

ASOLO TABLES, 1981. Another example of reasoning on the physical/mechanical characteristics of materials, the Asolo table series explores the exceptional resistance qualities of granite, utilized here as the sole material. Asolo: a top with two "eyelets" in which to fit two slab/uprights of the same thickness; the vertical blocking of the top is caused by the trapezoidal form of the uprights, which are inclined to increase the table's stability. Asolo: when one doesn't reach the "minimal" by following fashion but through knowledge of material, always ahead of the rest in terms of style...

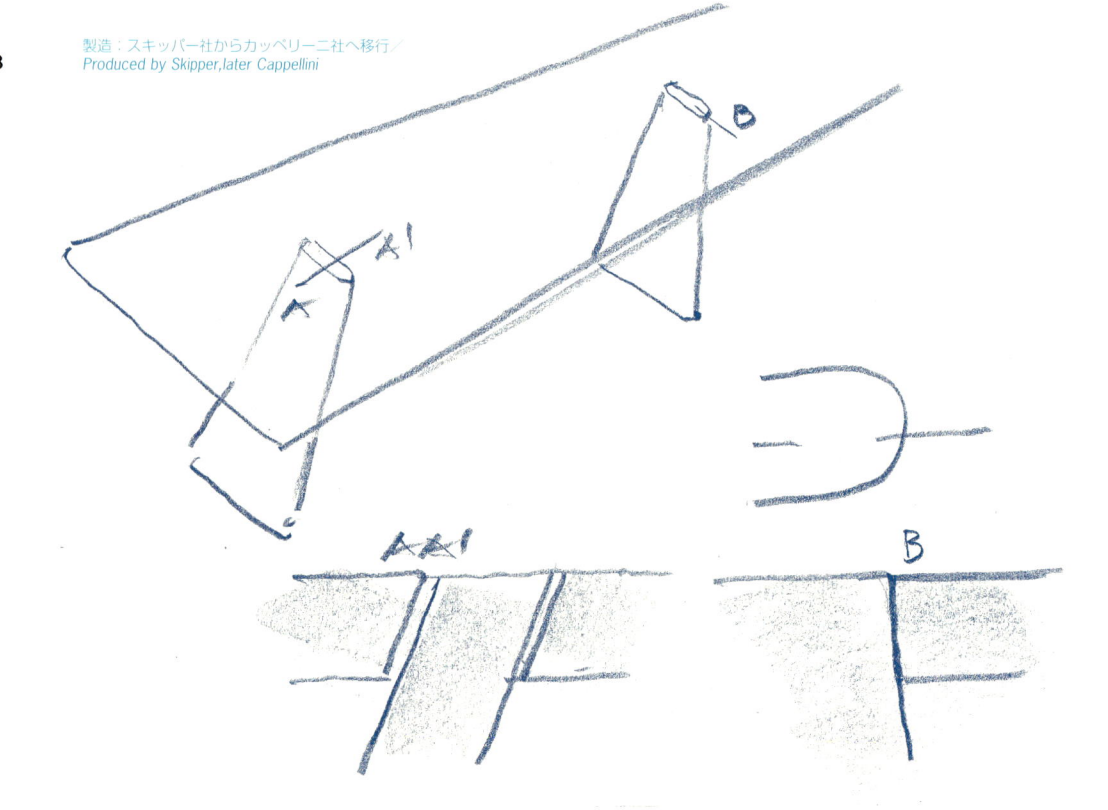

製造：スキッパー社からカッペリーニ社へ移行
Produced by Skipper, later Cappellini

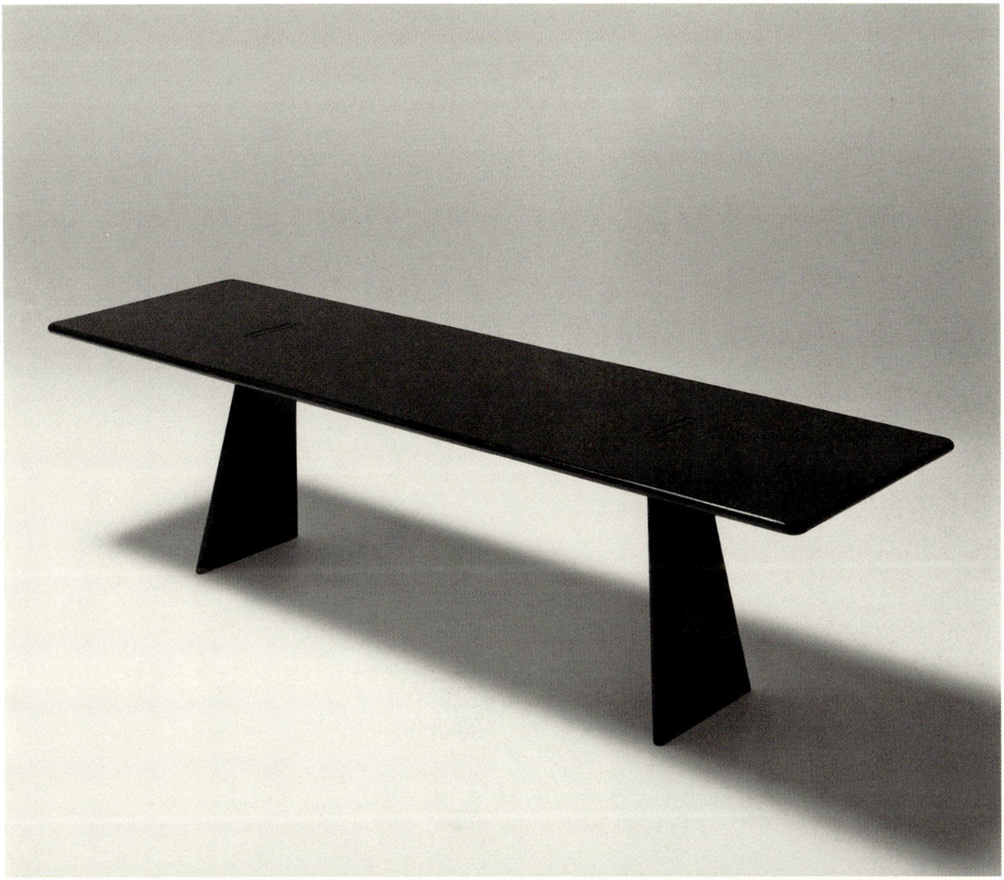
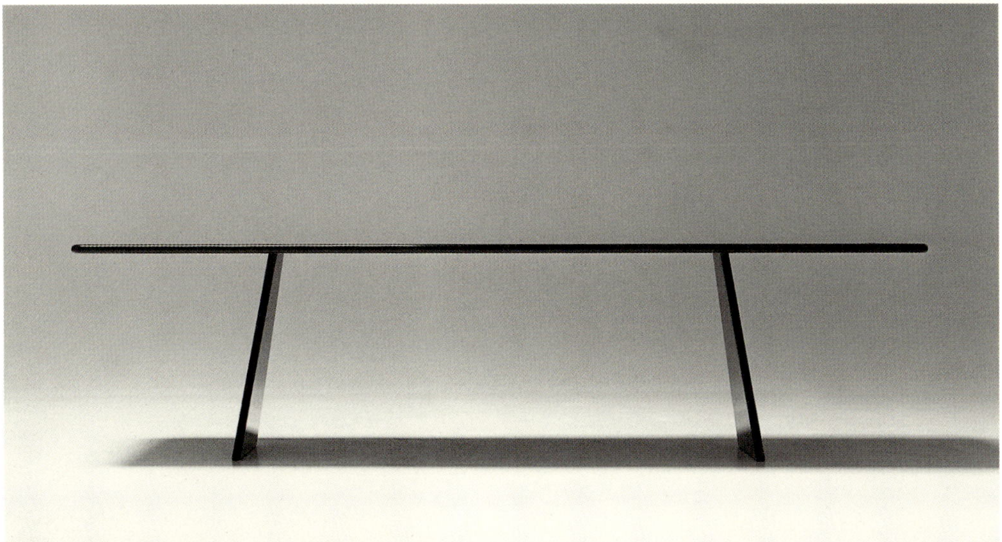

TAVOLI MORE, 1989

テーブル：モアー，1989年

御影石の天板とスチールパイプの脚だけで構成されるテーブル。天板に対して少しだけ傾けられた脚は、回転を防ぐために楕円形の断面で組み合わされている。テーブルの表面は、円錐状の切断面がその穴を塞いでいる。ほかにはなにもないシンプルなテーブル。

(Ka.M)

MORE TABLES, 1989. Tables with granite tops and tubular steel legs. The inclined position of the legs with respect to the top determines an elliptical interlock to prevent rotation, while the truncated conical section of that part of the leg vertically blocks the top. Nothing more.

製造：スキッパー社からカッペリーニ社へ移行 Produced by Skipper, later Cappellini

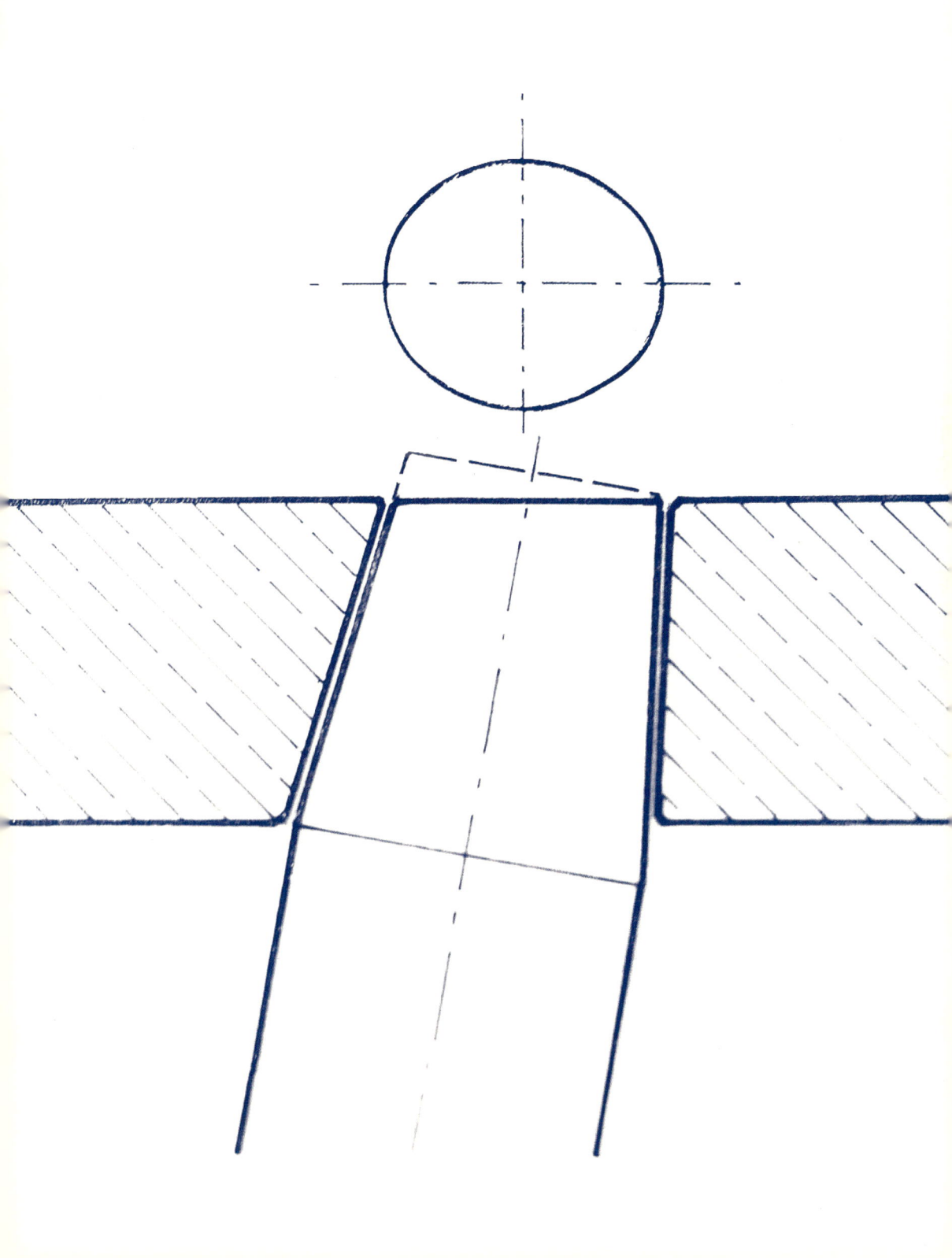

MOBILI IN COMPENSATO CURVATO, 1955

曲げ成型合板による家具，1955年

このプロジェクトは、ストゥール、ベンチ、テーブル、ソファベッドを含むたくさんのアイテムを想定したシリーズ。これらは、フィンランド産のカバを曲げ成型合板した縦部材と水平の帯状連結材、いろいろな素材による天板（天然木、ゴムと布地でカバーされたもの、ガラス、石、大理石、プラスティック板）、緊結用の真鍮製ボルトで構成されている。明快で、厳格なノック・ダウンシステムの採用など、アルヴァー・アールトを想起させる。　(Ke.M)

CURVED PLYWOOD FURNITURE, 1955. A project designed for mass production, including a stool, a bench, tables and a sofa-bed. Curved Finnish plywood for the vertical support elements and their connections, different materials for the horizontal surfaces (natural wood or wood covered in rubber and fabric, glass, stone, marble, plastic laminate), brass for the assembly bolts. A clear, rigorous, well-defined system, easily disassembled, that even impressed Alvar Aalto.

製造：フリジェリオ社／Produced by Frigerio　　　　共同者：ブルーノ・モラスッティ／With Bruno Morassutti

APPARTAMENTO MANZONI, MILANO, 1957

マンゾーニ通りのアパート／ミラノ，1957年

綿密にデザインされたインテリアのための洗練された小品。2枚重ねのベニア板が壁に沿って飾り棚になり、必要に応じて分岐し、カーブしながらバー・カウンターになっている。オープンなデザインによるソファは、いろいろな構成を可能にしている。カバでできた壁掛け照明にはテルモルックスのシェードが掛けられ、このソフトな部屋に明るさのアクセントを演出している。

(Y.T)

MANZONI APARTMENT, MILAN, 1957. Small, refined signs for a well-calibrated interior. Two overlapping sheets of plywood run along the wall to form a counter surface, splaying and curving to incorporate a bar unit. Upholstered elements with an open design allow for different compositions. A wall lamp with birch structure and "termolux" shade adds luminous accents to the particularly "soft" ambience.

共同者：ブルーノ・モラスッティ／With Bruno Morassutti

APPARTAMENTO BIGNARDI, MILANO, 1952

ビニャルディ通りのアパート／ミラノ, 1952年

軸回転とスライド機能をもつ4枚のパネルによる袖収納可動間仕切は、自由度の高い空間構成を可能にしている。アメリカ人画家ウィリアム・クラインによる白と黒とクリーム、そして黄色の抽象的なコラージュによる装飾が、さらに組合せの選択肢を増やしている。リーザ・ポンティは、雑誌「ドムス」で〈才能ある若手建築家〉の仕事として紹介し、「最小の装置による最大限の効果、絵画と彫刻と建築が融合した新しい成果である」と評している。このアパートメントのために製作された金属フレームと曲げ加工合板の棚板による本棚は、その後同様の技術で製作される家具シリーズの先駆けである。

(N.M)

BIGNARDI APARTMENT, MILAN, 1952. A diaphragm of mobile wings, Infinite Construction, composed of four pivoting, sliding panels to permit infinite configurations. The decoration – an abstract collage by the American painter William Klein in white, black, cream and yellow – multiplies the possible combinations. Lisa Ponti, presenting this project by the "talented young architect" in the magazine Domus, describes "a minimum machine with maximum effects, a new development involving painting, sculpture and architecture, together". For the same apartment a bookcase with a metal structure and curved plywood shelves appears to be the forerunner, by several years, of a series of furniture made with the same technology.

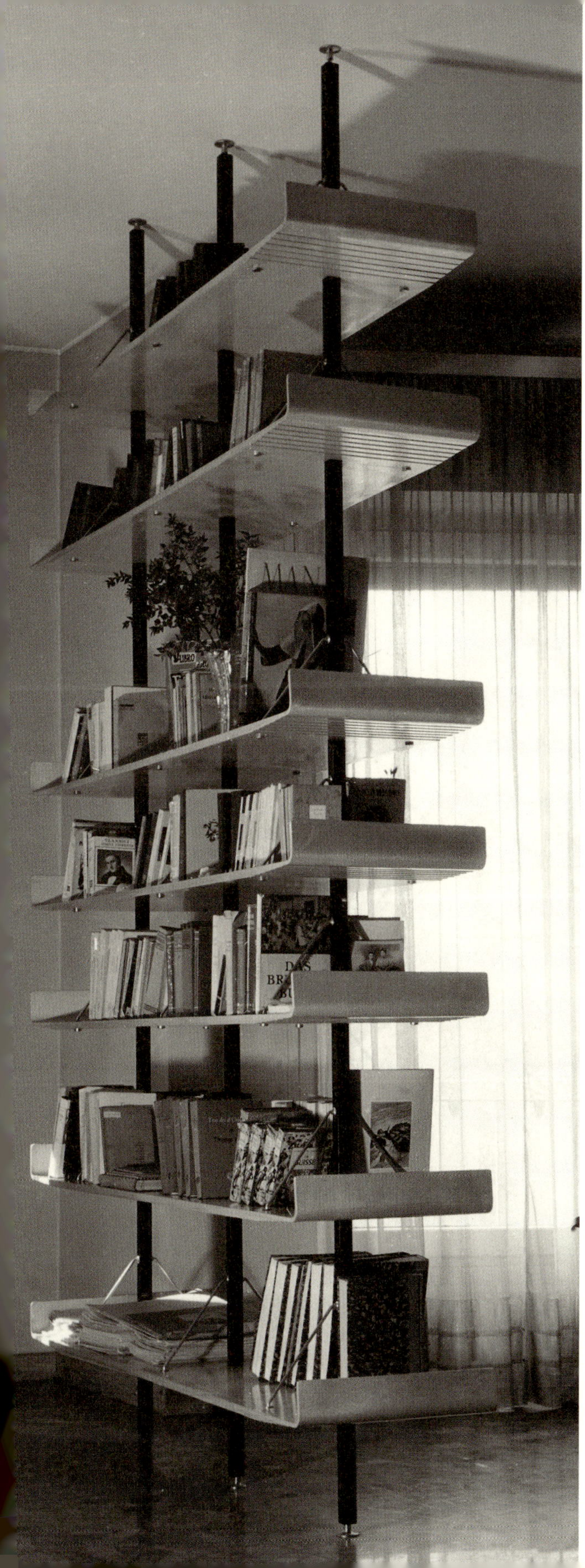

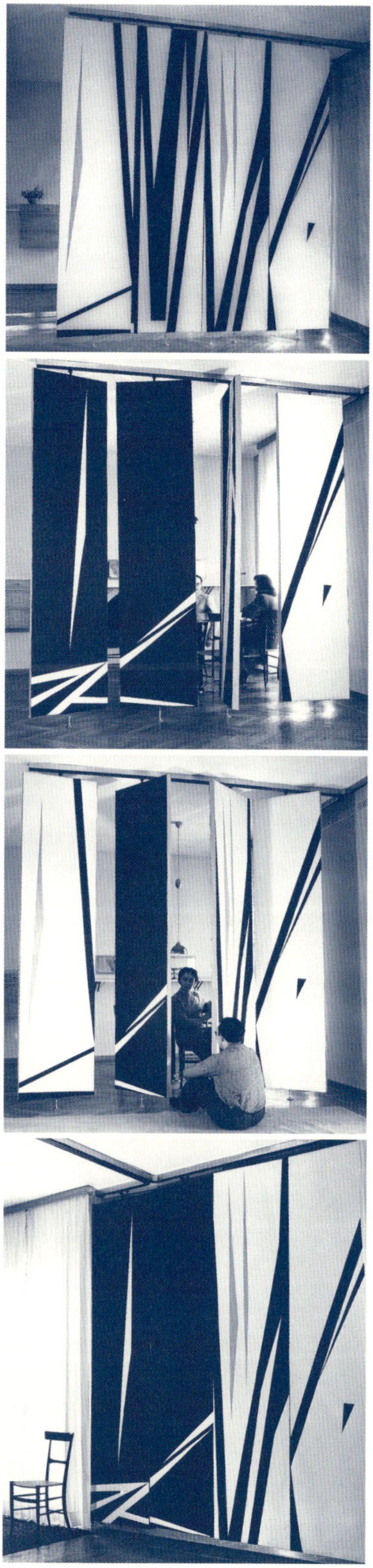

SISTEMA JUNIOR, 1966

システム家具：ジュニア，1966年

簡単に組み立て、分解が可能なこのシステム家具は、積層ベニア板でできている。当初は、子ども用（幼稚園や小学校で幅広く使用）に設計された。その後、寸法を変えて大人用もつくられた。「さまざまな組合せや素材の感触を楽しむことができ、その構成システムも明確に理解できるこの家具は、子どもたちに対する教育ツールにもなっている」

「システム家具：ジュニア」は、家具のタイポロジーの原形である。丸鋸で切断されただけのパネルは、過剰な表面仕上げもなく、金属金物も一切使わず、接着することなく、唯一各部材を嵌め込むだけで組み立てることができる。この家具はシンプルではあるが、陳腐ではなく、ミニマルではあるが、無個性ではなく、ドライで無装飾ではあるが無表情ではない。実に模範的な家具。 (I.M)

製造：カザルーチ社からカッペリーニ社へ移行（2002年）
Produced by Casaluci, later Cappellini (2002)

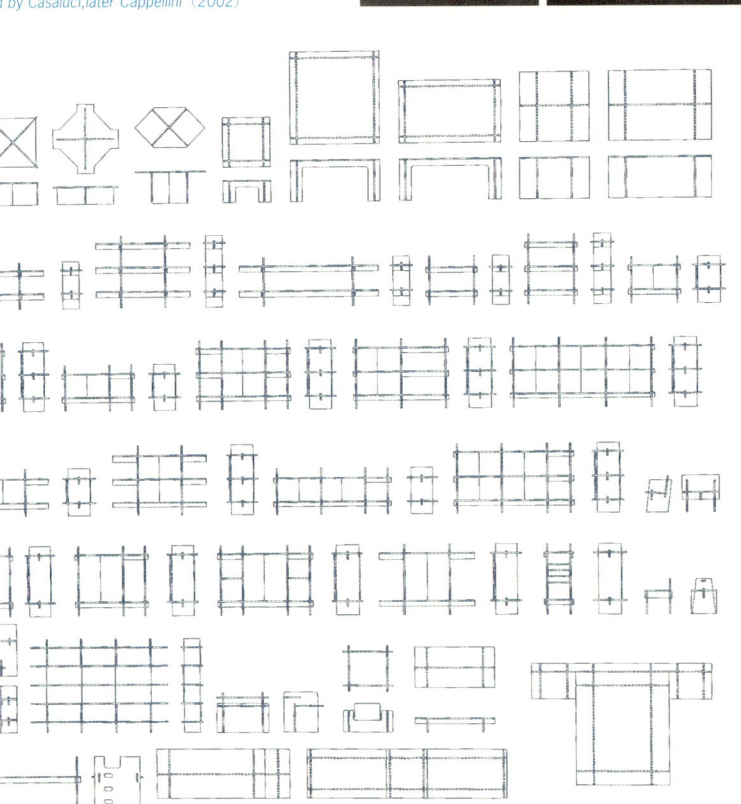

197

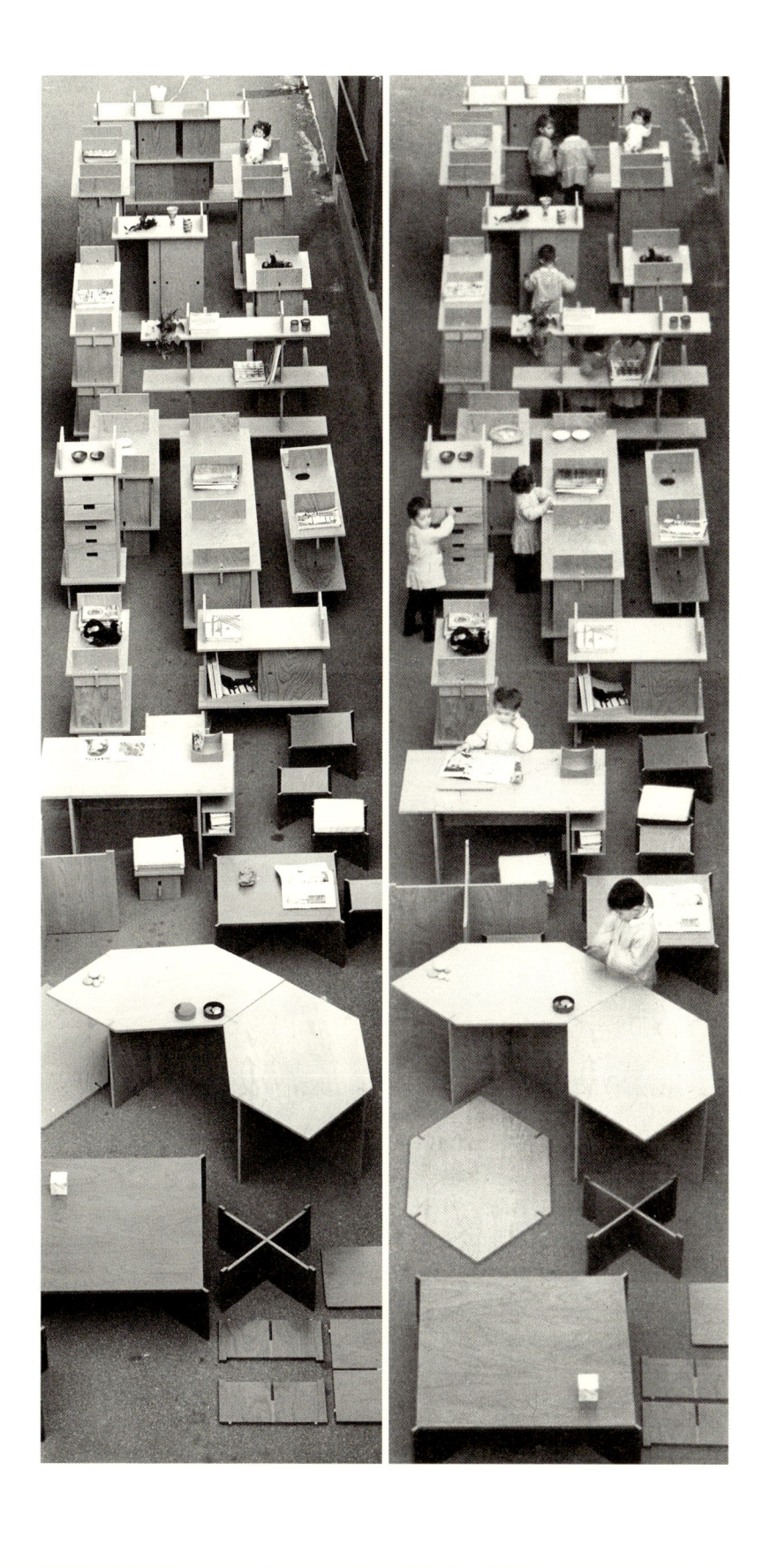

JUNIOR SYSTEM, 1966. A system of furniture for easy assembly and disassembly, in plywood, initially designed for children (and widely used in daycare centers and schools), and later adapted (in terms of size) for adults. "The possibility of combination of the elements, the direct contact the child has with the sincerity of the material and the clarity of the construction system add an implicit educational function to this furniture". Junior: an extensive primer of furnishing typologies obtained with cut, milled panels that can be interlocked together without the use of metal hardware and without further finishing. Objects that are simple but not banal, minimal but not anonymous, terse and composed, but not without character. Exemplary.

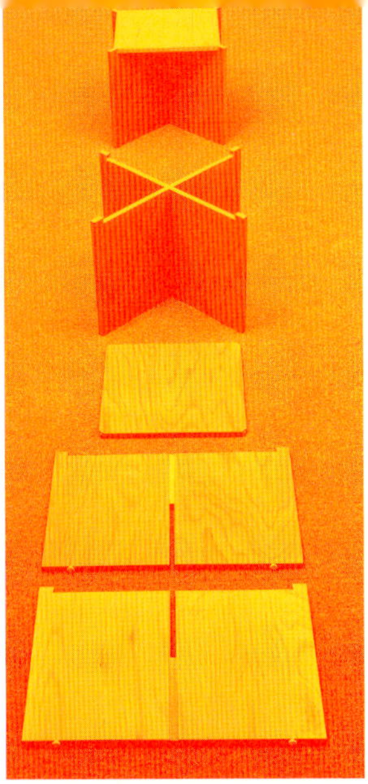

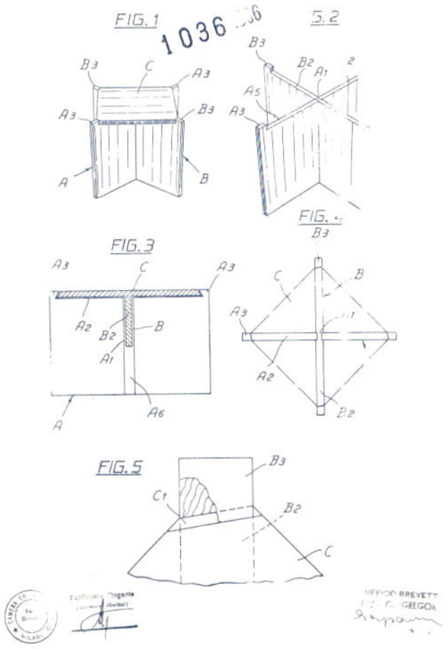
FIG.1
FIG.3
FIG.5

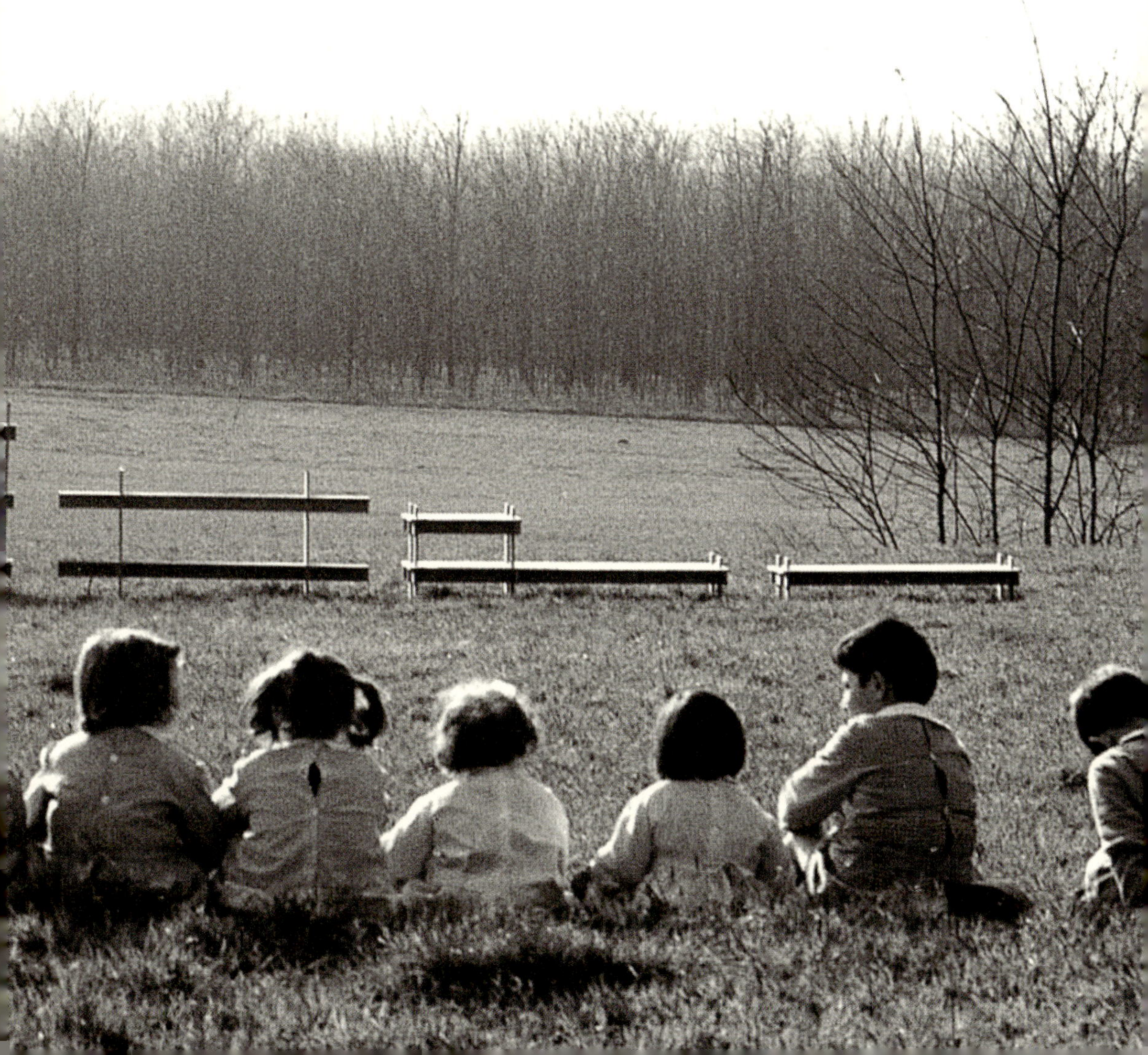

SISTEMA CUB8, 1967

システム：CUB8，1967年

このプロジェクトは、建築のプレファブリケーションの研究成果と知識をインテリアに転用した象徴的な例である。両面化粧張りされたパーティクルボードのパネルは、縁取したPVC押出成形材と一体化し、同一のパネルが隣接・結合（もう1つのC型をしたPVC押出成形材の素材特性である柔軟性を利用して、2つのパネルの縁材にカチッと嵌め込む）を繰り返しながら、最終的に計画された収納壁をつくり出している。線状のジョイントはパネルをシンプルに、かつ極めて高い展開の可能性を利用して、より複雑なシステムのエレメントにも応用が可能である。この押出成形材の応用は、パネル端部の仕上げが省けることと、厚さと重量を軽減できるために、インテリア部材に求められるさまざまな要求に応えることも可能にしている。「CUB8」はその名称も含めて特許を取得している。

(O.H)

製造：ポルトローヴァ社／Produced by Poltronova

CUB8 SYSTEM, 1967. An emblematic project for interior architecture that seems to transfer research and knowledge from the world of prefabricated construction. A section in extruded PVC utilized for the borders of panels of bilaminated wood chipboard permits them to be combined and joined (by means of another C section in the same material that interlocks by snapping, thanks to its elasticity, into the two adjacent sections) to create accessorized walls. A linear joint that transforms the mere panel to which it is applied into an element of a more complex system with great development potential. The application of the section to the border of the panel avoids operations of perimeter finishing and distributes stress along the entire piece, permitting reduction of thickness and weight. Cub8: a patented model and registered name. Really.

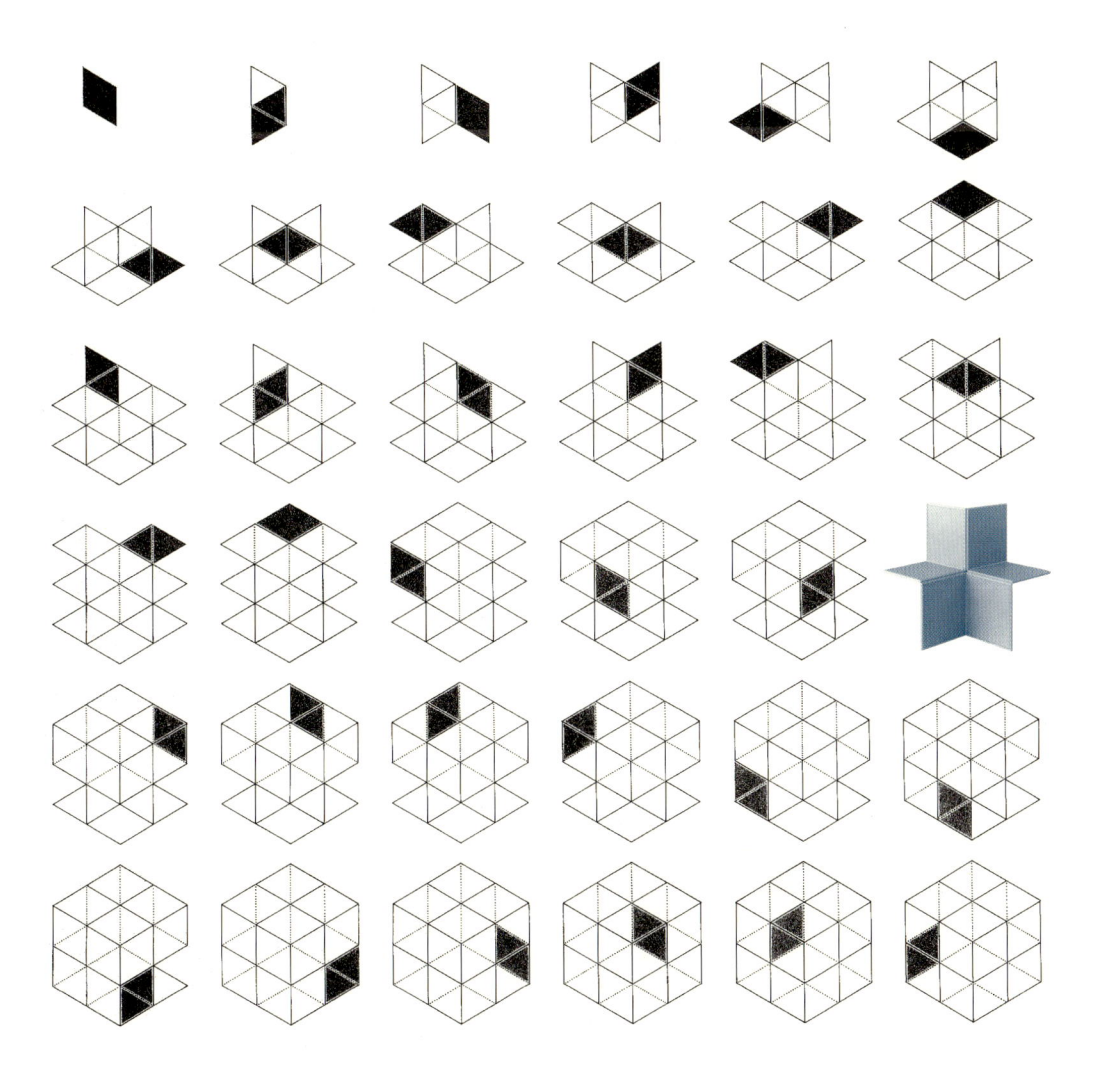

FIG. 2

FIG. 3

l'Ufficiale Rogante
(Caio Zanibelli)

UFFICIO BREVETTI
Ing. C. GREGORJ

202

スタディのためのスケッチ／Working sketch

SISTEMA IN/OUT, 1968

システム：IN/OUT，1968年

「IN/OUT」は「CUB8」の考え方を発展させて、PVCの押出成形部材だけで構成された収納棚のシステム。ハニカムの断面をもつパネル、四つ葉の断面形状の支柱、そしてこれらを連結する弾力性に富んだジョイントで構成されている。ほかに棚受け、蝶番、把手に使用される部材により、軽量で強靱、かつ耐久性に富む材料の特性を活かした最高のシステムが完成している。「IN/OUT」は「CUB8」と同様に特許と商標登録を取得しており、名称が示すように屋外でも使用することができる。さらに、2本の柱を連結して強固な二重壁をつくったり、パネル間に断熱材を入れることも可能である。

(M.T)

スタディのためのスケッチ／
Working sketch

IN/OUT SYSTEM, 1968. The evolution of the reasoning behind Cub8, In/Out is a system for accessorized walls entirely composed of elements in extruded PVC. A honeycomb-section panel, a quadrilobate section that functions as an upright, an elastic seal that attaches them together. Other accessories (shelf supports, hinges, handles) lead to the definition of a system that makes optimum use of the lightness, resistance and durability of its material. In/Out (like Cub8 a patented model and registered name) can also be utilized in outdoor applications, as the name indicates: by coupling two uprights it is possible to obtain a strong double wall, with the possibility of injecting insulation material between the panels.

特許用図面／Patent drawing

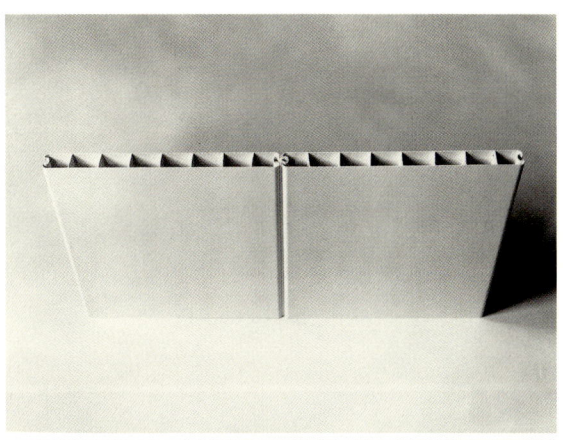

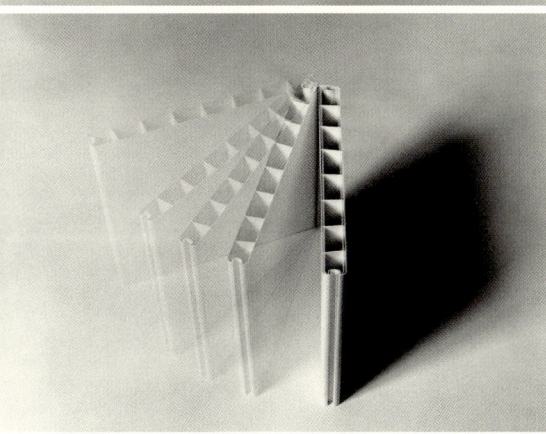

製造：ノル・インターナショナル社
Produced by Knoll International

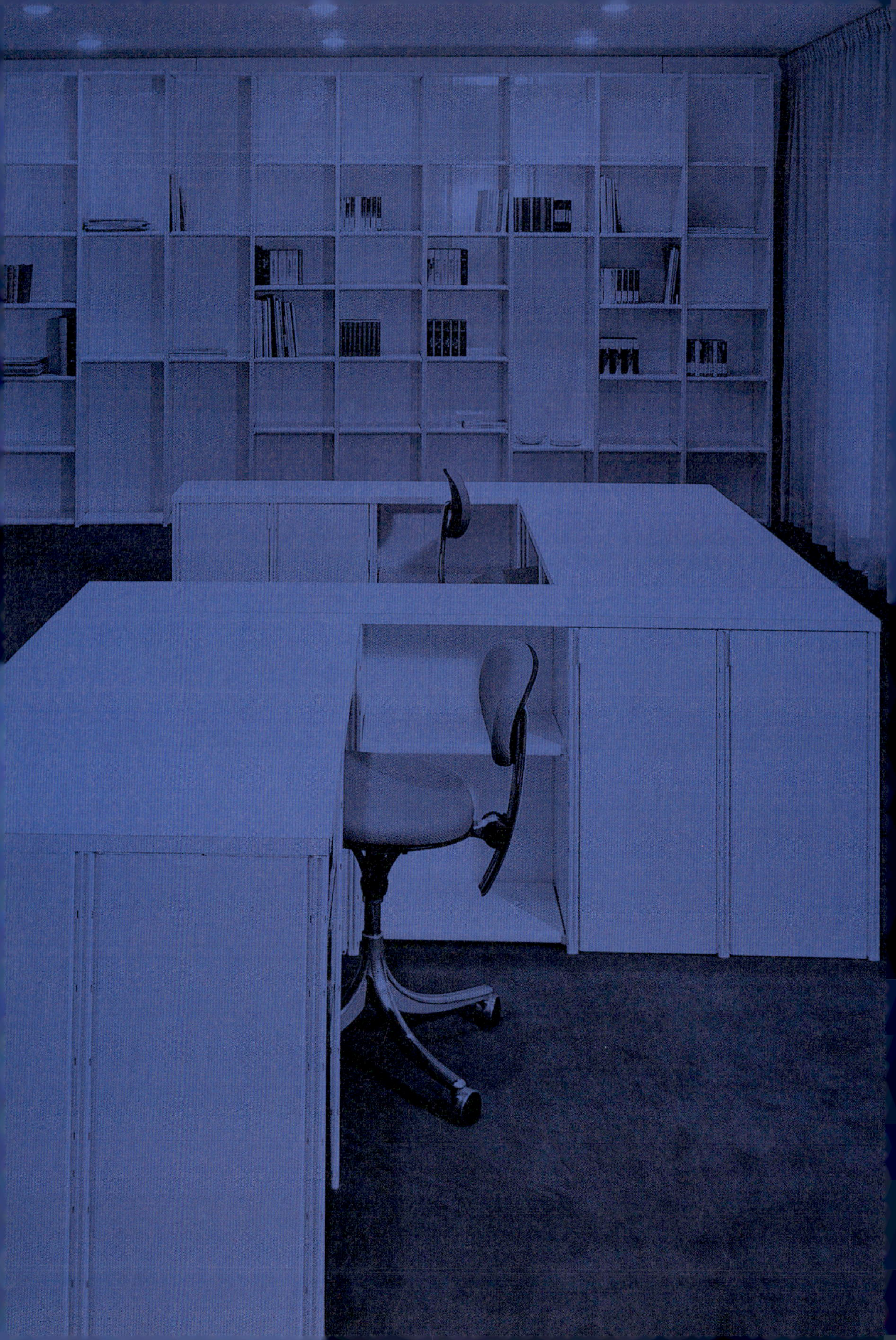

FIG.2

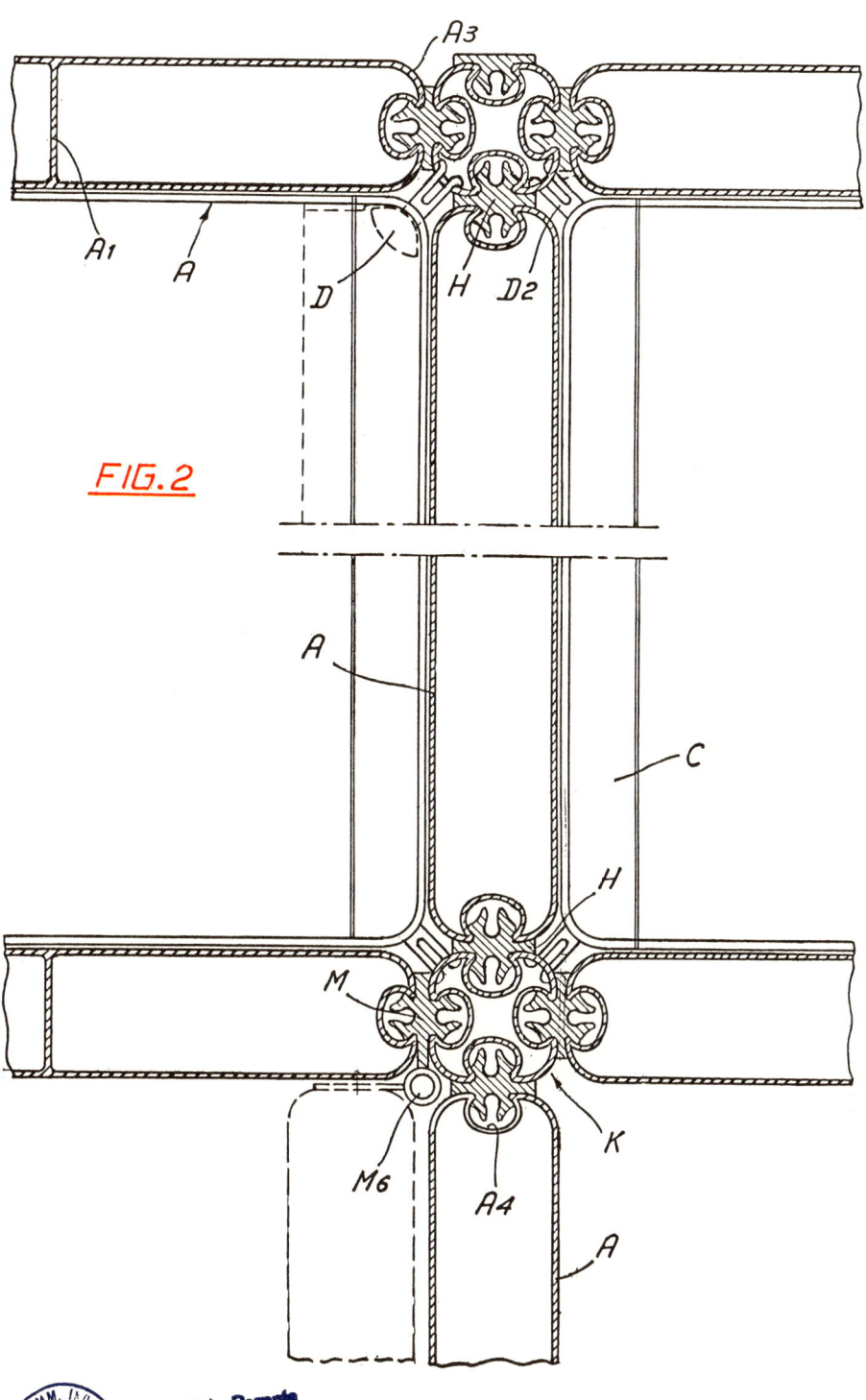

LIBRERIA ESTRUAL, 1981

書棚：エストゥルアル，1981年

この書棚は、側板と棚の2つの部材で構成され、アルミニウムと押出成形技術という単一素材、単一生産技術でつくられている。棚の断面にはリブが設けられ、耐荷重を増している。側板には、ドアとパネルの取付けも可能である。側板の最も幅広のものは、従来の鋳型でつくることは不可能であるが、2つの同一部材を組み合わせることで可能にしている。　(M.O)

ESTRUAL BOOKCASE, 1981. Just two parts, upright and shelf; a single material, aluminium; a single production technology, extrusion. The ribbed section of the shelf adds great load bearing resistance, while the particular design of the upright permits insertion of doors and panels. The greater lightness of the upright, which would be impossible to obtain with the traditional matrices, is the result of the pairing of two identical elements.

製造：スキッパー社．Produced by Skipper

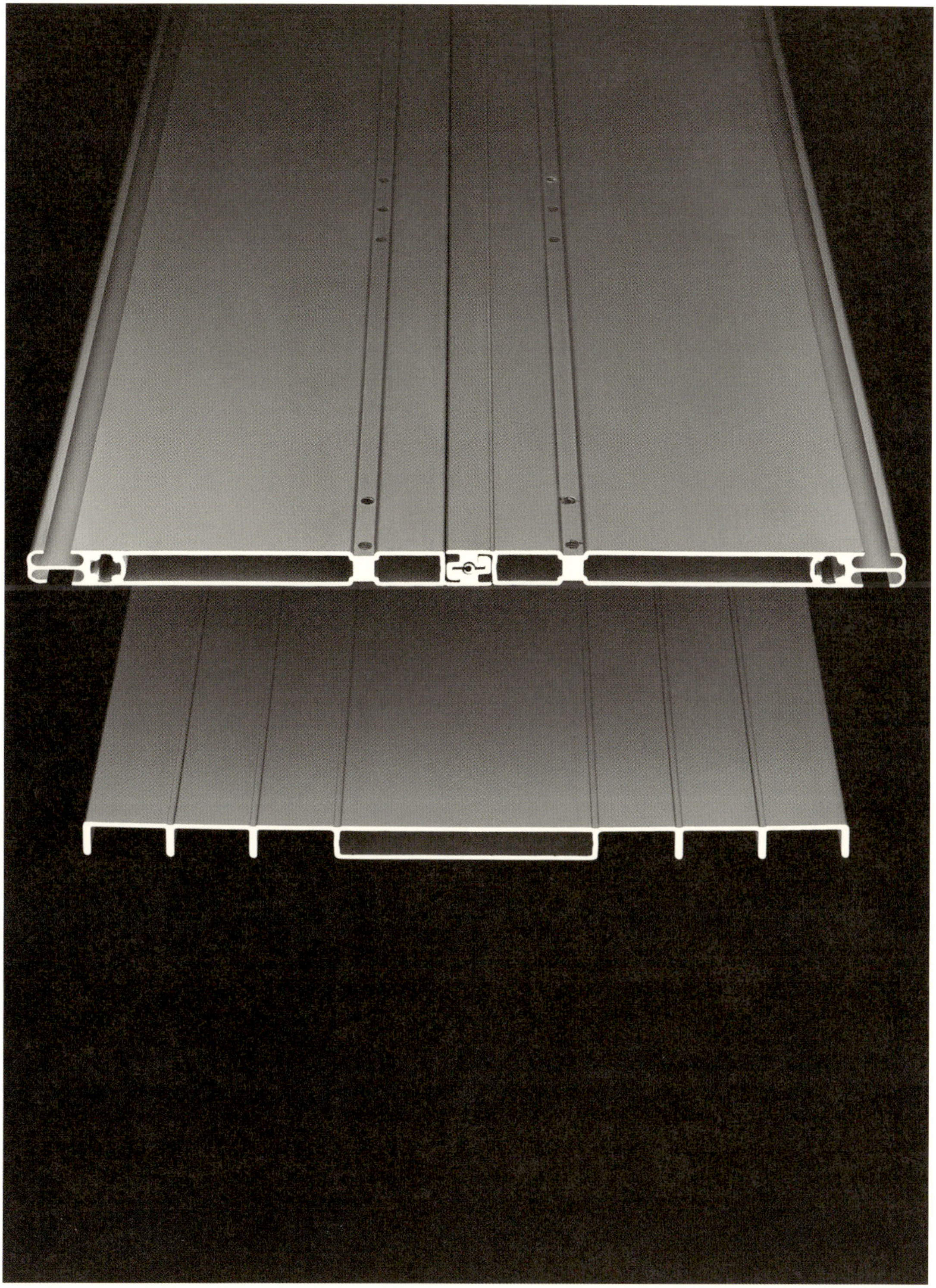

LIBRERIA YPSILON, 1996

書棚：イプシロン，1996年

厚さ1.2mmのスチール鋼板を、この書棚の名称にもなっているY字型（イプシロン）に折り曲げて、形成された部材による高い耐久力を有する書棚。

(K.H)

YPSILON BOOKCASE, 1996. A highly resistant form obtained by bending sheet metal with a thickness of 1.2 mm, in a design that gives the bookcase its name.

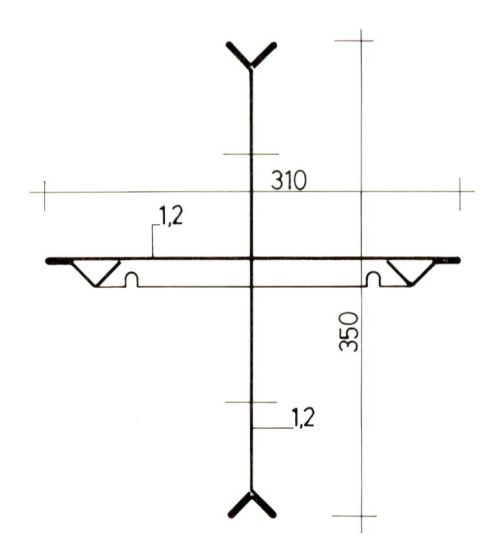

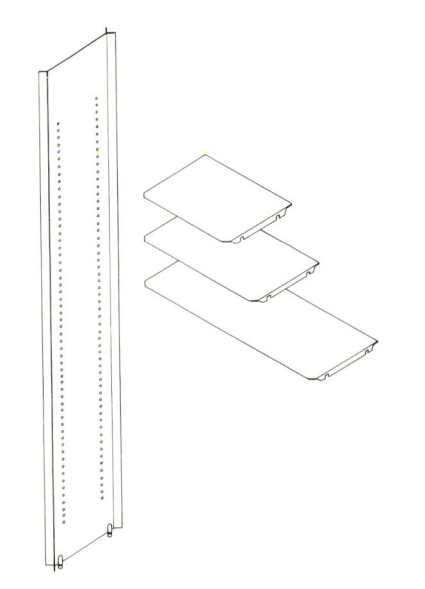

製造：バレーリ・イタリア社／*Produced by Baleri Italia*

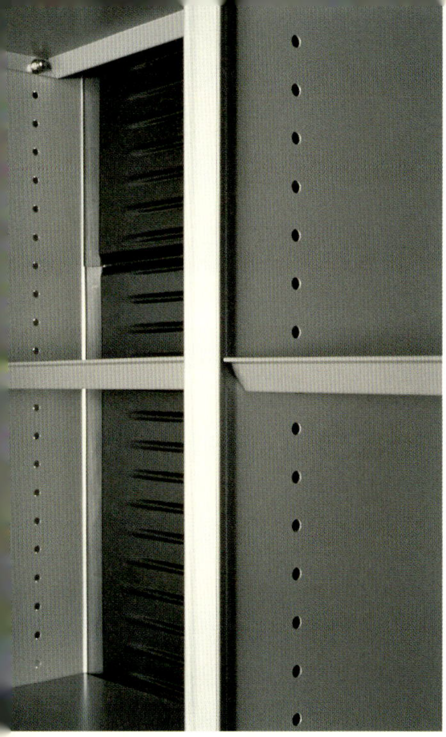

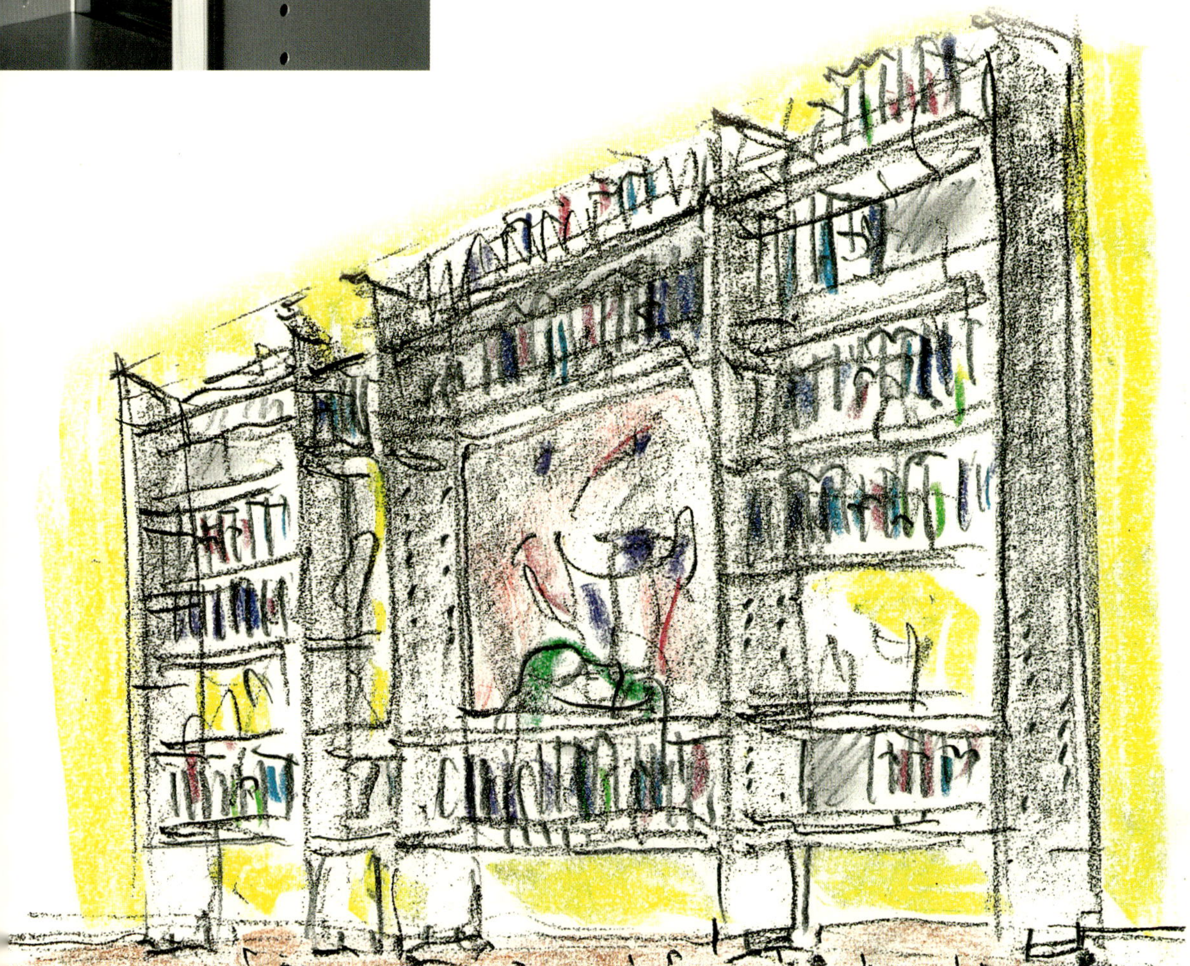

IMPIALLACCIATURE IN/IN, 1981

化粧用突き板：IN/IN，1981年

「IN/IN」には、半加工品として考案された工業生産寄木材である。あらかじめ着色された薄板を1枚1枚圧着し、そのブロックをさらに薄板に切断する。その切断面は必ずしも直角である必要はない。それらの板は何度もほかの板と寄せ合わされ、色彩と成型が掛算的に無限に増殖する幾何学模様の新しい化粧突き板が生産される。モニカ・ルッキは言っている。「切断は、破壊・裂傷・分裂や抗議のシンボルではなく、色彩・表現・探求を含蓄するものである」

(O.H)

共同者：イタロ・リヴェラーニ／with the collaboration of Italo Liverani　製造：アルピ社／Produced by Alpi

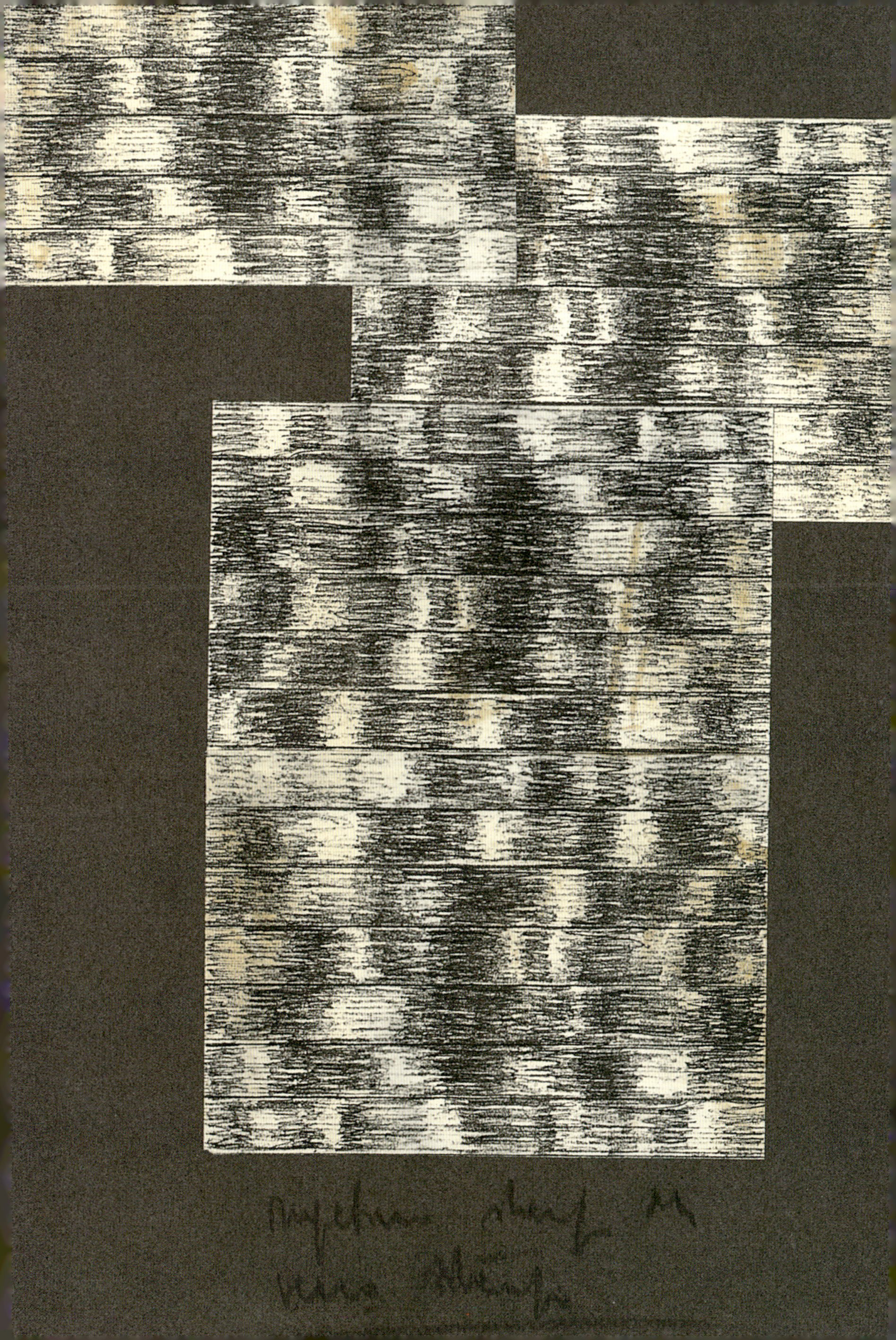

IN/IN VENEERS, 1981. In/in stands for Industrial Inlay, a way of thinking about semi-finished products. Sheets of pre-colored veneer are pressed together and then cut, not necessarily at orthogonal angles. The resulting sheets are then placed side by side to create a new kind of veneer in which a "geometric" design is multiplied in infinite configurations and chromatic effects. "The cut is no longer a symbol of breakage, laceration, division and protest, but takes on the connotations of research, expression, color" (Monica Luchi).

IMPIALLACCIATURE NEVER THE SAME, 1993

化粧用突き板：ネヴァー・ザ・セイム，1993年

「IN/IN」に続くこの製品「ネヴァー・ザ・セイム」は、自然の模様を模倣したものでもなく、幾何学模様でもなく、繰返し模様でもない。決して同じ模様がないのだ。製作過程は、ポプラの木（特に軟らかい木）の薄板を異なる色に染め、それぞれを重ね合わせて接着し、多少不規則にプレスをかけ、薄く切断する。こうして絶えず変化のある不規則な模様の化粧用突き板が生産される。

(Ka.M)

共同者：イタロ・リヴェラーニ／with the collaboration of Italo Liverani
製造：アルピ社／Produced by Alpi

NEVER THE SAME VENEERS, 1993. The ideal continuation of the In/in series leads to an industrial production of veneers that "without imitating nature" are nevertheless less geometric and repetitive. Never the same: sheets of poplar (a particularly soft wood) dyed in different colors, glued together, pressed between slightly irregular surfaces and subsequently cut to produce new veneer sheets with an unusual, constantly variable design.

217

ANELLO VERA LAICA, 2000

指輪：ヴェラ・ライカ，2000年

マンジャロッティは、自由な発想で、2人の人間の結合を象徴する伝統的な結婚指輪もデザインした。「ヴェラ・ライカ」は、それぞれ異なった2つの部分を嵌め込んで一体化する指輪である。接合部の特別なデザインは、指にしている間は分離することがない。

(K.H)

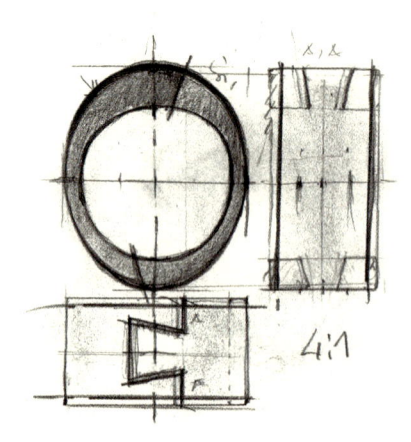

VERA LAICA RING, 2000. The secular thought of Mangiarotti focuses on a revision of the symbol of the union between two persons: the traditional wedding ring. Vera Laica is a ring composed of two interlocking parts. The particular design of the joint prevents the parts from separating when the ring is being worn.

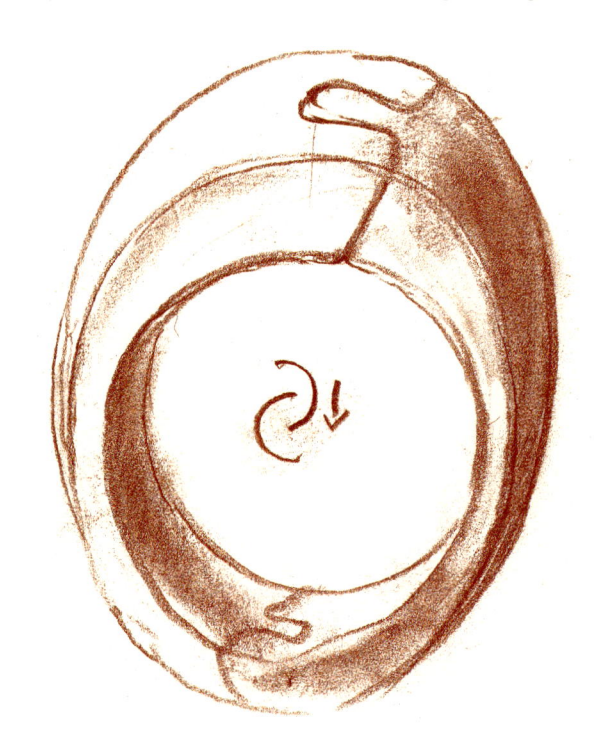

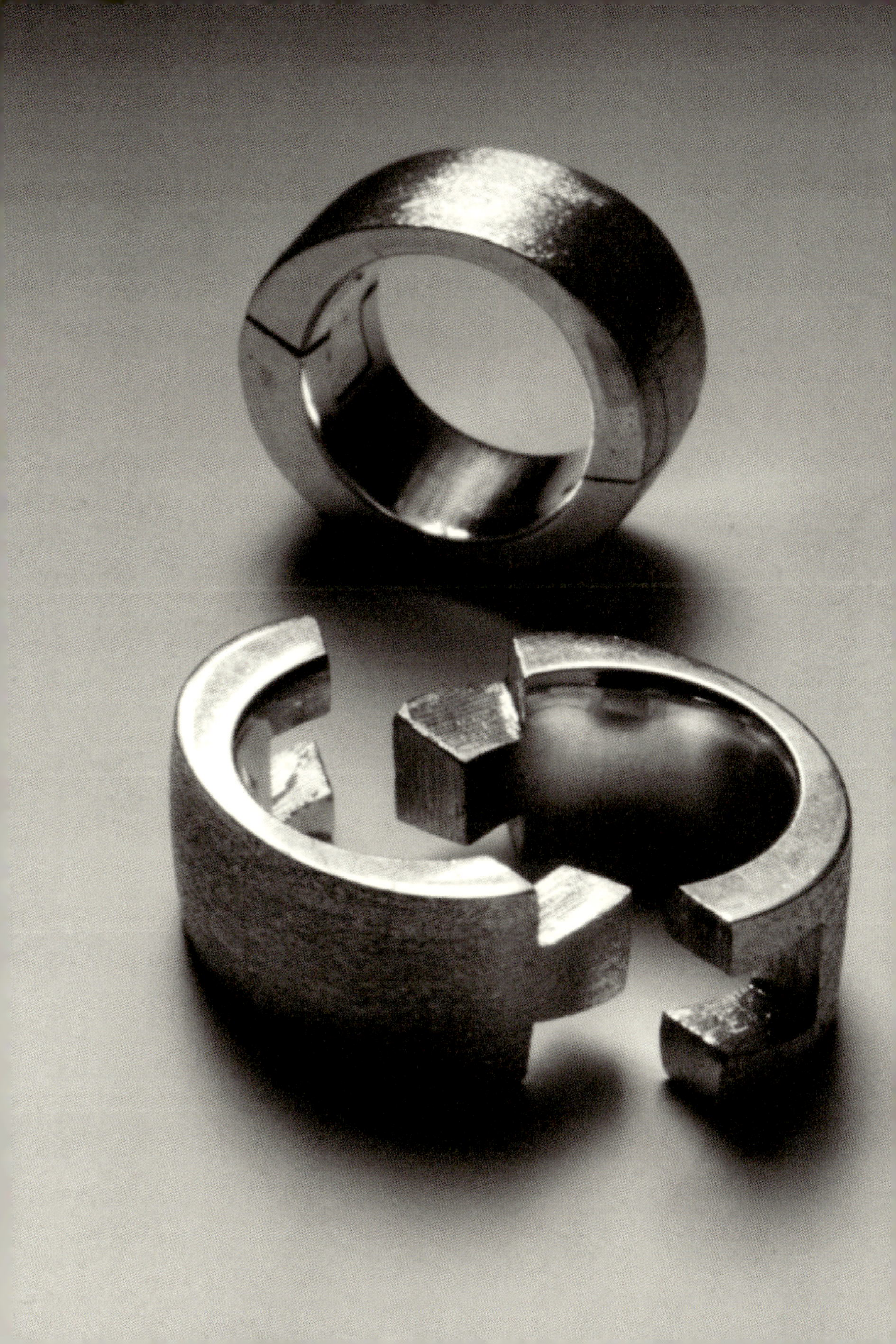

SUL DESIGN

デザインについて　フランソア・ブルクハルト

アンジェロ・マンジャロッティは、イタリアの「ベル・デザイン」の第1世代を象徴するほかの人たち（ベリーニ、カスティリオーニ、マジストレッティ、ソットサス、ザヌーソなど）と一線を画している。彼の特異性は、使われる素材が要求する特質や制約に応じてデザインを適応させることができる能力にある。彼は、素材がもつ固有の特性を活かして人工物をつくりあげる術を心得ている。例えばガラスではその本来の透明性、順応性、柔軟性を与え、また合成樹脂ではその弾力性を最大限に活かしている。

元来、建築から始まってプロダクトデザインの領域まで拡大してきたのは、同期の人たちと共通している。彼の場合は、特にプレファブと乾式工法、エンジニアリングによる構造上の問題解決が契機になっている。実際、彼の関心の核は工業化である。彼はさまざまな組立システムの技術から、建築にもプロダクトデザインにも使うことができ、特にインテリアデザインに応用できるモジュールやジョイントを考案している。これらの組立技術を活用して、マンジャロッティはさまざまな用途に応じていろいろなものを創作している。それは収納であったり、整理棚であったり、事務所用の家具であったり、家庭用の家具であったりする。彼がデザインしたキャビネット、本棚、オフィス家具は、いずれも典型的な工業的組立プロセスの結実である。

彼のデザイン理論は、最終的な作品の機能と用途に基づいている。しかし、その形態は、オーソドックスな合理主義思考、つまり素材を適材適所に使うことから生まれる純粋で単純な結果からではない。マンジャロッティの理論はもっとはるかに複雑で、発想する形態にも影響が及び、素材の物理的な組成から始まり、そのほか多岐にわたる要因を含んでいる。事実、マンジャロッティの作品にはたくさんの素材が使われていて、素材の実験と探求には多大な力が注がれている。

もう1つ彼の仕事で注目すべき特徴は、適切な素材の選択によって、作品の官能的な側面を導き出すマンジャロッティの能力である。その能力を支える、直観と強い表現力を備えた造形感覚によって、彼の作品は合理性と感性の領域に等しい力強さで存在感を呈している。

彼が現代的デザイナーと位置づけられる資質の1つは、時代の最新技術に精通している点である。例えば、NC制御の工作機械を使用した石材の切削などに見られる。ある領域で得た知識を別の領域に応用する能力によって、彼の活動領域は環境・建築からインテリア、プロダクトデザイン、アートまで、関わる領域のすべてを横断的に拡張していく。また、マンジャロッティの芸術作品は、具象・抽象の芸術世界と近似している点も特徴である。彼は造形に関して大きな自信をもっている。これは、彼が工業生産の領域で得た技術的・実用的な知識を統合し、完成させていることに裏打ちされている。

マンジャロッティは、デザイン界で独特の位置を占めている。この世界で彼は職人芸から工業文化までの幅広い領域で活躍し、圧倒的な存在感を得ている。工業的生産技術への関心と、芸術的表現の探求の2要素が、等しく彼のデザイン活動の原動力となっているという意味では、芸術性においても評価に値する作家である。

(M.K)

ON THE DESIGN

Angelo Mangiarotti stands apart from the other figures of the first generation of Italian "bel design" (including Bellini, Castiglioni, Magistretti, Sottsass, Zanuso) for his capacity to adapt the product to be designed to the characteristics and conditions required by the materials utilized. He knows how to restore the original natural character of the material to artificial objects, granting glass its transparency, malleability and flexibility, for example, or fully capturing the elasticity of plastic. Like his colleagues he came to product design through architecture, and in particular through industrial prefabrication and the techniques of dry assembly, resolving structural problems through engineering. The main focus of his interest is, in fact, industrialization: from the techniques of different assembly systems he creates modules and joints that can be applied both to architecture and to design, especially to design for interior architecture. By assembling these structures Mangiarotti creates different types of objects for different functions – to store, to file, for the office, for the home. His cabinets, his bookcases, his office furniture are the result of typically industrial processes of assembly. His design logic is based on the function and use of the final object whose form, however, is not the pure and simple result of an orthodox rationalism, of a rational use of the right material and the appropriate construction techniques. Mangiarotti's logic is much more complex, taking other factors into account, such as the physical composition of materials, which influences the form that emerges. The work of Mangiarotti is multi-materic, in fact, and demonstrates his great commitment in the area of research and experimentation starting with materials. Another noteworthy characteristic is Mangiarotti's ability to bring out the sensual side of objects through the correct choice of materials, sustained by an intuitive, highly expressive formal sensibility that places his works, in equal measure, in the sphere of rationality and that of subjectivity. One of the qualities that make him a timely designer is his gift of keeping up with the most advanced techniques in use in the field of material culture, as when he operates with the aid of numerically controlled machines for the cutting of stone. His capacity to apply knowledge acquired in one sector to work in another leads to a transversal practice that extends to all the fields in which he operates: environment, architecture, interior architecture, product design, art. The artistic practice of Mangiarotti is characterized by his closeness to the world of concrete and abstract art. This gives him great confidence in the making of forms, completing and integrating the technical and practical know-how he has acquired in the field of industrial production. In the world of design Mangiarotti has a particular position, making him an impeccable figure on a technical plane, active in different areas of artisan and industrial culture, but at the same time artistically qualified, because his research springs from an interest in industrial processes, but to the same extent from attraction to artistic expression. ■Francois Burkhardt

CONO-CIELO, 1987

天空の円錐，1987年

形態・技術・構法の妙技である。この塔は石材加工の現場に導入された新しい機械（NC制御）が生み出す可能性を探る思考過程から生まれたものである。デモンストレーション用の建造物であり、彫刻でもあるこの塔は、カラーラ大理石の1つの塊から切り出した部材を、段々に小さくなっていく切頭円錐のプロポーションで積み上げてできている。すでに世界の各地で展示されてきたこの作品は、単純に各部材を積み上げ、コーン型の足元と頂上（上に向かって石の厚さは薄くなり傾斜角度は急になる）をロープで引き締めるだけで組み立てられる、いたってシンプルな構成である。

(Y.T)

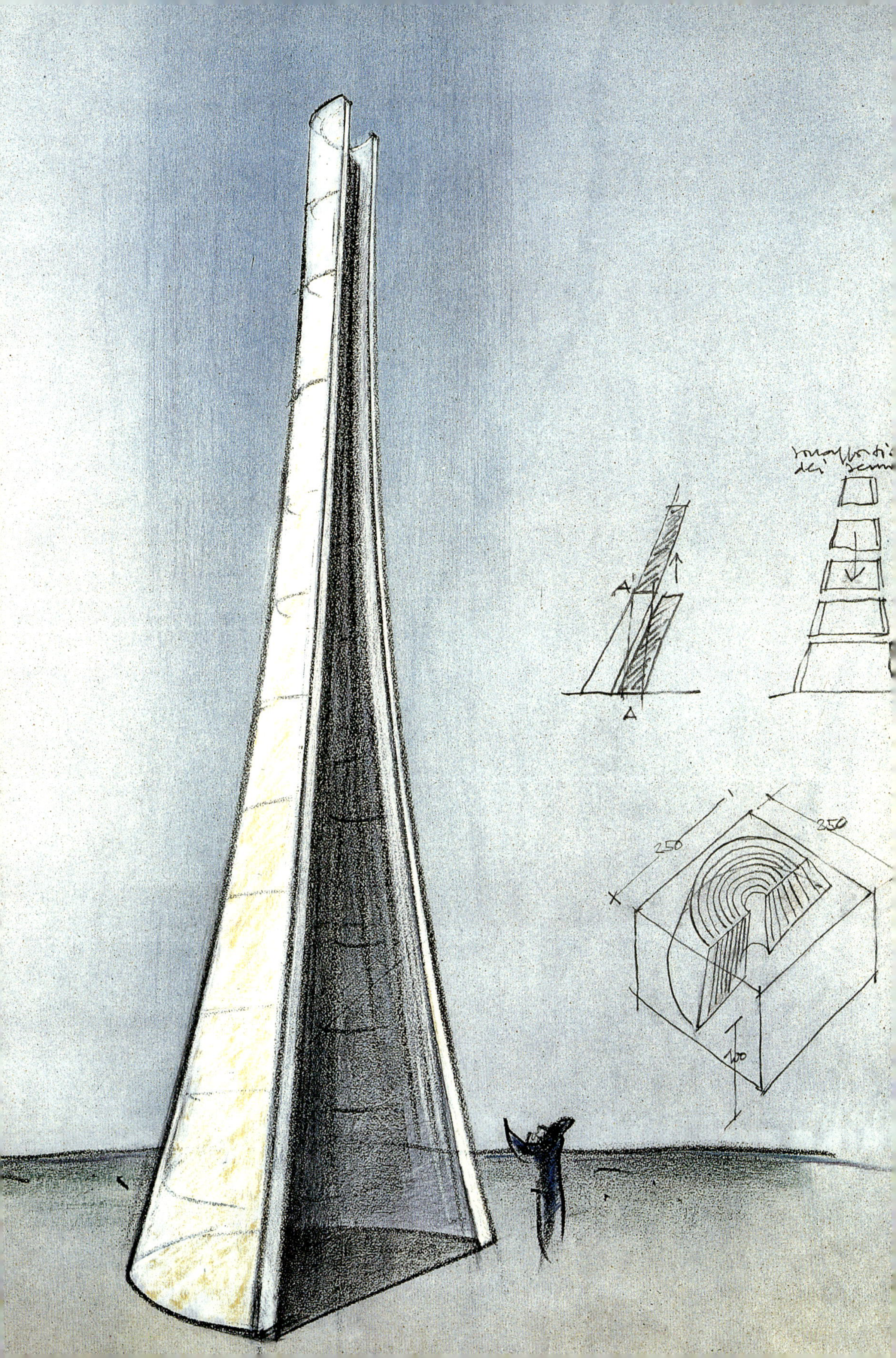
A
250
250
100

CONO CIELO, 1987. A feat of form, technology and construction achieved by reasoning on the possibilities offered by the new numerically controlled machine tools utilized in the working of stone. A demonstrative structure/scupture composed of stacked portions of truncated conical elements of diminishing size made with a single block of Carrara marble. A project that has been exhibited in many parts of the world, simply assembled by stacking the pieces (whose thickness and slope diminish toward the top) and placing a compression cable between the base and the top of the cone.

225

PRESENZE, 1999

プレゼンツェ(存在), 1999年

一辺35cmの正方形を底辺にもつ高さ250cmの大理石のブロック。各面は自由で流動的な曲線で4つにカットされている。あらゆる視点から無限にフォルムを変化させる彫刻。

(K.H)

PRESENZE, 1999. A marble block with a square base, measuring 35 centimeters on each side, by 250 cm in height. Four cuts with a free form on each side. The result: infinite presences for a sculpture that varies its profile, radically, from different vantage points. Effective.

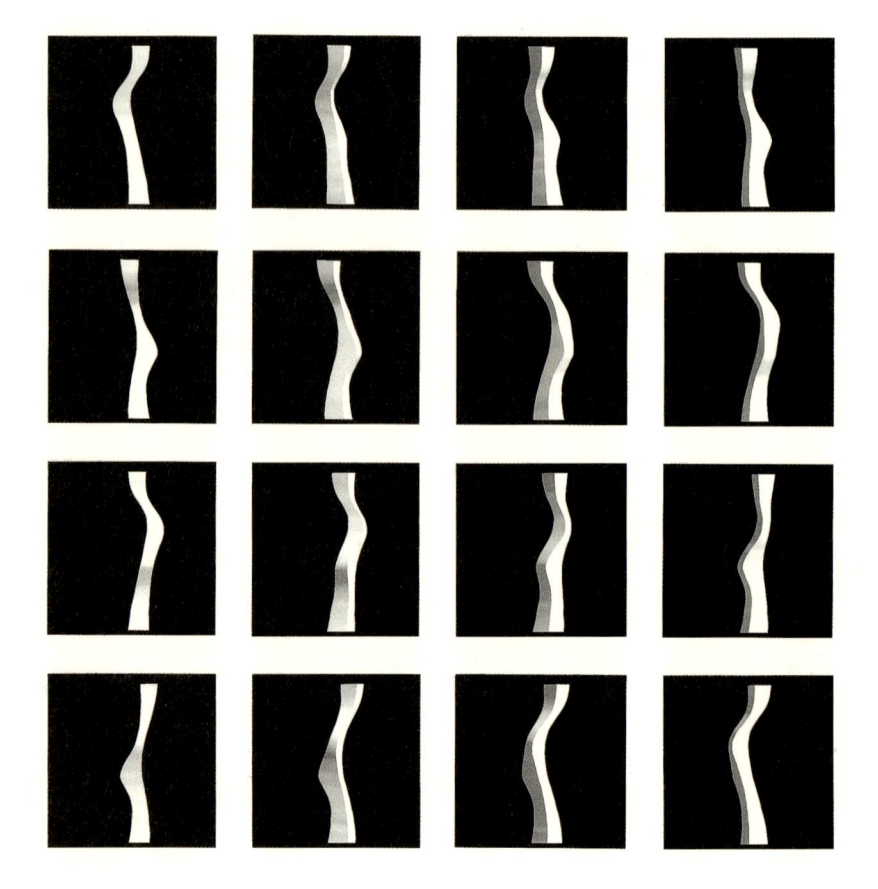

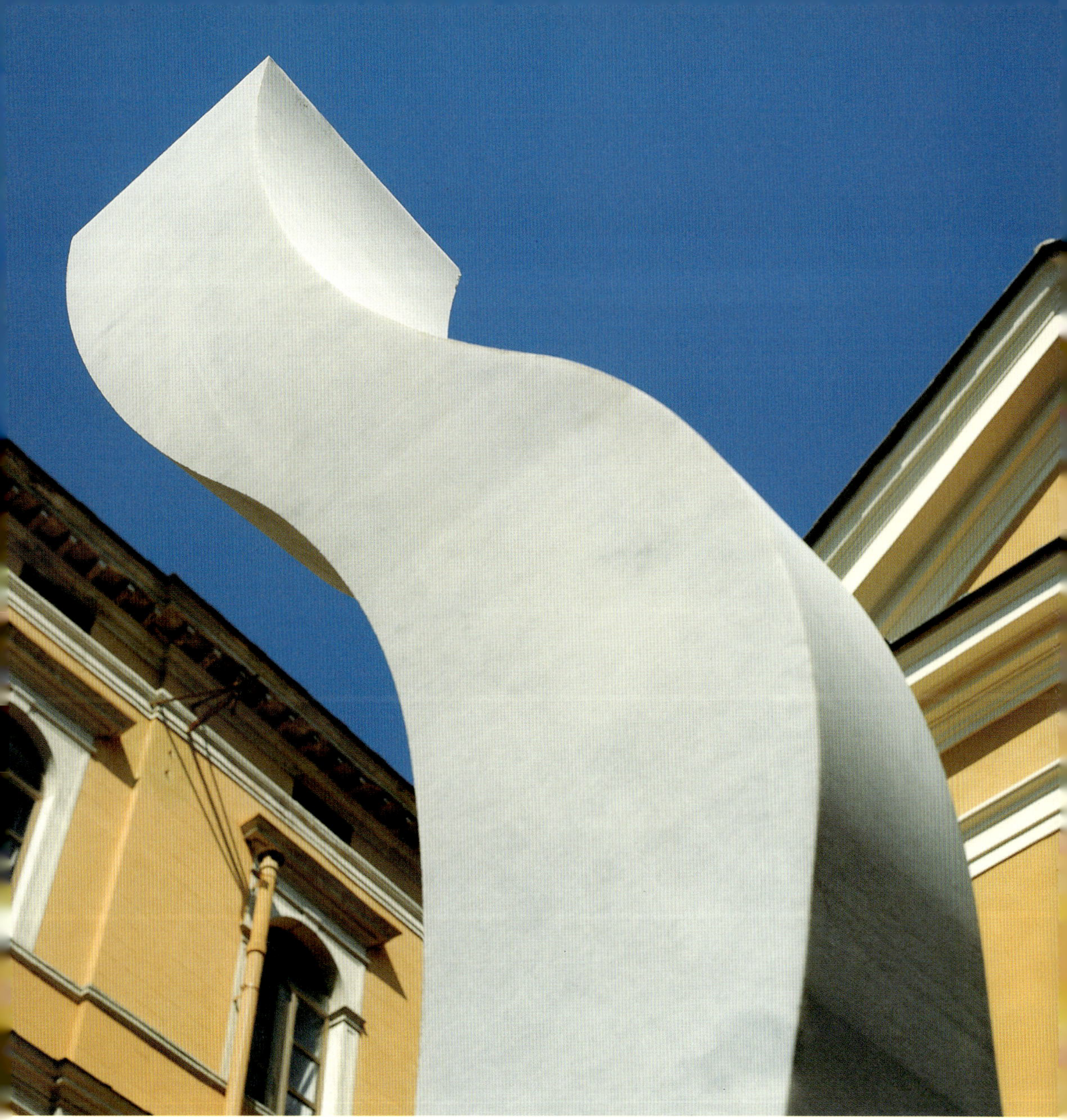

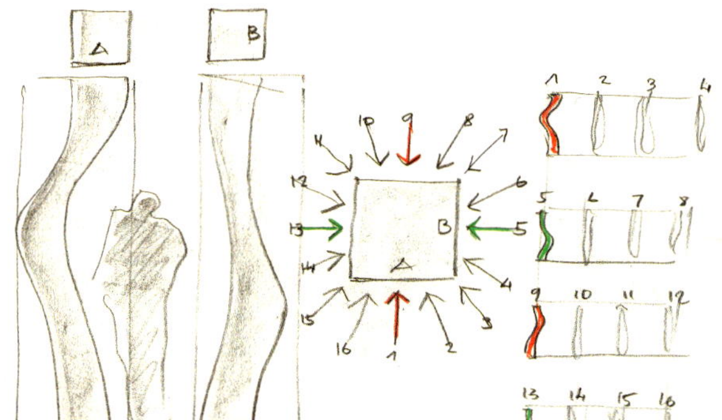
A
B
A
B
1
2
3
4
5
6
7
8
9
10
11
12
13
14
15
16

LA GALLERIA, MARINA DI CARRARA (MASSA CARRARA), 1999

ギャラリー／マリーナ・ディ・カッラーラ（マッサ・カッラーラ），1999年

大理石の1塊から、隣り合ったブロック間に同じ輪郭を生み出す、滑らかで連続性のある曲線によって切り出された7つの形体のギャラリー＝通廊は、公共公園内の小道に沿って互い違いに置かれている。「このギャラリーの中を歩くと、〈満ちていること〉と〈空であること〉は同じ価値をもつことを感じることができる」

(K.H)

LA GALLERIA, MARINA DI CARRARA (MASSA CARRARA), 1999. A Gallery of seven figures – created with a single block of marble, through fluid, continuous cuts that produce matching profiles between contiguous volumes – positioned alternately along the edges of a walkway in a public park. "The observer, walking through the work, can alternately perceive, with identical interest, solid and void volumes that assume an equal value".

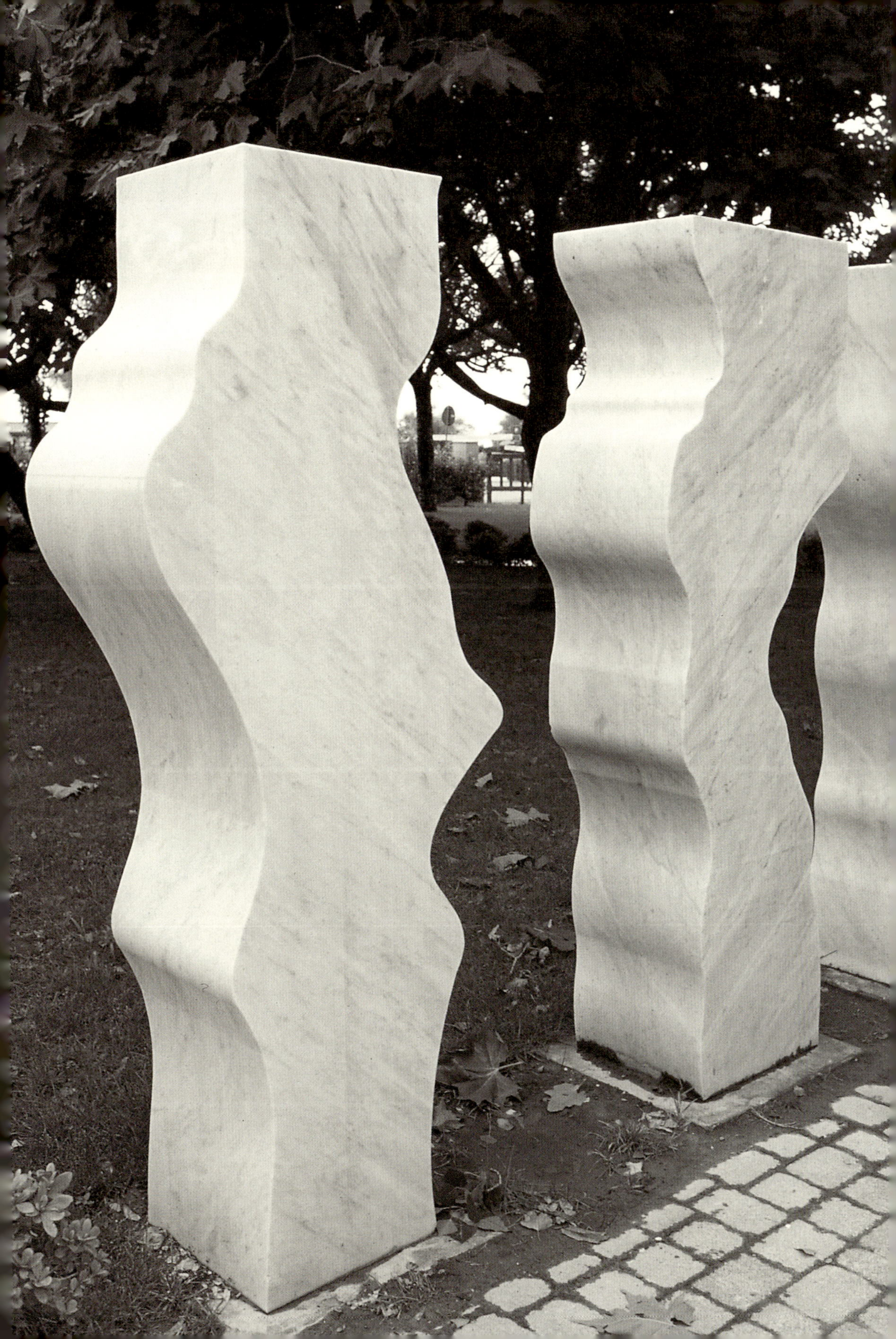

IL PERCORSO, MARINA DI CARRARA (MASSA CARRARA), 1999

軌跡／マリーナ・ディ・カッラーラ（マッサ・カッラーラ），1999年

NC制御の工作機械で実現した大理石の彫刻。あらかじめ描かれた軌跡を辿りながら、ダイヤモンドの糸が連続的にブロックを切り取っていく。切断の完璧性と連続性は、ブロックの広い面に沿って、前に出したり後退させたりしながら光／影、空虚な空間／満ちている空間の特殊な効果を創出している。

(K.H)

IL PERCORSO, MARINA DI CARRARA (MASSA CARRARA), 1999. A sculpture in marble designed to be produced by a numerically controlled machine which cuts the block with a continuous action following a designed/programmed sign/path (Percorso). The perfection and continuity of the cut make it possible to obtain parts that can run along the width of the block and which, protruding or receding, produce particular light/shadow and void/solid effects.

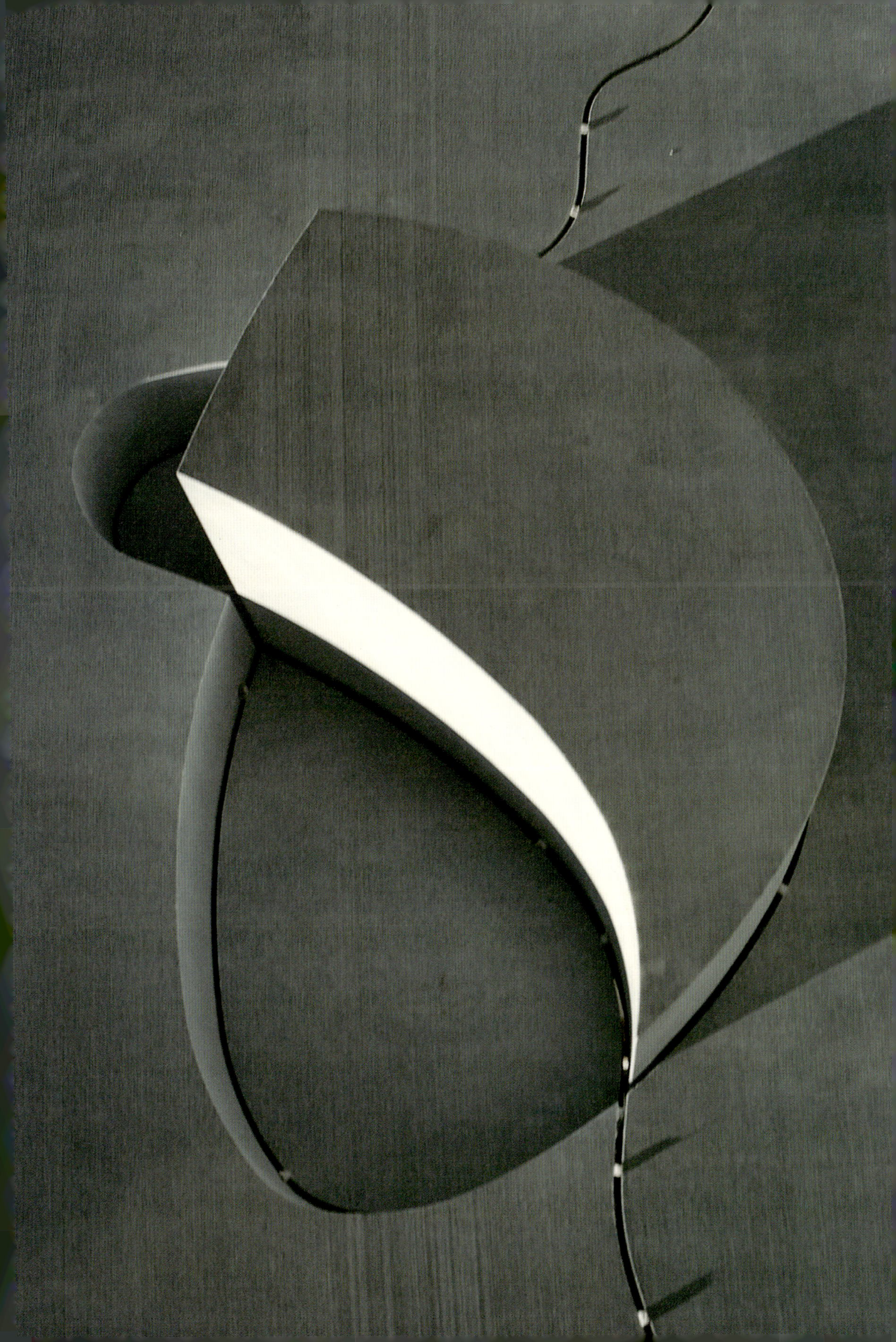

MONUMENTO AI CADUTI SUL LAVORO
APRICENA (FOGGIA), 2000

労働戦死者のモニュメント／アプリチェーナ（フォッジャ），2000年

アプリチェーナの石でつくられたモニュメントは、アプリチェーナの採掘場での労働戦死者を悼み思い出すため、街の前方の丘の上に建てられた。手で砕かれた石のブロックは、1つ1つ間を取って置かれている。ブロックとブロックの間の空間は、戦死した人々の生命を表現している。夜には居住地区の上空を投射しながら、光の帯がその空間を照らし出している。

(K.H)

DESIGN FOR A MONUMENT TO WORKPLACE CASUALTIES, APRICENA (FOGGIA), 2000. To commemorate workers who died on the job in the stone quarries of Apricena, a monument in the same material, positioned on the hill facing the city. Blocks of stone hewn by hand are placed at a distance from one another. The empty space between them dramatically represents the life of the deceased workers: at night a beam of life crosses the monument, projecting shadows on the houses.

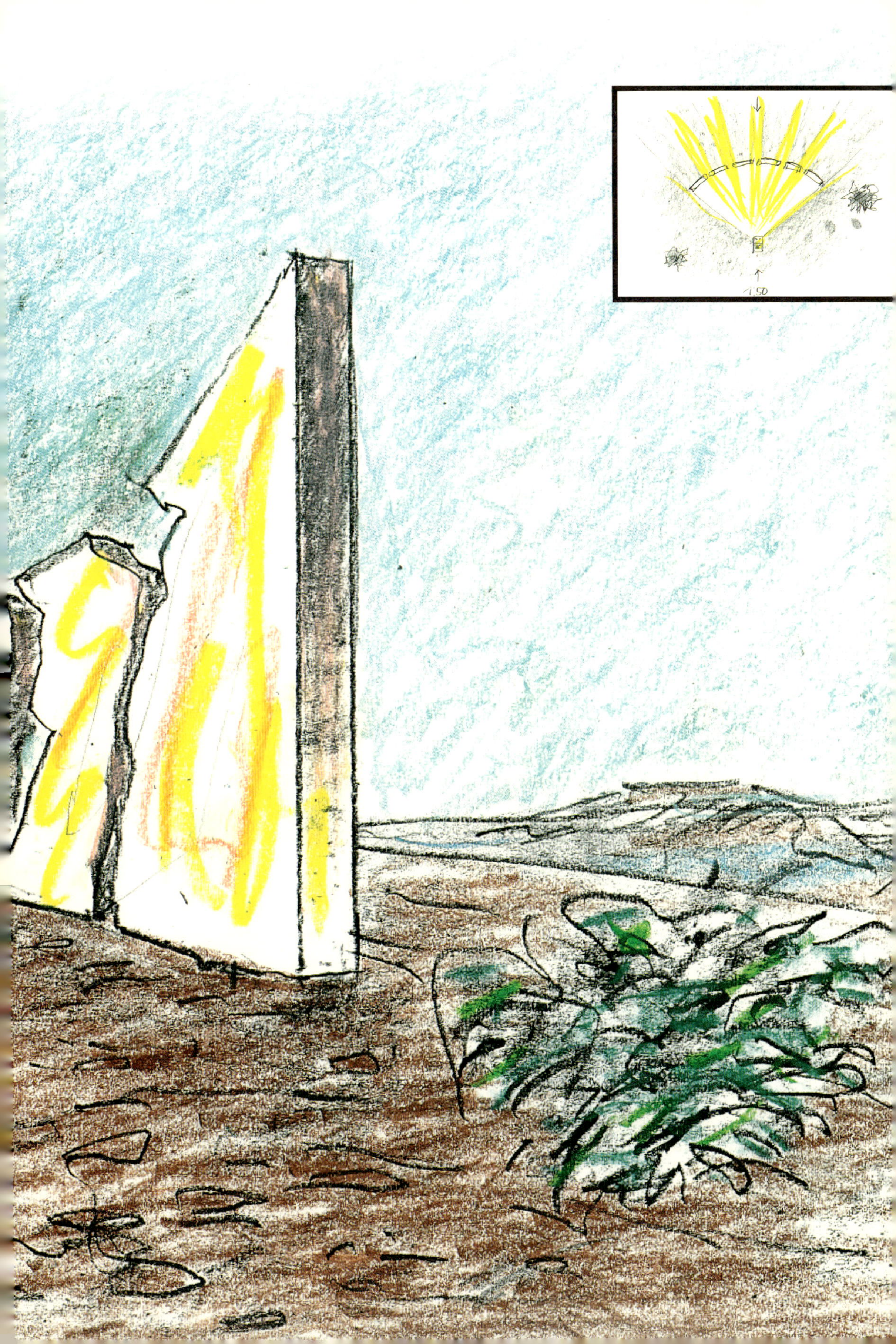
1,50

MASSACRO A SANT'ANNA
SANT'ANNA DI STAZZEMA (LUCCA), 2000

サンタンナの虐殺／サンタンナ・ディ・スタッゼマ（ルッカ），2000年

1944年8月12日、ナチスが560人の市民、なかでも老人、女性、子どもを殺害した。ルッカ県にあるアルピ・アプアネ町スタッゼマのサンタンナでの大虐殺を記憶にとどめるためのモニュメント。マンジャロッティ（彼は当時バル・ドッサラのパルチザンであり、パルティート・アツィオーネのメンバーだった）は、小さなアンナ・パルディーニ広場（一番若い、生後20日の犠牲者の名前がこの広場につけられた）に、簡潔で控えめながら強い表現力をもつモニュメントを建立した。「サンタンナの虐殺」は機関銃で発砲されたかのような穴をもつ、2×2mのコールテン鋼の板でつくられている。この作品にゴヤの厳しい「黒の時代」の銃殺の象形、またキュビズム画家ピカソの「ゲルニカ」に続く、抽象的かつ象形的な新しい表現方法を垣間見ることができる。形態と意味は「素材に魅せられた」マンジャロッティの思考を通して同一になる。素材／彫刻は、「人生のごとく」時間とともに変化していく。月日とともに、コールテン鋼が自ら望むような色に変化していくように。

(K.H)

MASSACRO A SANT'ANNA, SANT'ANNA DI STAZZEMA (LUCCA), 2000. A monument to commemorate the massacre of Sant'Anna di Stazzema, a village in the Apuan Alps in the province of Lucca, where on 12 August 1944 the Nazi-Fascist madness killed 560 civilians, most of whom were elderly people, women and children. For the small Piazza Anna Pardini (named for the youngest of the victims, born just twenty days earlier) Mangiarotti – who was a young partisan at the time in Val d'Ossola and a member of the Partito d'Azione – has created a terse, measured, discreet but strongly expressive sign: Massacro a Sant'Anna is a two by two meter slab of corten marked and perforated by "shots" that appear to have been made by a machine gun. After Goya's images of firing squads, the harsh prelude to his "black" paintings, and after the Cubist hypertext of Guernica, this is another, simultaneously abstract and figurative way of narrating, where form and meaning seem to coincide in yet another case of reasoning on the part of a "lover of material", a material/sculpture that "will change in time, like life", taking on the color chosen by the material itself

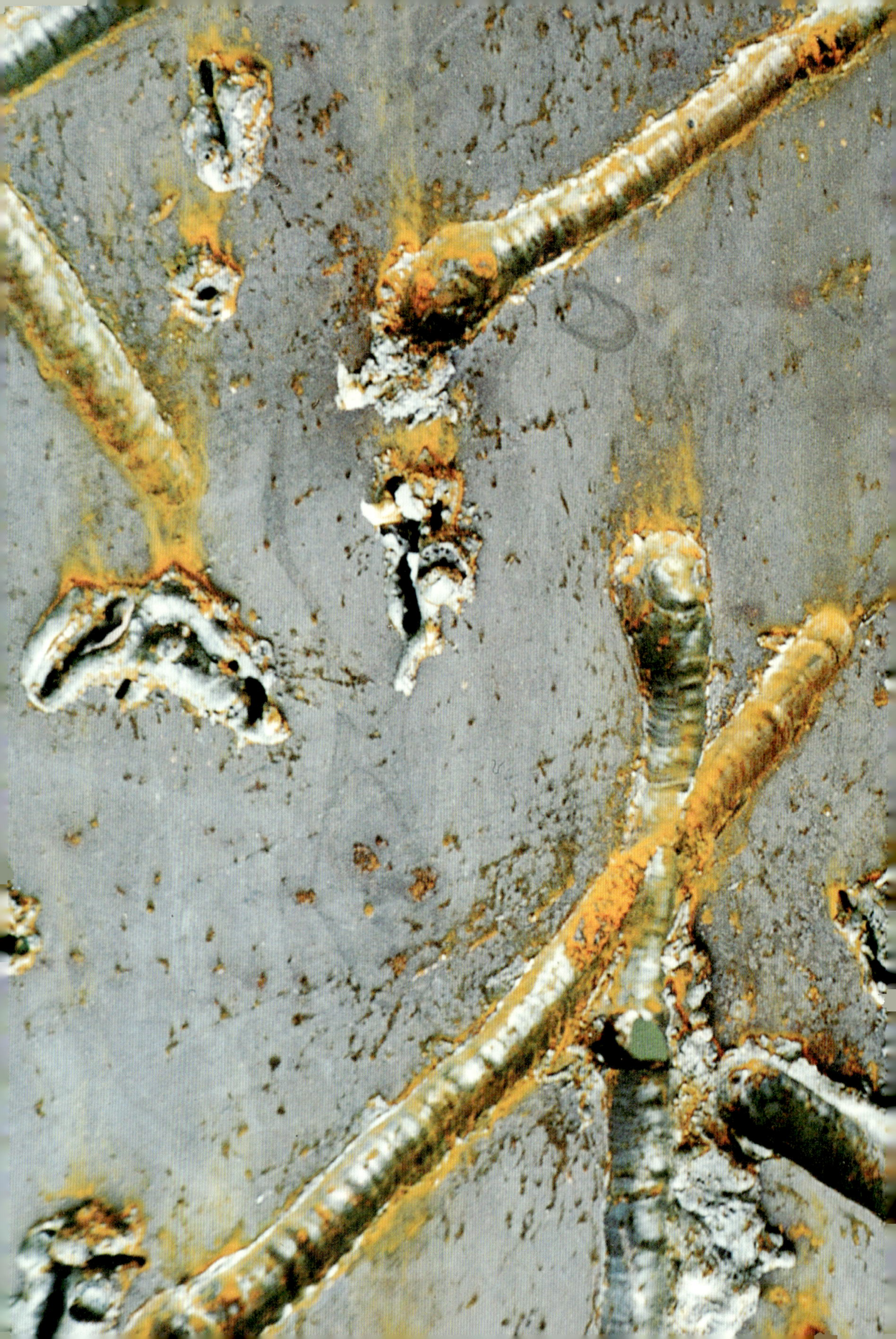

SULLA SCULTURA

彫刻について　ルチアーノ・カラメル

アンジェロ・マンジャロッティにとって、彫刻は長年取り組んできた表現形式であり、気まぐれな余芸などではない。それは少々毛色は違っているとしても、彼のデザイン・建築における総合的な探求の一部である。彼の彫刻には、素材の特性に基づく価値としての造形とその原理についての絶えざる考察が見られる。これは量的に仕事の大部分を占める建築・デザインの取組みと、まったく共通している。この姿勢は、造形を決める際にも、あるときは「自然発生的な」流れのレベルで起きる内在的な因果関係の現象と、またあるときは外部において、マンジャロッティ自身の言葉を借りれば「構造のもつ法則・原理による外的な刺激によって」引き起こされた状況と、整合性をもった形態がつくられる。

彼は、プロジェクトにおける機能的な側面と素材の選択とに、同等に重みを置く。このアプローチの「自然発生的な」結果として、成果の形が多様であることには必然性がある。これは非常に明確で、カッラーラで開かれた個展のタイトルに明言されているように、マンジャロッティは「彫刻のDNA」について自信をもって語れるのだ。こうした枠組みのもと、次に重要なのが意味性の表現である。マンジャロッティの彫刻は、決してトートロジー（同義反復）に陥ることはなく、かといって形態と素材の関係のみに依存することもない。これは、本書に掲載されたすべての作品について言えることである。本書で初めて紹介される最新作のうち数点には、それがことのほか強く表れている。ヴェルシーリアのナチ・ファシストによるサンタンナの虐殺の、犠牲者追悼のために立てられたコールテン鋼の平板はその好例である。この平板は、殺戮者たちが放った銃弾にちなんで、いくつもの穴に貫かれている。金属の素地と切り裂かれた傷口の色が、その恐ろしい出来事を圧倒的な力で生々しく伝えている。

ストラッツィオ、2001年、Strazio,2001

それは製作者個人の主張が一切介在しないことによって、さらに際立っている。これは極めて意図的であり、マンジャロッティは最近のインタビューで「物事をこれみよがしに主張しないでおくことは、偉大な謙虚さを示す行為だと思う」とコメントしている。

この作品と同じ2001年後半の作、「ストラッツィオ（拷問）」は、どちらかというと初期作品、特に「エクイリーブリ・グラヴィタツィオナーリ（重力の平衡）」と近い関係にあるが、旧作の静的な構成が引き伸ばされ、目を釘付けにし、苦悩を呼び覚ます効果を生んでいる。「形態／素材の平衡」は打ち消されるのではなく、逆に極限にまで押しやられ、その結果、自己の確実性を自問する西洋的良心のあやふやさ、頼りなさを感じさせるものとなっている。

この感覚は、近年の出来事を見るにつけ、ますます強烈に感じないではいられないものである。

「ストラッツィオ（拷問）」は2001年9月11日以前の制作で、本書で紹介するほかの作品もこの日よりさらに早い時期の作品だが、いずれも前提としてあらかじめ想定された平衡をもたないものばかりだ。これらの作品に示されているのは、ダイナミックな関係の探求である。それはエネルギーと物質と空間との力関係であり、内部と外部、空虚と充填の二重性と相互関係である。その関係は常に動き続け、私たちの西洋文明がもつ合理性は放棄せずとも、その検証性をもたない自明主義を否定し、むしろほかの文明、とりわけ東洋世界への傾倒を示している。そのことは、マンジャロッティの彫刻において強烈な明確さで表れている、マイナスの空間あるいは虚空に付与された意味の重要性を見れば明白である。

(M.K)

ON THE SCULPTURE

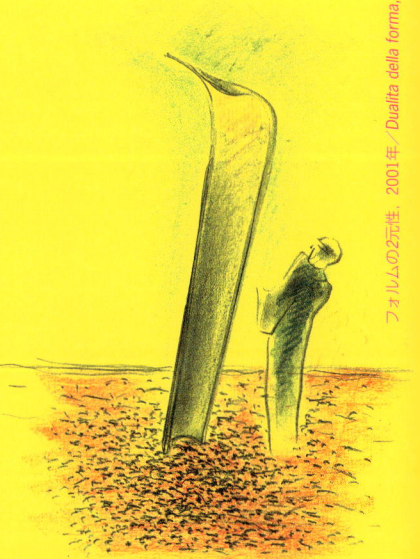

For Angelo Mangiarotti sculpture - a form of expression he has cultivated for years, not only in isolated episodes - is a coherent but diversified part of his overall research on design and construction. It is connected with the quantitatively preponderant practice of architecture and design by the constant consideration of the reasons behind the form as a value based on the characteristics of materials. Which contribute to determine the form in keeping with an endogenous phenomena of cause and effect, at the level of a "spontaneous" procedure, or one that is provoked outside "of external stimuli by a principle, a rule intrinsic to the structure itself", as Mangiarotti puts it. He considers the functional aspect of the project and the choice of materials to be of equal importance. The consequence, again "spontaneous", of this approach is that the results are necessarily diversified. So much so that Mangiarotti doesn't hesitate to speak of a "DNA" of sculpture, as explicitly expressed in the title of one of his exhibitions in Carrara. Within this framework the expression of a meaning is also important, which in the sculpture of Mangiarotti is never tautological, never based only on the form-material relation. This is evident in all the works reproduced in this volume. But in some of the latest works, seen here for the first time, it can be seen with special intensity. As in the slab of corten steel that commemorates the victims of the Nazi-Fascist massacre at Sant'Anna di Stazzema, in Versilia, a slab perforated by a series of holes that are reminders of the murderers' bullets. Where the color of the metal and its lacerations evoke that terrible event with absolute nudity, accentuated by the lack of any indication of the maker (this is intentional: "I think not signing things is a great act of civility", Mangiarotti remarked recently in an interview). In closer relation to earlier works, and in particular to the Equilibri gravitazionali (Gravitational Equilibria), the work Strazio (Torture), also from the second half of 2001, nevertheless stretches the static arrangement, causing effects of anguishing engagement. The form-material equilibrium is not negated, but pushed to radical limits in which we seem to sense the dubious self-questioning of the occidental conscience with respect to its certainties, a sensation that is only more evident in the wake of recent and current events. Strazio was made before 11 September 2001, and other works presented in this volume, sculptures that do not postulate preconceived equilibria, are earlier still. These works reveal a pursuit of dynamic relationships, in the tension between energy, matter and space, in the dualism and interaction between interior and exterior, void and solid, in an always active condition that avoids renunciation of the rationality of our culture, but counters its axiomatic lack of verifiability with greater attention to the oriental world, among other things. As can be seen in the equal importance attributed to negative space or emptiness, strikingly evident in the sculpture of Mangiarotti. ■Luciano Caramel

reggere - portare - aspirare

一体型システム、2000年／*Monolite, 2000*